CAREER CHALLENGES

CAREER CHALLENGES

Straight Talk about Achieving Success in the
Technology-Driven, Post-COVID World of Work

3RD EDITION

FRANK BURTNETT

ROWMAN & LITTLEFIELD
Lanham • Boulder • New York • London

Published by Rowman & Littlefield
An imprint of The Rowman & Littlefield Publishing Group, Inc.
4501 Forbes Boulevard, Suite 200, Lanham, Maryland 20706
www.rowman.com

86-90 Paul Street, London EC2A 4NE

British Library Cataloguing in Publication Information Available

Library of Congress Cataloging-in-Publication Data
Names: Burtnett, Frank, 1940– author.
Title: Career challenges : straight talk about achieving success in the technology-driven, post-COVID world of work / Frank Burtnett.
Other titles: Career errors
Description: Third edition. | Lanham : Rowman & Littlefield, [2022] | Revised edition of: Career errors : straight talk about the steps and missteps of career development. | Includes bibliographical references and index.
Identifiers: LCCN 2022023358 (print) | LCCN 2022023359 (ebook) | ISBN 9781475868074 (cloth) | ISBN 9781475868081 (ebook)
Subjects: LCSH: Career development. | Vocational guidance. | Work-life balance.
Classification: LCC HF5381 .B793 2022 (print) | LCC HF5381 (ebook) | DDC 650.1—dc23/eng/20220718
LC record available at https://lccn.loc.gov/2022023358
LC ebook record available at https://lccn.loc.gov/2022023359

Dedicated to three role models who taught me the importance of respect, loyalty, and hard work.

Rose Marie Best was a single, working parent for much of her life, and she balanced the challenges of career with her responsibilities as a parent and a daughter. The victim of gender discrimination her entire career, she was never deterred from doing the best job she was capable of doing and displaying maximum loyalty to each of her employers. She taught me the meaning of work.

Thomas Gray, my father-in-law, immigrated to the United States from England as a young man. After serving in the US Army in World War I, he spent his working life in the coal mines of Pennsylvania. Tom was a stellar example of what it means to turn in a good day's work and seek the best for one's family. He was a humble man who lived by example.

World War II took my father, Sergeant Francis E. Burtnett, from me when I was four years of age. However, his prewar experiences portray a man dedicated to his work and being successful at it. One can only wonder what career heights he would have achieved had he not been taken at such a young age.

Each is sadly missed and remembered for the impact they have had on my life and the example they set for their children, family, friends, and coworkers. They were the best of the Greatest Generation.

Contents

Preface

Career satisfaction and success are predicated on the management of a series of unique factors and conditions that occur over the life span. As simple as that may sound, few have scrutinized the career development process in detail or comprehend how its positive navigation can impact the totality of the life experience.

People at every life stage can be their own worst enemy when it comes to making mistakes about their personal career and education development. These errors and omissions first slow and then impede career satisfaction and success. Worse, they place the individual somewhere they don't want to be, with no clue as to how to escape. Such was a premise of *Career Errors: Straight Talk about the Steps and Missteps of Career Development*, the title of the first two editions of this book.

This edition, *Career Challenges: Straight Talk about Achieving Success in a Technology-Driven, Post-COVID World of Work*, addresses those errors but also takes the reader deeper into the positive navigation for the new and emerging challenges that impact career growth, mobility, and maintenance. While the standard for career entry and progression once meant the acquisition of a knowledge base and skill set for a preferred occupational interest area, the world of work today demands that workforce members continually adjust to challenges and changes throughout their working lives.

Add to all of the personal factors that contribute to successful career development the myriad challenges and changes that must be accommodated, and you begin to grasp why good management and control are so vital in the contemporary world of work. *Career Challenges* will address many of the life lessons that need to be mastered. Most notable among these are the unforeseen parade of adjustments the workforce has had to adapt to as the technological revolution continues and the unexpected impact that a global dilemma like the coronavirus pandemic would thrust upon work, the worker, and the workplace.

Warren Bennis, organization consultant and scholar, once offered some powerful food for thought when he wrote, "Leaders are people who do the right thing; managers are people who do things right." Throughout your personal growth and development, both aspects of the Bennis admonition need to be addressed. You must assume both a leader and a manager posture because career success depends on your doing the right thing and doing things right.

As you pass through the various life stages, you often become the victim of things you can't control. At other times, you ignore things that can be controlled or deal with them incorrectly. Errors of any type or magnitude can have a destructive effect on both your career and education.

Everyone reading this is at some stage in the career development process. In some instances, you will have to look backward, sideways, and forward because any look to the future must occur with your possessing an understanding of the past and the present (where you have been and where you are now) and the power you possess to influence that future.

The process called career development is just that—a progression of experiences and events over time. It progresses in a cyclical fashion during which the main character—you—goes round and round with multiple entry, exit, and reentry points. Having not done things right the first time doesn't mean it has to be that way the next time. From the time you start preparing for your chosen career until the last day you work, mistakes are likely to happen. This book examines the experiences of ordinary people, as witnessed personally or shared with the author by hundreds of professional counselors, and offers a variety of approaches or strategies for dealing with them.

To fully understand the context of how work and the workplace influence your life, you need to understand what the author means when he uses the terms *job*, *occupation*, and *career*. A job is a distinct position that you will assume multiple times in your life. An occupation represents a larger body of jobs that differ from each other in the unique knowledge, skill, and competence you must possess to perform it. Career is a larger body of life and work experiences that includes all of the jobs and occupations that you have and will perform over time. It is something that you prepare for, enter, and proceed through over many years.

Each of the five sections of this book examines a different aspect of the life experiences and the issues or concerns that are likely to surface during that time. Those sections are:

Part 1—Entering, Reentering, and Moving About in the World of Work

Part 2—The Initial Steps

Part 3—Achieving Career Satisfaction and Dealing with the Occasional Crisis

Part 4—Winding Down and Exiting Your Career

Part 5—Challenges to Career Development in the Future

Career Challenges is not suggesting perfection as the only solution to career success and satisfaction. Albert Einstein, considered by many one of the most brilliant characters in the history of civilization, once said, "A person who never made a mistake—never tried anything new." Past, current, and future errors and setbacks can be your best teachers. Learn from them!

Frank Burtnett, EdD

Acknowledgments

Throughout my career, I've been fortunate to have been exposed to a number of knowledgeable and competent individuals with whom I share a common interest in helping people achieve their full educational and career potential. They have taught and guided me in understanding the career development process and the transitions that must be navigated successfully to achieve life–work balance. Two people, in particular, have shared their knowledge and experiences in a way that have affected the content of this book.

Edwin L. Herr, distinguished emeritus professor of education at the Pennsylvania State University, served as my mentor and friend for four decades. Ed continually impressed me with his scholarly writing and research, as well as the sensitive and caring manner in which he has helped countless students learn how to become effective counselors. The counseling profession is fortunate to have had a man of his character and energy serve in a variety of American Counseling Association (ACA), National Career Development Association (NCDA), and Association for Counselor Education and Supervision (ACES) leadership roles.

Similarly, Conrad Taylor helped me to understand the role of search and staffing professionals in serving the public good. As president and chairman of the board of the National Association of Personnel Services (NAPS), Conrad was recognized as a staunch advocate for professional and ethical standards and the education of those helping candidates for employment enter, grow, and move about the American workplace. His work has stood as a model for everyone who works in the search and staffing industry.

Over my career, some of my best teachers have been my counseling students, and while many have taught me important things, one has made a special contribution to this book. Lauren Sadighi, a graduate student in counseling at Marymount University in Arlington, Virginia, read development drafts of the first edition of this work and offered many suggestions on how to make it better. I'm indebted to her for a comprehensive and candid assessment of my writing.

Frank Burtnett, EdD

PART I

ENTERING, REENTERING, AND MOVING ABOUT IN THE WORLD OF WORK

CHAPTER 1

Challenge: Understanding the Career Development Process

Life is a succession of lessons which must be lived to be understood.

—HELEN KELLER (1880–1968), AN AMERICAN AUTHOR,
POLITICAL ACTIVIST, AND LECTURER, AND THE FIRST DEAF
BLIND PERSON TO EARN A BACHELOR OF ARTS DEGREE

OKAY . . . YOU DON'T HAVE TO ASSUME FULL RESPONSIBILITY FOR WHAT you don't know about the career development process. Others are equally guilty. Schools, colleges, and the workplace itself could have done more to teach or explain the career development process—the path that all people follow from the day they are born. But they didn't, and now it's up to you to see where you have been and where you are now, and then determine where you want to go.

The career development process represents a series of stages during which you identify, select, prepare for, enter, and progress through an occupation or career. Along the path, you have held or will undoubtedly hold numerous jobs. It is important to recognize the order of the events and the tasks that you must perform to ensure success.

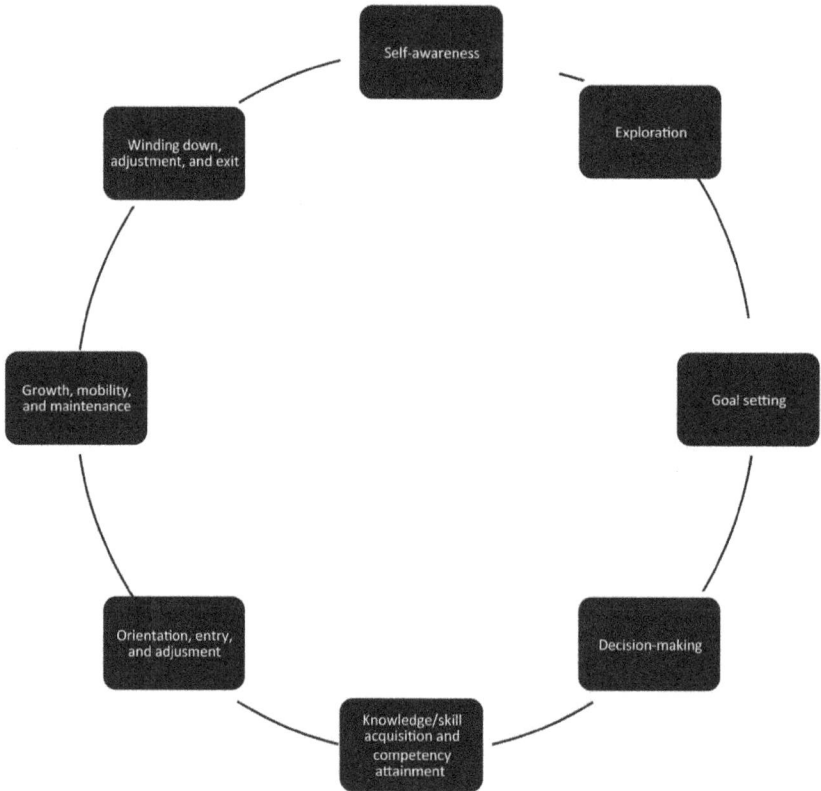

Figure 1.1 The Career Development Process

CAREER DEVELOPMENT: A SERIES OF STAGES

The following stage definitions will bring the career development process into focus.

Self-awareness

This initial stage represents the time when you acquire and sustain a "sense of self" by examining your aptitudes, achievements, interests, personality traits, values, and lifestyle preferences. It is the stage where you are able to answer the "Who am I?" question. During adolescence and young adulthood, that sense of awareness is forming and emerging as a by-product of the maturation process.

Any assessment of this nature must, however, be viewed as a snapshot in time. It must be revisited periodically to make certain you have kept up with the changes that are brought on by your growth, maturity, and the environment in which you function.

Exploration

During this stage, you create questions and search for answers that broaden your career understanding and allow you to set goals. When a student explores, the goals are often tentative and not realized until further along in the school or college experience. In young adulthood, the goals harden somewhat and become genuine direction for the explorer.

It goes without saying that we live in a changing, dynamic world in which the work that people must perform and the way that they must respond to their employer's demands are undergoing constant change. Many occupations today don't look anything like they did five or six decades ago. Today, robots and machines do things that people were once employed to do.

Existing occupations change and sometimes disappear. New occupations emerge and offer new opportunities. For this reason, career explorers must be vigilant and assertive in their search and discovery strategies, keeping one eye on the "here and now" and one on the future.

Once in the workforce, exploration will continue as you grow and change and new options become visible and attainable. This stage also represents a time when you relate what you have learned about yourself personally to the investigation of the career and education options you are considering. Information consumption is an essential element of the exploration stage.

Goal setting

Self-awareness and exploration of options will undoubtedly resonate with you and lead to the setting of actual goals. While a considerable amount of goal setting happens in adolescence and young adulthood, it is an action that can arise at any point in the career development process.

Goal setting typically occurs in phases—immediate, midterm, and long-term—each representing the objectives you would like to achieve during that period. Each goal must be evaluated to determine if you are overaspiring or underaspiring—the former tied to setting the career bar too high, the latter to setting it too low.

Decision-making

Rather than a stage or phase, decision-making represents the events that you experience any number of times throughout the career development process—intervals when you must choose from various options you have identified. Your decisions vary from selecting courses to study in school to choosing the right internship experience in college to eventually choosing the occupation or field that will become your career.

Decision-makers cannot expect to be correct 100 percent of the time. Because many decisions are correctable, it's important that you have a follow-up mechanism at work in your life skills that will allow you to reconsider decisions without too much damage or disturbance to the career development process.

You make dozens, if not hundreds, of decisions throughout the career development process. The best decision-making occurs when you are aware of the decision that must be made and have the opportunity to consider the range of options that exist, including the outcomes or consequences of each choice.

Knowledge/skill acquisition and competency attainment

Following each education or career decision, you will take deliberate steps toward implementing the decision and evaluating it once made. Typically, this involves an action to acquire the knowledge and skills needed to move into and become successful in the career. It involves your following the education or experience path (i.e., career training, college, graduate/professional school, etc.) that is most likely to help you achieve your goal or goals.

In some instances, the study may be generic (i.e., liberal arts study, etc.), preparing you for additional study that becomes more career focused. Through education and "hands-on" work experiences (i.e., internships, part-time employment, etc.), you develop a recognizable competency level, which can be placed on your resume or employment application and used to procure employment.

To be certain, full competency in any given career is not achieved instantly, but basic competencies reflect what you are capable of doing and will be viewed favorably by employers. The study of accounting, for example, begins with the study of general principles. Eventually, it will lead to a more specific application of those principles into a specialty like public accounting, management accounting, or auditing. Each will provide entry into the occupation of accountant, as each will show prospective employers the knowledge you have acquired and the competencies you possess. Throughout this stage, you are likely to face a number of implementation decisions, each significant in the achievement of career and education goals.

Orientation, entry, and adjustment

The orientation stage is a "bridging" time, a period of transition when you relate where you are with where you want to be in the immediate future. It is a time of renewed examination of your abilities, interests, personal characteristics, and preferences while dealing with a new set of options and decisions.

This is the period when you identify, secure, and move into a job or occupation. It is a time when you will learn and use job-seeking strategies (i.e., resume writing, interview skills, etc.) in order to be proactive in the employment search. As a new or rookie employee, you will experience a period of adjustment to your work role and the adapting of your knowledge and skills to the specific work setting.

Growth, mobility, and maintenance

The longer you work in your chosen career and achieve a measure of success, the greater the likelihood that you will receive added responsibilities and rewards, including promotions and salary increases. Such adjustments are usually accompanied by the need for continued learning in order to stay abreast of the knowledge, techniques, and tools in your career field.

Figure 1.2 Achieving Career Competence

Work experience strengthens the opportunity for mobility, whether within your current setting or in situations with other employers. Throughout the work experience, the maintenance of knowledge and skills will lead you to improved competence.

Maintenance is the period in your career when you face the changes (i.e., emergence of new technologies, tools, etc.) that will have an impact on your work or the manner in which you do it. If you demonstrate a willingness to learn new things and an ability to adapt to change, you stand the greatest chance of career growth and mobility, and you will be less likely to be affected negatively by economic setbacks like recessions or other challenging times.

Winding down, adjustment, and exit

This is the time in your life when you elect to ease up on the accelerator and even apply the brakes as it relates to your career. This stage should never be construed as final or the end of anything. Deceleration is simply the act of slowing down, making changes in time devoted to work, reducing the tasks that are performed, and adjusting to a revised work style (i.e., three-day work week, telecommuting, etc.). It also will afford you greater time for family, friends, and leisure pursuits.

As the latter stages of your career approach, you are likely to face a good news–bad news contradiction. The good news is that people are living longer, healthier lives and you may want to work longer than seniors did a generation or so ago. The bad news is that some employers may not want you any longer. Older, experienced workers are sometimes viewed as more expensive than younger, fresh talent and find resistance in their desire to continue working. Federal law prohibits discrimination in the workplace on the basis of age, but it appears in more places than you might realize.

GETTING A SENSE OF PERSONAL CAREER DEVELOPMENT BEGINNING WITH GREATER SELF-AWARENESS

A full understanding of career development will not occur until you engage in some personal pulse-taking. No two individuals are ever at the same place at the same time. You will likely launch, land, launch again, and land again many times over the course of your career. And different people navigate the process at different speeds.

People have personalities. Careers and occupations have personalities, too, a factor that you must consider before venturing in the direction of a career where you will spend the next twenty-five, thirty-five, or more years. Conduct any self-awareness exercise as if you're looking into a mirror. In addition to personality, examine your aptitudes, achievements, interests, values, and lifestyle preferences. And don't do it just once; return occasionally and look again at the characteristics that define you, characteristics that may have changed as a result of age, maturity, and life experiences.

Let's take a minute to examine up close the elements that define you and make you unique.

Aptitudes

Aptitudes represent your capacity for learning and your natural ability to do something. When someone makes the statement "She's a born mathematician" when referring to the ease with which you relate to the study of mathematics or "He's a natural," when describing how you take to a particular sport, they are usually speaking of your exceptional aptitude. Others may have a superior capacity for writing, science, or other studies. Often, these aptitudes extend to skills like interacting with people, conducting research, or similar proficiencies.

Achievements

Your achievements are the measured accomplishments in your life, those things that you have excelled at or done well. In school, progress is measured regularly and reported in the form of grade reports or test scores. In athletics, achievements are measured by a stopwatch, statistics, or records.

9

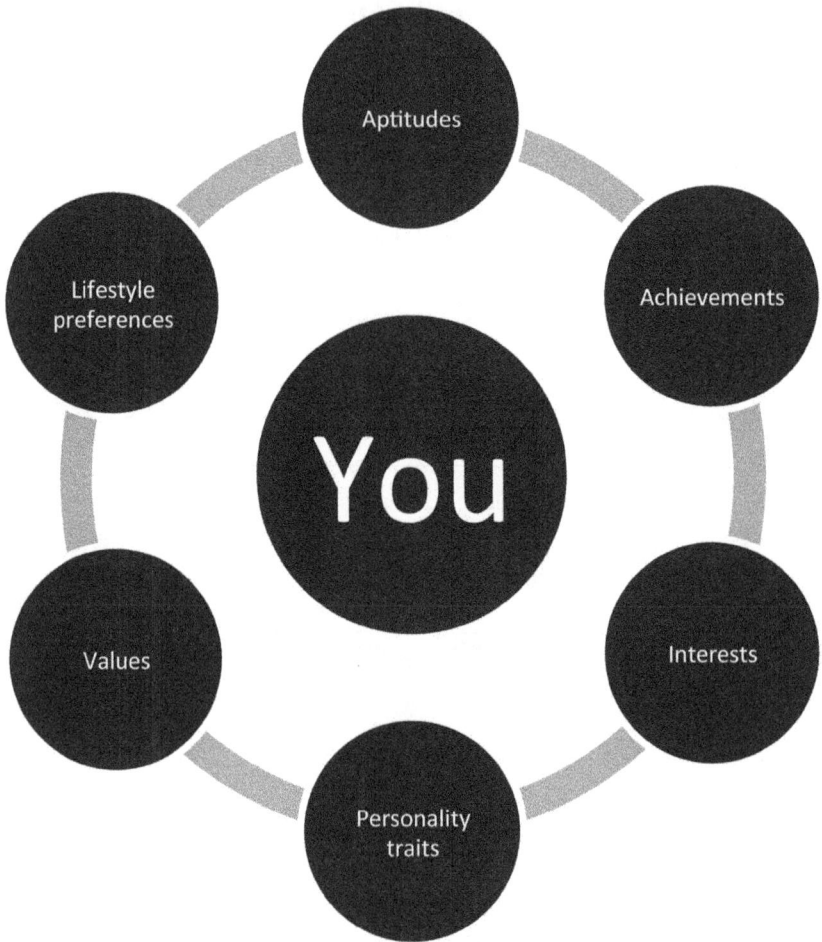

Figure 1.3 Elements of Personal Awareness

In music, art, or theater, your achievements may result in praise or recognition for a job well done or an award for an outstanding performance. It is possible to achieve or become accomplished in something for which you have little or limited aptitude. This is usually the result of commitment, concentration, and hard work.

Interests

Interests are the things you like to do. They command your time, arouse your curiosity, and generally leave you with a good feeling for having done them. Sometimes, interests are related to aptitudes and achievements because they represent areas where you have devoted study and attention and earned some degree of success. Other interests, like cooking, playing an instrument, or pursuing a hobby, are outlets or diversions from the things you have to do. Often, however, an interest can be nurtured into something more permanent—like when an interest in photography leads to a career as a photographer.

Personality traits

The characteristics that make you different from another are your personality traits. In psychology, personality is defined as the total physical, intellectual, and emotional structure of a person, including aptitudes, abilities, and interests. Words like *outgoing, quiet, inquisitive,* and *creative* are characteristically used to describe a person. Assessing and understanding personal traits can help define career characteristics and workplace environments consistent with your personality.

Values

Values are the aspects of life that you hold in esteem, things you would prefer if an option were available. They are also the principles or ideals that you are committed to or stand behind. Often, your values are rooted in your faith, culture, or family traditions. A sense of self-awareness would be incomplete without some analysis of your values and how each relates to your personal and career development. For example, prestige and status may be important to you but mean less to a close friend, classmate, or coworker.

Lifestyle preferences

As all of these characteristics emerge and take hold, your lifestyle preferences begin to take shape. These are the ways you prefer to use your time. You may prefer the "hustle and bustle" of city life, while others prefer the slower-paced atmosphere offered by smaller communities or rural areas. You may become passionate about your career and throw yourself into your work, often spending hours upon hours in your career pursuits. Others may prefer to escape regularly and pursue noncareer things away from work.

If you value time and don't want to spend it sitting in traffic or traveling a long distance to the workplace, you may elect to seek employment where technology will allow you to telecommute either full-time or part-time. Doing so allows you to exercise a preference that is important to you. As you move into and through adulthood, these preferences become even more pronounced and play a major role in your behavior.

You will have a greater chance of succeeding in your career and education pursuits if you find living, learning, and workplace environments that are compatible with your aptitudes, achievements, interests, personality traits, values, and lifestyle preferences, ones that will assist in achieving stated goals.

Many personal characteristics are apparent and straightforward and seem to have been around forever. Others will appear as we learn and mature and engage in new and different life experiences. A thorough and ongoing self-assessment, like the image seen in a mirror, keeps that examination in perspective. Personality traits emerge at different times, and interests appear and disappear as we grow and mature and expand our life experiences, a factor that will impact our identity across the life span and dictate continued self-study.

THE CYCLICAL NATURE OF THE CAREER DEVELOPMENT PROCESS

The career development process is a cyclical one—not a linear one. It is not unusual for a person to return to an earlier stage and address it again. Your approach the second or third time may be different from an earlier one. Often, this recycling is self-imposed as you learn new things about yourself and seek to amend your life–work situation to reflect your current conditions. Sometimes, the recycling is not voluntary but imposed by a circumstance (i.e., termination of employment, impending job obsolescence, etc.) that dictates that you take stock of your current situation and move purposely in a new or different direction.

Eventually, all of the exploring, deciding, and learning prepare you to enter and progress through an occupation or career. When you piece together a series of employment experiences, over time, you are creating a career, a body of work that reflects much more than the routine day-to-day occupational experiences. Your career represents the totality of your education and work experiences, one upon which you are proud to place your personal signature.

Dignity in all work

As you look at the American and global workforce, do so with a respect for all careers. John W. Gardner, secretary of health, education, and welfare during the mid-part of the last century, was extremely prophetic when he spoke the following:

> *The society which scorns excellence in plumbing as a humble activity and tolerates shoddiness in philosophy because it is an exalted activity will have neither good plumbing nor good philosophy: neither its pipes nor its theories will hold water.*

There is dignity in all work.

STRAIGHT TALK ABOUT THE CAREER DEVELOPMENT PROCESS

Gaining command of the career development process is an essential ingredient in the achievement of career satisfaction and success. Learn everything there is to know about the process, and be sensitive to the stages as they occur or reoccur in the life cycle. And don't fall into the "been there . . . done that" trap. Failure to understand the career development process is like trying to find an unfamiliar location without a GPS or a map. Getting lost is inevitable.

CHAPTER 2

Challenge: Making Quality Decisions

Making good decisions is a critical skill at every level.

—PETER DRUCKER (1909–2005), AUSTRIAN AMERICAN
MANAGEMENT CONSULTANT, EDUCATOR, AND AUTHOR WHO
INVENTED THE CONCEPT KNOWN AS "MANAGEMENT BY
OBJECTIVES"

LOOK BACK AT THE RECENT CAREER AND EDUCATION DECISIONS YOU
have had to face, and ask if you made the right ones. Look even further
back—at decisions you made three, five, or more years ago—and ask if
you are satisfied with the outcomes. As stated earlier, rather than a discreet stage in the career development process, decision-making occurs
many times, with each decision varying in importance and impact.

Mistakes occur in decision-making when you don't gather quality
or sufficient information or you engage in bad behaviors (i.e., don't
allow sufficient time) that result in errors. Any of the above can alter the
options that you will eventually attempt to consider as a decision-maker.
While you cannot be expected to get every decision right the first time,
the reality is that many people are incredibly bad at making decisions and
the consequences can be devastating.

You don't like what you are studying or where you have chosen to
go to school. You allow an outside force to influence too heavily what

you are going to study and the career you will enter. You don't prepare adequately to compete in a competitive job market. You accept a job that you feel is below the expectations you have set for yourself or that limits your growth and development. Or worse, you are unemployed or hate the work you are doing. Each could be the consequence of faulty exploration and terrible decision-making.

Before examining these and other poor decisions that dot your past, let's examine a decision-making model put forth nearly 250 years ago by none other than American Founding Father Benjamin Franklin. In 1772, the English scientist, educator, and theologian Joseph Priestley wrote to Franklin seeking his assistance with a decision he had to make.

Rather than advise Priestley on his particular decision or make his decision for him, Franklin chose to offer his personal guidance on how a good decision is made.

What Franklin suggested to Priestley was nothing more than what today is called a "pros and cons" list in which the decision-maker places the pros of a question on one side of a piece of paper and the cons on the other. Following a day or two of thought as to whether the list was complete, Franklin suggested a return to analyze the reasons for or against an action or behavior.

When such analysis finds that a reasons for or against an action are equal in value, Franklin suggests they neutralize each other and should be eliminated. This intellectual exercise forces the decision-maker to stop and consider the consequences associated with the positive and negative aspects of each option. As pros and cons are eliminated from the list, Franklin believed, the remaining options should point the decision-maker toward the best action. Finally, following some additional time for consideration and reflection, the decision-maker should act.

Critics of Franklin's model point to personal prejudices and biases as flaws in his process and that is why, they suggest, personal decision-making needs a healthy dose of external information before some aspects of the model can truly work.

Following is a multistage model created by the author that includes but expands upon the Franklin model. You may wish to use it to navigate the decisions that are going to impact the remainder of your education and working life. Before you get too concerned about applying a nine-stage model to every decision and the time that might assume, recognize that once it is learned, this model becomes a fixed cognitive process with the brain doing most of the work.

STAGE 1: KNOW THERE IS A DECISION TO BE MADE

On the surface, this stage may seem peculiar, but think about all the times someone made a decision for you and you were the last to find out about it. It means taking control instead of leaving it to others or happenstance. Think back to the time you were in late middle school or early high school. You found yourself studying Spanish (or another language). Do you remember how you landed in Spanish? Did you have a rationale for selecting this subject? Was it the foreign language everyone was studying? Did someone other than you place Spanish on your course schedule?

Situations like these occur all the time and point to the need for you to take control and become engaged in the decisions that have an impact on your life.

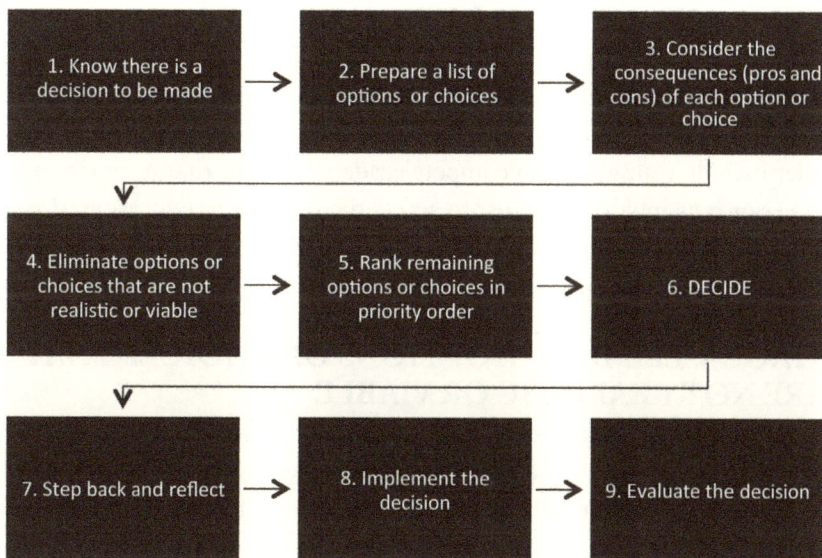

Figure 2.1 Model for Career and Educational Decision-Making

STAGE 2: PREPARE A LIST OF OPTIONS
OR CHOICES

Decisions in your career and education are like the intersections of streets. If you want to get somewhere and there is more than one way to get there, the Franklin model suggests that you have to know the options before you. Based on the totality of your life experiences—meaning your exposures to and awareness of a certain number of occupations and careers—your ability to learn about new and different occupations and careers is limited. Whether a first job or an employment change off in the future, the number of options you have to choose from may be intimidating.

Career exploration begins with a review of careers you know about and moves on to others that interest you. Finally, exploration generates new understandings, and you shouldn't close the options door until full consideration has been given to all that you know and have learned. Exploration will also yield something else, namely, the careers and occupations that you do not wish to consider at this point in your life.

STAGE 3: CONSIDER THE CONSEQUENCES (PROS
AND CONS) OF EACH OPTION OR CHOICE

With every career option that you consider, there are likely to be both positive and negative consequences, the consideration of which can affect how long it will actually take to make the decision. Other factors to consider include your ability to compete academically for that occupation or career or how much it will cost to access the training or education. If you are considering a career makeover, you have to determine the extent to which any decision will affect you and your family.

STAGE 4: ELIMINATE OPTIONS OR CHOICES THAT
ARE NOT REALISTIC OR VIABLE

A major part of decision-making is the "weeding" of options that are not realistic or viable. If an option appears too easy or seems too good to be true, it likely is and needs to be examined further. If the option appears unattainable, give it a good review before removing it from the conversation. After this exercise, eliminate any options that are not worthy of additional consideration.

STAGE 5: RANK REMAINING OPTIONS OR CHOICES IN PRIORITY ORDER

Ranking the remaining options by priority is the beginning of true decision-making because you will now attach a value to those that remain. It is also a time when you must consider the investment you must make in order for the decision to be realized. If the decision is yours, you will be responsible for making it work. You must take "ownership" of the decision as a part of your investment. With every decision, there are multiple investments, including energy, time, expense, and ego.

Decision-making requires an investment of energy. The information-gathering process, along with the requisite ranking and prioritizing, will all place demand on you. After the decision has been made, it must be implemented, and another energy commitment must be made. Next, each judgment intersection you pass through involves an investment of time, most of which cannot be recouped if a poor decision has been made.

Decisions can also be costly, as in the example of the tuition, room and board, and fees paid to a college where you aren't likely to achieve academic success or earn a degree. Faulty decisions can also be dangerous as in your terminating employment prematurely while you seek to explore new options or do a career makeover. Energy, time, and financial loss can be added to your list of life experiences, but their impact slows or prohibits what might have been achieved if a good decision had been made.

Set aside the expenditure of energy, time, and money and consider the ego bruising that occurs when you make a decision that cannot be realized. Enrolling in a college or training program and then discovering that the academic requirements exceed your capabilities leave little option other than to admit failure. Such an admission is often the pill you have to swallow in order to clear the path to a new, different, and better decision.

Like choosing the wrong turn at a highway intersection, correcting a poor decision will require you to stop and return to the decision point and start all over again. In some instances, going back to square one can be avoided if you can successfully amend your action and make a successful shortcut to where you need to be. Poor decisions, especially those that you don't discover soon enough, are often like quicksand. They bog you down in a quagmire from which you will have difficulty escaping. Good decisions, on the other hand, set you free and place you on a positive course toward the future.

STAGE 6: DECIDE
It's time. You're ready. Nothing more needs to happen. Decide!

STAGE 7: STEP BACK AND REFLECT
Reflection, especially the immediate variety, is a healthy way for you to evaluate what you decided. Decisions have to be digested, whether the next day, next week, or later. Reflection allows you to make adjustments before too much energy, time, or expense has been committed to any action. It can also protect any ego investment you have made. Decision-making can be an anxiety-producing event or series of events in your life, and standing back to assess the decision made and the direction that needs to be taken to implement the decision is a sound strategy in what is sometimes a complex and angst-ridden process.

STAGE 8: IMPLEMENT THE DECISION
Each decision requires that action be taken by the decider. If you have decided to change jobs, the search for a new one dictates immediate action. If a choice has been made to attend a particular college or grad school, an application must be secured, completed, and filed. The more decisive and pronounced the action or actions, the quicker and more efficiently you will begin moving toward the benefits that your good decision will yield.

STAGE 9: EVALUATE THE DECISION
As you head down the runway in a new direction, it is mentally healthy to engage in a long-term evaluation of your choice or choices. Identify the indicators that will tell you that desirable outcomes will be achieved as

the result of the decision. Was the right decision made? If so, keep moving forward. If not, determine what needs to occur in order to amend, correct, or move in an altogether different direction.

The effects of bad decisions can be enormous. Don't sentence yourself to four or more years of college or a lifelong career that isn't what you want. Never allow decisions to imprison you in the way a judge sentences a guilty person to incarceration for committing a crime.

ROLE OF CAREER AWARENESS IN EXPLORING OPTIONS AND MAKING DECISIONS

Individual differences, along with other important factors such as age, experience, and maturity, are going to demand that you acquire quality information in order to become a quality decision-maker. Career counselors have long recognized that self-awareness has an incredible influence on who you are, where you are, and what you want to do. But always remember, any pulse taking you do represents a single point in time in a very dynamic period of personal growth and development. Add to the equation the vast number of opportunities that lie before you, and it is little wonder why decision-making often becomes intimidating and anxiety producing. The options and choices are astounding.

Before it was replaced in the late 1990s by O*NET, the U.S. Department of Labor's *Dictionary of Occupational Titles* (DOT) listed 12,741 occupations. Driven by skills rather than tasks and delivered in a more user-friendly internet format, today, O*NET (http://www.onetonline .org) collects and disseminates information for just under 1,000 occupations that are performed in the United States. Add to this information base the more than 4,100 degree-granting colleges and more than 10,000 accredited career-preparation institutions, and the enormity of the information becomes apparent.

Before the advent of the internet, decision-makers were often limited in their access to accurate and timely information. Today, that problem has been solved, and a new one has emerged—information overload. The vast array of career and education opportunities gives credence to why the "What do you want to be when you grow up?" and "Where do you want to go to school?" questions are often the two most difficult you may ever be asked.

LIFE EXPERIENCES, VALUES, AND LIFESTYLE PREFERENCES AFFECT DECISION-MAKING

Whatever the career and education decision, there is no one-size-fits-all decision-making strategy. Two people facing the same decision are going to approach it differently and likely elect to follow different paths—even if it is toward the same goal.

Consider the simple task of purchasing a tube of toothpaste. Different people apply different personal attributes and characteristics to their purchase. One buyer retrieves their favorite brand from the shelf and heads for the checkout counter. A second buyer, possessing a discount coupon, decides to try that brand. A third buyer enters the store, sees a display for a toothpaste brand right next to the checkout counter, and makes a speedy purchase.

All three buyers are doing the same thing—purchasing a tube of toothpaste. Buyer #1 expresses loyalty and trust by going with a brand used consistently over time. Buyer #2 displays thrift in selecting a brand that is on sale or less expensive with the coupon. The last, Buyer #3, sees an opportunity to get their toothpaste from a convenient display, pay for it, and exit quickly, thereby minimizing time in the store. Each is displaying a value associated with their personality and behaving accordingly.

Another example of options driving people to employ their decision-making skills and attitudes is the popular Baskin Robbins ice cream stores, where the consumer has the opportunity to choose among thirty-nine different flavors. Ice cream stores are a great place to watch different decision-makers in action, including the risk takers who experiment with the flavor of the month and the traditional ice cream lover who rarely strays too far from their favorite flavor. With an ice cream cone, the positive or negative consequences are immediate. You like the flavor, or you don't.

PRINCIPLES OF SUCCESSFUL CAREER DECISION-MAKING

Sound decision-making results when a number of basic principles are in place. Adherence with these principles will maximize options and make decision-making more relevant and efficient. Following are thirteen principles that, if followed to some measure, will result in improved decisions:

1. Have a goal, including both career and education objectives.

2. Learn as much as you can about yourself.

3. Learn as much as you can about options and choices.

4. Determine "fit" when choosing a career or education path.

5. Create a path toward your career goal and objective and make decisions to get you to the first destination, next destination, and, ultimately, the full goal.

6. Learn as much as you can about the employment marketplace where you will eventually work and move about.

7. Create the best tools (i.e., resume, interview skills, etc.) to have in your job search toolbox.

8. Give yourself the appropriate amount of time to consider options and make quality decisions.

9. Minimize the importance of money, prestige, size, and brand, and again look for the best "fit."

10. Make decisions with an appropriate amount of help from family, friends, and educators, but know when those characters become distractions and need to be turned off. Spouses, partners, and others who will be influenced by the results directly should be involved in your decisions.

11. Manage your career and education. Don't let them manage you.

12. Become a lifelong learner by honing your knowledge and skills in the workplace competencies that will enhance options.

13. Refine and grow your career as you move into, though, and eventually, exit it.

THE INFLUENCE OF FREEDOM, POWER, AND CONTROL OVER DECISION-MAKING

Freedom, power, and control are elements of decision-making. You need to know that each exists, and refuse to relinquish them at any time. Freedom during adolescence expands in young adulthood and matures when schooling ends and you enter the workforce. Students have a reasonable measure of freedom, similar to that of single young adults. Married workers and those with dependents have less freedom to make decisions when the consequences influence others.

Another factor that influences freedom for many is debt. Paying off college student loans is often inhibiting. It can limit graduate school options and force you to consider job decisions differently than if you were free of debt. As you get older, the responsibilities of life (i.e., caring for senior parents, grandparenting, etc.) can also have a significant influence on freedom.

If you begin and proceed through adulthood with a full recognition of the power you have as a decision-maker and the control you possess in determining direction, you become an effective career manager. If you abdicate your control or abuse the power, you will likely find yourself somewhere you don't want to be, doing something you never intended to do.

EXAMPLES OF DECISION-MAKING MISTAKES

Following are a number of mistakes cited by working adults discussing unhappiness with the outcome of their decision-making experiences. Some of these mistakes occur while you are a student. Some arise when you enter the workforce. Some happen in both environments.

- This job isn't me—Failure to factor self-awareness into the decision-making process.

- I didn't even know that major even existed—Failure to base decision on good information.

- Everyone was applying there—Following the crowd and doing what others are doing.

- I felt pressure to make a decision—Deciding too fast and/or procrastinating too long.

- Wrong school studying the wrong subject—Lack of or faulty exploration of education options.

- I'm lost in this place—Failure to investigate school or work setting/environment.

- My job is taking me nowhere—Breakdown in examination of growth opportunities.

- If I had only known then what I know now—Jumping in over your head.

- But the salary looked great—Reliance on a single element in making the decision.

- I'm not getting any interviews—Failure to create an effective resume or use good search tools.

- How did I get here?—Clueless about how decision was made or who made it.

- Why are these things happening to me?—Loss of control and power.

- No one would tell me what to do—Abdicating a responsibility that is totally yours.

- This process is wearing me out—Inappropriate use of human energy.

- Every day gets worse than the day before—Imprisoned by lack of exit options.

- This job is killing my personal life—Failure to address and control life–work balance issues.

- I feel like a ship without a rudder—Failure to use professional counselors and other career helpers.

While the above circumstances represent some you have already faced or may face in the future, the list is not exhaustive, and you will likely be able to add a couple of your own.

STRAIGHT TALK ABOUT MAKING GOOD DECISIONS

Approach all decisions using a systematic model for quality decision-making. Your model should include achieving the necessary level of self-awareness, gathering all appropriate information, and determining and prioritizing options. It concludes when the decision is made and then evaluated over time.

Quality decisions must be personal decisions, not a rush to join the masses in the most popular path selection. The oft quoted words from the Robert Frost poem—"Two roads diverged in a wood, and I . . . I took the one less traveled"—humanizes the need to express one's individuality in their decision-making.

Fully understand the power and control you have over your personal career destiny and never relinquish either. Make your personal decisions, taking into account the energy, time, money, and ego that you must invest, but also be cognizant of the effect your decisions may have on others.

Refine your personal decision-making model as you grow and develop and apply it throughout life in all career and education decisions.

CHAPTER 3

Challenge: Conducting Effective Searches at Every Career Stage

If you don't know where you are going, you might wind up someplace else.

—YOGI BERRA (1925–2015), ALL-STAR CATCHER FOR THE NEW YORK YANKEES, MANAGER OF THE NEW YORK METS, AND MEMBER OF THE MAJOR LEAGUE BASEBALL HALL OF FAME

MODERN TECHNOLOGY HAS CHANGED THE WAY PEOPLE STUDY THEMselves and the world of work, acquire occupational knowledge and skill sets, and then move through the various transitions that must be navigated during the career development process.

The ability to conduct a good search is an essential behavior that you must perform at any number of points throughout your career development process. A failure to conduct a thorough search will inhibit or limit options and result in career blindness.

The range of searches you will face will vary from what occupation or field you want to select as your life's work to where you will study to acquire the knowledge or skills needed in that occupation to where the job opportunities exist once you are ready for employment. Searches occur at all stages in the career development process, from the initial ones that will start you off in the world of work to those that will continue across the life span and ensure your career growth, mobility, and maintenance.

CHALLENGES OF A GOOD SEARCH

If there was ever a place where the "tip of the iceberg" metaphor was applicable, it most certainly can be seen in searching for career and education options. Explorers are likely to be limited initially by their worldview and life experiences. The colleges you know about are the ones that are local or have a national reputation or possibly one that a friend or family member attended.

The career exposures you have had are also limiting. The teacher, physician, salesclerk, television news reporter, and FedEx delivery agent are visible because your path has intersected with theirs on countless occasions. Less visible, like the underwater mass of the iceberg, are careers like cytotechnologist, gaffer, actuary, shipwright, and hundreds of others.

Even more daunting, because any visibility will have been recent, are careers like transcultural anthropologist, analytics engineer, and sustainability czar that are just emerging. Finally, there are those occupations for which there are not many inhabitants like oil well firefighters, CEOs (of anything), college presidents, and professional athletes. Regarding the latter, while more than 551,000 boys and girls played basketball at more than 1,850 U.S. high schools in a recent year, any of those athletes with professional ambitions would have been vying for positions on just thirty National Basketball Association (NBA) and twelve Women's National Basketball Association (WNBA) teams. Looking at occupations and careers requires an assessment of how competitive those positions are and just how many or few people will get to them.

In addition to the emergence of new careers, explorers have to contend with new titles being established for old ones. The secretary of yesteryear is the administrative assistant of today. The same is true for librarian who is now the media specialist and the bartender who today goes by the mixologist title.

Other positions have been retitled to be contemporary in perspective or to make the title gender free as in the firefighter (fireman), flight attendant (stewardess/steward), and sales associate (salesman/saleswoman).

Finally, many firms and businesses have become unusually creative in titling certain occupations as in the food preparer at Subway being called a sandwich artist and receptionist at Houghton Mifflin Harcourt publishing company in Boston now being referred to as the director of first impressions. To avoid heading down the wrong path or eliminating a career or occupation from consideration because it has an unfamiliar name, research is essential.

Another difficulty in conducting a good search is how far you are removed from the occupations you might like to know about and consider. A college student in Nebraska may have an interest in biology or biology-related careers, but how far will she have to travel to see and learn about marine biologists. A person interested in astronomy will have difficulty exploring that field if he doesn't have access to a university or research planetarium.

The nemesis of a good search is "not knowing what you don't know." Paths that are concealed will be paths you may never travel. Whether it is electing where to study, what to study, where to work, or how to fulfill one's potential, that which is out of view will likely never appear among the options you're considering and thereby eliminated from consideration.

CAREER EXPLORATION: AN ART OR A SCIENCE?

Since career exploration is considered by many to be both an art and a science, look first at what that means. Any definition of art will include the elements of creativity, design, and fabrication. Science, on the other hand, is defined as an object of study that is governed by a set of rules. Writing is an excellent example, as good writers are creative and their work is guided by the rules of grammar, spelling, and punctuation. Successful career explorers are the ones that are creative and inventive while following a certain order in conducting or managing their search.

America and the world community afford explorers thousands of education, training, and retraining opportunities leading to countless careers and employment settings. The days of the learner having to go to an institution or campus as their only means of acquiring knowledge and skills have been complemented by internet and IT mechanisms that bring learning to the learner. What we know about careers and education can only be defined as a point-in-time reference to an ever-growing, ever-changing, and complex information universe.

To illustrate the challenges associated with conducting a good search, consider how many children in elementary school at this very moment will prepare for, enter, and pass through occupations and careers that didn't exist the day they started to school. Some occupations like journalist, electrician, and dental hygienist seem to have existed forever. Many have existed over time, but represent ones with which you have had little contact and know little about. Others like app developer, social media manager, data miner, and cloud solution architect are new occupations and destined to be followed by many like them.

Educators are constantly being challenged to prepare their students for the "real world." Similarly, people who are currently unemployed or feel underemployed are constantly searching for whatever knowledge, skills, and competencies will lift them from their plight.

In a never-ending discussion about the attributes needed to be successful in any workplace, some employers have gone on record as suggesting that applicants have generic skills and abilities, rather than specific occupational skills. What generic skills are they talking about? The following skills, often cited by human resource managers, represent the characteristics that are likely to afford you the greatest opportunity in many career fields, including those that have yet to come into view:

- Knowledge generation—Knowing how to question and explain
- Critical and analytical thinking—Reflective reasoning about beliefs and actions
- Problem solving—Using sound methods to arrive at effective solutions
- Networking—Joining with like-minded people to recognize, create, or act upon opportunities
- Flexibility—Adapting to challenges and changes as they are introduced in the work and the workplace, as well as the ability to work independently or unconventionally should the need arise

- Written and oral communication skill—Competence at using the written and spoken word to interact with colleagues, clients/consumers, and the general public
- Leading and teaming—Recognizing personal strengths and those of others and blending for the good of the cause
- Teaching—Facility for causing something to be learned by others
- Cultural sensitivity—Awareness of and ability to work in a diverse environment
- Entrepreneurism, drive, and self-regulation—Independent inner force that leads to task, job, occupation, and career success
- Curiosity and imagination—Ability often described as thinking "outside the box"
- Technology understanding and application—Command of the technological tools of the present and future
- Global awareness—Interests that have no geographic border or planetary restrictions
- Commitment to career growth—Engaging in learning, experimentation, and investigatory behaviors that confirm your ambition to be the best at what you do

Just as these characteristics are welcomed in the contemporary workplace, equally important is keeping a watchful eye toward the future so as to identify and master what the occupations of tomorrow are going to require for entry and progression to career growth and satisfaction.

The skills identified above represent the personal attributes that are needed in many work environments today, talents that employers, managers, and supervisors would like to see in candidates for employment and promotion. The more of them that the individual worker possesses, the greater their chance of moving into and upward in existing and emerging careers.

People who possess these skills have to convey or demonstrate their presence before and during the job search or change process. Work this information into the resume, application, and cover letter and encourage references to speak of your unique skills when contacted by employers. When an opportunity presents itself during the interview, weave any thoughts about your skills into the questions you are asked and the discussion that is occurring. Be prepared to cite examples of how and where you have applied the skill previously.

Viewed from another perspective, the occupations and careers of the future—the ones that haven't been created yet—are going to demand an assortment of skills for entry and progression.

Some educators, including those who want schools and colleges to do more to get students ready for the workplace, are suggesting that students not prepare for occupations or careers, but rather with skills and competencies that allow the skill possessor to move directly into new occupations and careers as they are emerging.

LIMITING SEARCHES TO THE COMFORABLE AND THE KNOWN

If, as an explorer, you limit yourself to career and education options that you feel comfortable with or the ones that are known to you, an incredible number of options are taken off the table. Never allow your searches to be conducted within such boundaries. Step out and seek information about the unfamiliar and the unknown. Chapter 4 will present a number of new and emerging careers that you may wish to consider.

Beyond limiting your occupation and career search, examining only the comfortable and known means that many education and training options will never be considered as well. Remove any blinders and considerable a variety of education paths to the world of work.

SEARCHING ACCORDING TO A SET OF RULES

Whatever the search, adherence to the following rules will produce the best results.

Allow sufficient time to conduct an effective search

No search, whether career, education, or employment, can be done haphazardly, recklessly, or "on the fly." Allow whatever time is needed to do what needs to be done and then maintain a calendar that produces positive results. The architecture of every search begins with a blueprint or plan and a milestone calendar for accomplishing every task.

Look beyond the obvious and familiar

The circumstance that will eliminate more options than you may wish to purge is restricting the size and scope of your examination of careers. Horse owners often use blinders to restrict the animal's vision and minimize distractions. Don't look into your future the same way. Remove any blinders and don't be afraid to "think outside the box." Occasionally put the blinders back on as you narrow choices and make decisions.

Involve others in the process

Anyone conducting a career search will find signals like the growth, decline, and sustainability of occupations and the emergence of new ones throughout the world around them. Proponents of involving others in the search process support the use of "shadowing" experiences where explorers engage in the casual pursuit of information and in internships where the experience becomes more formal. Utilizing workplace and education networks (formal and informal) and maintaining active membership in professional and trade organizations are outstanding mechanisms for engaging others in the search process. And don't minimize what you can learn from friends, family, and educators.

Take the competition pulse throughout the process

The Bureau of Labor Statistics (BLS) of the U.S. Department of Labor does an excellent job of keeping the nation informed about workplace competition via the *Occupational Outlook Handbook* (http://www.bls.gov/ooh). The profiles featured here cover hundreds of occupations and offer detailed occupational descriptions, work environment summaries, and compensation information to name a few. Each profile also includes BLS employment outlook projections and anticipated changes for that occupation for the 2020–2030 decade.

Use the professional assistance of counselors and recruiters

There is a vast pipeline of professional people whose work is devoted to helping others with theirs. These helpers range from the counselor in the education setting (school or college) to the human resource expert in an employee assistance program to a recruiting specialist, sometimes referred to as a "headhunter," with a general or setting-specific (i.e., engineering, health and medicine, information science, etc.) search firm. Each can play a role in searches for entry occupations, as well as offer guidance for those examining later career options.

Use good resources (human and nonhuman) to gather information

Every search you conduct demands that you absorb as much as you can about the careers being performed in the world before you, the education and training needed to enter those careers, and the settings or environments in which the work is conducted. Information acquired through experiential learning can play a vital role in setting goals and direction and taking important steps into your career future.

To do this you must identify and use the best human (i.e., people, educators, counselors, people practicing the occupation, etc.) and nonhuman (i.e., publications, guides, websites, DVDs, personal assessment inventories, etc.) resources available. And all of these resources have to be current, accurate, and free of bias.

Relate self-knowledge to career and education knowledge

Astute counselors will often tell you that the first stop in the search process is to stand before a mirror. Who are you? What to do you like and what are your preferences? What are you able to do now or willing to learn? What are your short-term and long-term career goals? The answers to these and other questions will serve as the foundation for an effective search.

Act affirmatively and realistically

Sorry, but this has to be said. Approach every search from a "glass is half full" perspective and remain positive throughout, even when setbacks occur. Should rejection or difficulty occur, continue to act resolutely and resist adopting a "the world is against me" posture. Searchers possessing an affirmative and realistic sense of personal awareness stand the greatest chance of success.

Now that you've examined the rules of conducting an effective search, consider the various places where those guidelines must be applied. Over the course of your life, you will need to conduct one or more—some multiple times—of the following searches:

- Long-term career choices
- Education or training programs that will prepare you for occupation entry or reentry
- Employment once you are ready to go to work
- Learning opportunities that will add to your occupational knowledge and enhance your skill set
- Employment adjustment should you become the victim of job loss, obsolescence, or furlough
- Employment to ensure your growth, mobility, or need to change

A poor career choice may place you in a dead-end position that feels more like prison than a career. If you conduct a lousy education or training search, you are likely to enroll somewhere where you won't be successful academically or will hate every minute while you are struggling to be successful. If this mistake carries over to the job search process, it can be even more destructive. You may not find a job you like, and worse, you may not find a job.

THE IMPORTANCE OF NUMBERS TO CAREER EXPLORERS AND JOB CHANGERS

Your brain could become numb reading the pages and pages of statistics that the U.S. Department of Labor and Census Bureau generate about the workforce and opportunities that exist now and are projected for the future. The appendix contains a selected number of the statistics and projections that may be useful to the career explorer or job changer. Included are lists of the most populated occupations, largest career groupings, fastest growing occupations, and occupations expected to decline.

SEARCHES OCCUR AND THEN REOCCUR

You've conducted a good career search, spent the appropriate time acquiring occupational knowledge and skills, and are now ready for entry level placement. You've spent minimal time in your occupation and now are ready to seek growth and advancement via a new position. Your career or occupation comes to an abrupt halt for any variety of reasons (i.e., recession related downsizing, termination, etc.), and you need to search for a "bridge" job to sustain you or get you to the next reasonable position on your career path. Each of the preceding circumstances sends you into a new search mode, one that has you looking for a place in the work world that will permit entry and passage to a point of satisfaction.

STRAIGHT TALK ABOUT CONDUCTING AN EFFECTIVE SEARCH

Become a lifelong student of the workplace, devote whatever time is required, and learn the tasks that must be performed to conduct an effective search. Learn how to examine your personal abilities and traits and conduct periodic assessments to keep up with who you are today.

Be careful not to overaspire (i.e., aim beyond your abilities and aptitudes) or underaspire (i.e., not take all of your interests, preferences, and talents into account) as you conduct the search. Become of student of the search process. Reflect on every good search that you conduct and be prepared to put that learning to work when you face the future searches you are certain to encounter.

CHAPTER 4

Challenge: Broadening Career and Occupational Knowledge

You miss 100% of the shots you don't take.

—WAYNE GRETZKY, FORMER NATIONAL HOCKEY LEAGUE
PLAYER, COACH, AND HOLDER OF THE ALL-TIME PROFESSIONAL
HOCKEY SCORING RECORDS. KNOWN AS "THE GREAT ONE," HE
PLAYED TWENTY SEASONS FOR FOUR NHL TEAMS.

THE INITIAL MISCALCULATION THAT MANY PEOPLE MAKE IN THEIR career or occupational search is to look at the future from a point that is far too narrow. At a time when you should open your future to a world of opportunities and new things, too many limit their searches to things they already know something about. Career explorers must do a great deal of digging to unearth the invisible occupations and careers that were mentioned in chapter 3. A mining technique used by many is to focus on clusters of occupations that make up a specific career group, rather than examining a specific occupation like engineer, graphic artist, journalist, or medical technician.

Following is a list of the twenty career clusters, originally developed by the U.S. Department of Education and then refined by other organizations and agencies, that group hundreds of different occupations into clusters. For each cluster, the reader will find a sampling of the representative occupations, as well as a number of new and emerging careers.

CAREER CLUSTERS

Advertising, marketing, and public relations

Representative occupations: Advertising director, commercial artist, image consultant, graphic designer, market analyst, media representative, opinion pollster, publicist, and technical writer.

New or emerging occupations: Consumer connection director, global marketing consultant, mass target developer, product/service evaluation specialist, social networking analyst, and survey researcher.

Agriculture, food, and natural resources

Representative occupations: Agricultural engineer, agriculture inspector, agriscience educator, agroforestry engineer, agronomist, blacksmith, commodity broker, crop duster, farmer, greenhouse manager, livestock production manager, purchasing agent/buyer, seed production specialist, veterinarian, and veterinary technician.

New and emerging occupations: Animal geneticist, aquatic farming engineer, plant breeder, storage and hygiene officer, and supply chain operations coordinator.

Architecture, building, and construction

Representative occupations: Architect, building engineer, building inspector, carpenter, civil engineer, construction engineer, cost estimator, electrician, heating and ventilation technician, landscape architect, plumber/pipefitter, and surveyor.

New and emerging occupations: Energy efficiency engineer, historic preservation engineer, restoration engineer, and space utilization specialist.

Arts, entertainment, and humanities

Representative occupations: Actor, actress, animator, artist, camera operator, casting director, cinematographer, choreographer, conductor, director, graphic designer, illustrator, lighting technician, musician, photographer, producer, publicist, and sound technician.

New and emerging occupations: A and R (artist and repertoire) administrator, festival manager, grants specialist, and video game developer.

Banking, finance, and investments

Representative occupations: Accountant, actuary, appraiser, auditor, bank manager, broker, budget analyst, commercial loan processer, controller, consumer loan manager, credit analyst, foreclosure manager, investment adviser, mortgage loan processor, real estate appraiser, securities analyst, teller, and underwriter.

New and emerging occupations: Compliance officer, forecast analyst, and index analyst.

Business, management, and administration

Representative occupations: Accountant, administrative assistant, auditor, billing and coding specialist, business machine technician, chief executive officer, chief financial officer, customer service representative, entrepreneur/independent business owner, human resource director, office manager, and systems analyst.

New and emerging occupations: Acquisitions tax manager, business risk consultant, chief learning officer, employee wellness coordinator, ethics officer, teleconferencing director, and workforce compensation specialist.

Communications and media

Representative occupations: Broadcast technician, camera operator, cartoonist, editor, interpreter, newspaper reporter, photographer, proofreader, television/radio reporter, sound/audio technician, videographer, video editor, and writer.

New and emerging occupations: Satellite telecommunications engineer, social media developer, strategic communications manager, and video service technician.

Education and training

Representative occupations: Educational technology specialist, ESL educator, instructional assistant, librarian/media specialist, principal, professor, psychometrician, school counselor, school psychologist, and teacher.

New and emerging occupations: Curriculum integration specialist, distance learning/remote education manager, education assessment consultant, grant writer, and school or college safety/security director.

Environment

Representative occupations: Air quality scientist, demographer, forester, forestry technician, geologist, meteorologist, oceanographer, park ranger, soil scientist, and water treatment plant operator.

New and emerging occupations: Conservation officer, energy efficiency and solutions engineer, sustainable landscape designer, and wildlife rescuer.

Government and public administration

Representative occupations: Archivist, assessor, cartographer, city/town manager, civil engineer, demographer, economist, foreign service officer, home economist, judge, librarian, mental health counselor, military officer, noncommissioned military specialist, postal worker, public health officer, and urban planner.

New and emerging occupations: Federal relations manager, federal grant administrator, and government business development specialist.

Health and medicine

Representative occupations: Audiologist, biochemist, biomedical engineer, dental hygienist, dentist, dietitian, EEG technician, EKG technician, epidemiologist, health services administrator, home health aides, hospital administrator, laboratory technician, medical assistant, medical illustrator, medical librarian, medical technician, nurse, optician, optometrist, orderly, pharmacist, physician, physician's assistant, physical therapist, podiatrist, radiological technician, rehabilitation counselor, and surgeon.

New and emerging occupations: Cardiac perfusionist, diagnostic radial sonographer, environmental health nurse, health counselor, diagnostic medical sonographer, medical research analyst, and medical science liaison.

Hospitality, leisure, and tourism
Representative occupations: Athletic (golf, tennis, etc.) professional, camp director, chef, concierge, curator, flight attendant, hotel manager, maître d', museum educator, security manager, spa/recreation director, tour director/guide, travel agent and waiter/waitress.

New and emerging occupations: Gaming facilities manager, seasonal recreational facilities manager, senior exercise specialist, and theme park designer.

Human and social services
Representative occupations: Anthropologist, career counselor, day care director, marriage and family therapist, priest/minister/rabbi, psychologist, social worker, and youth activity director.

New and emerging occupations: Bereavement and hospice counselor, futurist, transcultural anthropologist, and volunteer coordinator.

Information technology
Representative occupations: Artificial intelligence engineer, computer equipment technician, data entry technician, data miner, IT technician, programmer, systems engineer, and webmaster/designer.

New and emerging occupations: Artificial intelligence specialist, cloud solution architect, computer security specialist, data securing engineer, fiber optics technician, data mining specialist, social media architect, and wireless communications specialist.

Law, corrections, safety, and security
Representative occupations: ATF (Alcohol, Tobacco, Firearms and Explosives) agent, CIA (Central Intelligence Agency) agent, corrections officer, court stenographer, emergency medical technician, FBI (Federal

Bureau of Investigation) agent, firefighter, forensic scientist, paralegal assistant, police officer, security officer, U.S. customs agent, and warden.

New and emerging occupations: Crime scene investigator, DNA technician, and forensic psychologist.

Manufacturing and industry

Representative occupations: Assembler, ceramic engineer, chemist, designer, distribution manager, equipment operator/technician, industrial engineer, machinist, manufacturing engineer, mechanical engineer, metallurgist, millwright, occupational health/safety inspector, pattern maker, quality control engineer, production manager, purchasing agent, safety engineer, test technician, and tool and die maker.

New and emerging occupations: Automation and robotics engineer, merging markets manager, resident assessment specialist, sustainability engineer, and utilization review coordinator.

Personal services

Representative occupations: Attorney, caterer, counselor, florist, hairstylist, interior decorator, mortician, personal trainer, and realtor.

New and emerging occupations: Image consultant, music/dance therapist, personal nutritionist, personal shopper, self-education teacher, and senior care attendant.

Sales and service

Representative occupations: Advertising representative, cashier, credit analyst/officer, customer service representative, inventory control specialist, purchasing agent, retail/wholesale facility manager, and retail/wholesale salesperson.

New and emerging occupations: Call center agent, customer service engineer, logistician, purchasing pattern analyst, product supply engineer, and territory miner.

Science, technology, engineering, and mathematics

Representative occupations: Actuary, anthropologist, astronaut, astronomer, biologist, botanist, chemist, entomologist, geographer, geophysicist, laboratory technician, mathematician, meteorologist, research scientist, and technical writer.

New and emerging occupations: Bioinformatics scientist, biostatistician, data analytics specialist, and space psychologist.

Transportation and distribution

Representative occupations: Aeronautical engineer, airport facility manager, air traffic controller, cartographer, chauffeur, dispatcher, distribution engineer, driver, flight attendant, flight operations director, inventory analyst, navigator, pilot, safety engineer, shipping director, TSA (Transportation Security Administration) agent, and warehouse manager.

New and emerging occupations: Digital inventory analyst, parabolic engineer, and safety systems analyst.

Note: The occupations identified above have been placed in the cluster where they represent a significant number of employment opportunities. In reality, many of the newly created positions (i.e., director of remote operations, webmaster, etc.) are emerging in multiple career clusters and settings.

CURRENT CAREER CONCENTRATION

You may have observed that many of the new and emerging careers are situated in the science, technology, engineering, and math (STEM) fields; the health and medical professions; and personal and health care work. There are multiple causes for this concentration. First, the information and technology revolution has had a tremendous impact on career creation. Second, because the demographic trends show people living and remaining active longer, there is a greater need for health, social, cultural, education, and related services to respond to their needs. Finally, the work performed by "first responders" across the world of work has been the subject of considerable and deserved attention during recent times, a factor that has influenced their popularity.

Do not consider the preceding groupings to be an exhaustive list of occupations for the cluster. While the entire list may seem overwhelming at first, the mix of existing and new careers in each field is designed to get you to think about clusters and work environments, rather than occupations, in the beginning. Your personal research is certain to discover many more.

MOVING FROM CAREER CLUSTERS TO AN OCCUPATION EXAMINATION

Later in part 1 (chapter 6), strategies will be presented for you to use in getting answers to your occupational questions. The career cluster examination provided broad, basic information, and you are ready to dig deeper into the various clusters to identify specific occupations.

There are twelve "core" research areas that will help you create a profile for any occupation you are examining. Don't rest until you have answered every question that is important to you. Also, remember that occupations bearing the same title (i.e., chemical engineer, civil engineer, environmental engineer, etc.) are performed in different work settings. Each could generate a slightly different profile.

The research areas that should guide your study of occupations include:

1. Nature of the work or role definition—What is the general nature of the work? What are the duties or responsibilities of people performing this occupation?

2. Settings where work is performed—In what work environments (i.e., hospitals, education institutions, retail outlets, manufacturing centers, etc.) are you most likely to find this occupation? Could this occupation be performed under a telecommuting arrangement?

3. Worker characteristics and traits—What are the individual characteristics or personality traits most commonly associated with people who perform this occupation?

4. Location—Are these occupations more likely to be found in a concentrated region (i.e., Southeastern states, Silicon Valley of California, etc.) or in a particular community type (i.e., urban, rural, university setting, etc.) of the country or dispersed across the globe?

5. Education and training—What are the traditional or typical education paths to this occupation? Can you prepare for entry through any other route? To what extent are internships and related work experiences a part of the education and training process?

6. Supply and demand—How much competition (current or future) exists for people in this occupation?

7. Change potential—Is this a volatile occupation and more subject to change than others? How will technology impact people in this occupation in both the short and long term?

8. Credentials and requirements—Does this occupation have any special requirements (i.e., licensing or certification, physical strength, education attainment level, etc.)?

9. Compensation—How are people in this occupation compensated? Beyond salary and benefits, does this occupation present any unique benefits (i.e., travel opportunity, tuition assistance program, on-the-job training, etc.)?

10. Opportunities for career growth and mobility—Will meritorious achievements and length of service (seniority) result in both tangible and intangible benefits? Do career lattices and ladders exist?

11. Career relationships—What occupations are similar to this one? Who do people in this occupation interface with on a regular basis?

12. Life–work balance—Will this occupation present the work and nonwork conditions that will allow you to achieve the life–work balance you desire? Are or will there be opportunities to modify schedules and time commitments and to disengage as you grow older and see retirement in your future?

Several hundred career profiles or descriptions have been prepared in a manner similar to this one and are contained in the online edition of the *Occupational Outlook Handbook* of the U.S. Department of Labor.

Career explorers will find this valuable resource at http://www.bls.gov/
ooh/.

STRAIGHT TALK ABOUT THE IDENTIFICATION
OF CAREERS

The identification of your future occupation and career is something
that is going to require both your formal and informal attention. Start
by examining the big picture and consider the use career clusters as the
launch point for your research. As you gather information and refine your
interests, move on to the study of specific occupations.

Determine the characteristics and conditions required of your future
occupation and career and use the questions you create to filter the information you are gathering. Take whatever time is required to conduct a
comprehensive search. Use quality information as your compass to navigate your way through the maze of information you will undoubtedly
encounter.

CHAPTER 5

Challenge: Seizing Education, Training, and Retraining Opportunities

A career is something that you train for and prepare for and plan on doing for a long time.

—Sonia Maria Sotomayor, Associate Justice of the Supreme Court of the United States and the Court's first Hispanic and third female justice

The path to every career or occupation passes through doors of one or more schools, colleges, graduate schools, or career training programs. These may include an apprenticeship program in boatbuilding at a maritime institute on the coast of Maine, a series of courses in childcare at a Virginia community college, a baccalaureate or graduate degree program in business at a California university, an employer/industry-based certificate in information management with the Microsoft Corporation, or a professional degree in medicine from the Penn State College of Medicine. The education and training possibilities open to you are limitless.

Increasingly, job seekers and changers are being queried about the skills they possess more than the degrees, diplomas, certificates, and other badges that have been traditionally used to determine readiness and suitability for employment. Human resource managers at firms like Amazon, Apple, Google, IBM, J. P. Morgan, Verizon, and Walmart are placing greater emphasis on skill set evidence when screening applicants.

This emphasis on competency has employers seeking to measure the knowledge and skill set competence possessed by candidates for employment and what, if any, additional learning will ease the onboarding process and maximize the performance and productivity of the new hire. The less time it takes to bring the new hire to maximum performance and productivity the better.

Similar demand for education and training were inspired by the coronavirus pandemic. Even when occupational roles remained for the most part intact during the COVID-19–driven workplace shakeup, many firms, institutions, agencies, and organizations had to engage in emergency training exercises for employees to learn and master the techniques and tools they would be required to use when the traditional workplaces were abandoned. Likewise, training or "refresher" courses were installed in many instances to combat any "learning loss" brought on by furloughs and other pandemic work interruptions experienced by the workforce.

A CAREER CONSTANT: LIFELONG LEARNING

If there has been one dramatic shift in how work, workers, and workplaces are different today, it might be the early and ongoing emphasis on continuing education as a mechanism for employers to use to sustain a competent roster of employees.

Readers who have already passed through the basic education (sometimes referred to a preservice) pathway to employment are going to find lifelong learning a constant in their personal career growth and maintenance. Similarly, job changers may face learning and study challenges in their path to maximum mobility. Even the individual approaching retirement and wanting to start a small business may need to engage in the study of business ownership and management practices. There is no avoiding it—education and training are in your future and you are going to be a student again many times.

THE RELATIONSHIP OF EDUCATION AND TRAINING TO CAREERS

Education explorers at every point in their personal career development have an incredible amount of control over the choice process, a factor that is not understood by some and not acted upon by others. A veteran college admission officer once remarked that there are ultimately four decisions made when choosing from education and training options.

The choices of where to explore, where to apply, and where to enroll if accepted are in the hands of the student. The college, school, or training entity decides what students it wishes to admit. The same applies to all forms of education and training and at every level of preparation.

How important is education to job, occupation, or career? A recent CIRP Freshman Survey conducted annually by Higher Education Research Institute (HERI) at UCLA reported that students consider their own learning and future career opportunities very important reasons to go to college. Specifically, the respondents ranked the following reasons the most important: Learning more about things that interest them (87 precent), ability to get a better job (82 precent), gaining a general education and appreciation of ideas (80 percent), and getting training in a specific career (76 percent). The most recent findings of the HERI Freshman Survey can be found at https://www.heri.ucla.edu/infographics/TFS-2020-Infographic.pdf.

As a student or employed individual, you must respect the power that you possess in giving direction and taking action in any education or training decision. Like other searches, timing is a critical factor in gaining and maintaining personal control. By starting early, allocating appropriate attention to all of the information-gathering, decision-making, and application-filing tasks, you are exercising the type of control that will produce the best results.

If there is a preamble for the education search process, it is that rarely is there a single education and training route to your learning objective. There will most likely be many, and searching for perfection will be a very challenging exercise.

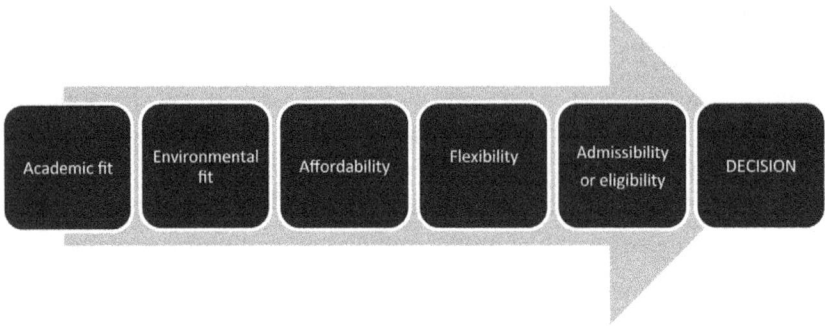

Figure 5.1 Factors That Influence Education Decisions

FACTORS THAT INFLUENCE EDUCATION, TRAINING, AND RETRAINING DECISIONS

A number of factors should be used to examine education and training options. Used properly, they will result in quality learning and study decisions. They include the following.

Academic fit

Since education institutions and training programs differ, fit means being challenged and being able to meet the challenge. Don't place yourself in an educational environment where you will simply coast along with little difficulty, and don't bind yourself to the constant pressure about whether you're going to succeed or fail. Academic or study fit should be your number one criterion in the selection of any education or training experience.

Environmental fit

Choosing a college or training program is often like looking for a new home. For those going to college or graduate school, a college campus is going to be your home for a significant portion of the foreseeable future. Try to find an environment where you will feel comfortable as a citizen, a place that presents the social, cultural, and lifestyle comforts that you desire. Find a place that meets your career aspirations and needs and don't spin your wheels looking for the "perfect" fit. The important element here is to look for things you want and things you want to avoid. When you find the right balance in those elements, you probably have found an education or training option worthy of a closer look.

Affordability

The cost of college or graduate school and most focused career training programs today cannot be dismissed as a factor in the selection process, but you should attempt to separate financial issues, to the extent possible, in the early stages of the search process and focus on the other elements affecting your decision. Certainly, affordability will have an impact on students already burdened with debt or possessing personal and family responsibilities that limit decision-making. It has also been put forward as one of the reasons college enrollments have dipped during the coronavirus pandemic.

Many employers support education and training by offering tuition reimbursement programs to reduce or eliminate costs. These programs usually require the student to show evidence of satisfactory completion of their studies and may require the participating employee to sign an agreement to continue their service for a period of time following their experience or reimburse the employer for the costs of their education.

Before dismissing a college, graduate school, or career training opportunity from consideration in the exploration process, you should gather as much information as is available about all forms of financial aid. This includes scholarships, fellowships, work-study programs, internships, and employee assistance programs.

Student loans for education purposes may also represent a viable option for those students requiring financial assistance to engage in their postsecondary education studies. Student borrowing, however, has become a subject of national concern, as loan debt is producing negative effects on borrowers entering and proceeding through the world of work.

Students at any educational level are encouraged to seek the guidance of trusted financial advisors and financial aid officers in order to proceed sensibly and cautiously in their borrowing behaviors.

Borrowers may be eligible for loan forgiveness programs if their study leads to a career or occupation in an area of high need or demand or they elect to work in a geographic area (i.e., inner city, rural region, etc.)

where significant worker shortages exist. When all financial aid options are considered, some schools and study programs, which first appear unaffordable, may in fact be more reasonably priced than you thought.

Flexibility

If you are currently working and looking at the possibility of mixing graduate study, college study, or career training opportunities with your demanding work schedule, flexibility is going to be an important factor. It will affect what you will study, where you will study, and just how deep you will be able to jump into the education experience. In some instances, employers offer schedule flexibility or leave that permits employees to engage in external studies that will add to their occupational knowledge and skills.

Many colleges and training programs recognize the needs of working learners and have adapted their programs (i.e., class schedules, web-based distance learning opportunities, etc.) to accommodate employed individuals. A growing number of higher education institutions, especially community colleges, now offer campus daycare services for parents that want to continue their studies.

Admissibility or eligibility

One of the things you will learn in your exploration of education, training, and retraining options is how you "match up" with the requirements for admission or eligibility for participation. Try to create a profile of existing students or training program participants and how closely you resemble them in your academic and experiential characteristics. Otherwise, you may be "chasing windmills" like Don Quixote. When you mirror the academic and personal characteristics of previously enrolled students, you will likely be regarded as admissible or eligible.

GETTING ANSWERS TO EDUCATION, TRAINING, AND RETRAINING QUESTIONS

When exploring education and training options, you will have an opportunity to ask a lot of questions in order to find the opportunities that meet the academic, environmental, financial, and flexibility requirements that you've determined to be important. The decision whether to apply will be tied directly to the information that is collected and the impressions that are made during this evaluative process.

TYPES OF INSTITUTIONS AND TRAINING PROGRAMS

Just as there are a limitless number of career opportunities for you to consider, a significant number of learning venues will prepare you for entry and movement within them. When you consider the full assortment of education, training, and retraining opportunities, you'll understand why it is so important to do a good job of exploring.

After high school, you can continue your education at a four-year college or university, a two-year community, junior or technical college, or a specialized career or vocational institute. Later on, you may wish to pursue additional study at a graduate or professional school. While you are working, there may be opportunities to return to higher education for specific career-oriented study, and you may also elect to participate in industry (e.g., Amazon, Microsoft, etc.) or professional and trade association (e.g., American Bar Association, National League of Nursing, National Association of Realtors, etc.) sponsored training.

As technology applications have emerged and expanded in the ways we live our lives, so have such innovations led to greater variety and number of vehicles for learners to use in their desired educational experiences. When the coronavirus pandemic called for social distancing, schools,

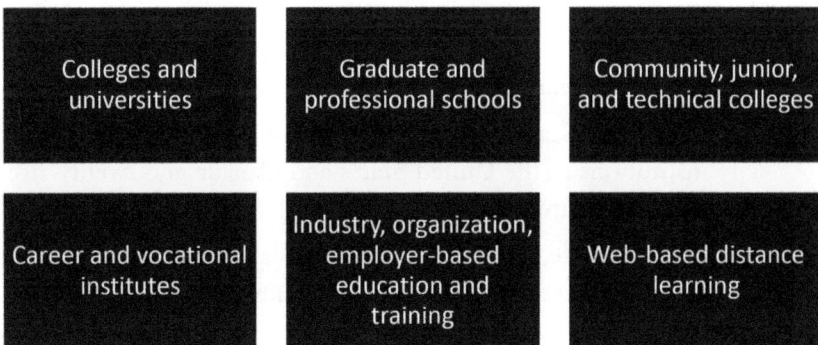

Colleges and universities	Graduate and professional schools	Community, junior, and technical colleges
Career and vocational institutes	Industry, organization, employer-based education and training	Web-based distance learning

Figure 5.2 Types of Education and Training Programs

colleges, and other educational entities of every form turned to remote education as they primary mechanism to address the issue.

In the ensuing period, additional technology applications have been discovered and used by the various types of institutions and training programs engaged in learning and instruction. Distance learning emerged as a solution to a problem and remains as a viable alternative to traditional in-person learning.

Four-year colleges and universities

- Represent approximately 2,000 U.S. four-year colleges and universities.
- Typically prepare graduates in professional studies (e.g., engineering, business, education, information sciences, etc.) or the more general study of liberal arts.
- Majority of four-year institutions are either privately or publicly supported.
- Admission is competitive, meaning students must meet specific institution-defined requirements for entry.
- Bachelors or baccalaureate degree is awarded to students satisfactorily completing four years of study in a defined course of study.
- A growing number of institutions, many that are proprietary or for-profit in structure, are moving into the world of distance learning and offering students the opportunity to earn a degree via the internet.

Graduate and professional schools

- The Council of Graduate Schools represents more than 500 graduate institutions in the United States and Canada and twenty-five international institutions.
- Master's, doctorate, and professional (e.g., law, medicine, veterinary science, etc.) degrees are awarded to students satisfactorily completing a defined course of study.

- Permit degree holders to extend and focus study (e.g., MBA, etc.) following the undergraduate experience.

- Admission is extremely competitive.

- Majority of the graduate and professional schools' function within privately and publicly supported institutions.

- A growing number of graduate schools, especially those at the master's level, present their programs in a manner that makes them available for working students who wish to study part-time.

Two-year community, junior, or technical colleges

- Represent approximately 1,300 U.S. institutions.

- Associate degrees or program of study certificates are awarded to students satisfactorily completing a defined course of study.

- Education programs prepare students to go directly into the workforce or transfer to a four-year institution to complete degree aspirations.

- Situated in local city, community, or regional environments.

- Institutions represent a mix of publicly and privately supported colleges. The number of degree-granting proprietary (for-profit) institutions has grown in recent times.

- Admission is open, but some study areas (i.e., nursing, graphic art, health technologies, etc.) may be more selective than others.

- Programs typically lead to an associate degree or specialized certificate.

Career or vocational institutes

- Represent approximately 9,000 accredited career, technical, and vocational institutions, offering more than 500 specialized courses and 200 career programs.

- The majority of these institutions are proprietary or for-profit in structure.

- Training is focused and varies in duration, from a few weeks to a year or more in length.
- Completion of a course of study often results in the awarding of a certificate by the institution or the preparation for a government-issued license or certificate (i.e., practical nursing, childcare attendant, etc.).
- Admission is open. Some study areas will set enrollment or admission requirements.
- Study is often characterized by a "hands-on" or "learn by doing" approach and may require an internship or field experience.
- Diplomas and/or certificates awarded to students who complete defined programs.

Industry-/organization-/employer-based education and training programs

- Operate to respond to the training and retraining needs of individuals in specific occupations and career fields.
- Many function as formal industry apprenticeship programs and are governed by industry standards with respect to study focus and skills taught.
- Typically award certificates of completion and/or participation.
- Training may be required to sustain employment status or achieve promotion.
- Can be offered by large businesses and firms or by professional and trade organizations.
- May offer education experiences for initial work entry or continuing education for those already in the workplace.
- Completion often results in compensation enhancement and/or promotion opportunities.
- Admission can be both selective and open. In some instances, industry training providers will travel to a particular business and

firm under a contract arrangement to provide on-site or in-house training.

- Some have unique names and identities as in the McDonald's Corporation's "Hamburger University" and the Ringling Bros. and Barnum & Bailey's "Clown College."

Web-based distance learning or remote education opportunities

- These are offered by a variety of postsecondary institutions, professional/trade organizations, corporate entities, and/or combination of sponsors individually or through partnerships and alliances.
- Programs allow students to determine the scope of subjects to be studied, ranging from training in short-term specific topics to comprehensive courses of study leading to certificates and degrees.
- Students can often dictate the pace of the educational experience.
- Employers often allow employees to engage in distance learning activities during work hours.
- Degrees, certificates, and other formal recognitions typically awarded to students meeting study requirements.

CERTIFICATION, LICENSURE, AND EMPLOYER REQUIREMENTS

A considerable number of occupations and careers are governed by certification and licensure requirements that you must adhere to in order to enter and progress in the field. Some require both industry or professional certification and the achievement of a state-issued license. Often, these same credentialing and licensing bodies dictate the continuing education requirements necessary for certificate or license maintenance.

Occupations such as nurses, accountants, teachers, electricians, psychologists, and civil engineers are among the hundreds of occupations for which a certificate or license is required. Other employment requirements are set by the employing body that dictates the proof of knowledge, skills, and competencies that they want in their employees. It should be noted that occupational license requirements are not consistent from state to state and there is no guarantee that a license you attain in Nebraska will be recognized in New Hampshire.

It is important to note that the subject of credentialing is one that educational institutions, employers, and other relevant contributors are examining regularly in order to develop alternative routes to many of the traditional pathways to the world of work. All parties appear to be aimed toward greater flexibility for prospective students while ensuring that professional, trade, and business standards are maintained.

Another issue to consider is whether the institution where you plan to study has been appropriately accredited by the governing body that oversees standards for the preparation of those engaged in a particular career. Ask if both the program and the institution itself are accredited by the appropriate credentialing body. Individuals who study at nonaccredited institutions may find employment difficult or impossible to obtain.

CHARACTERISTICS OF EDUCATION PROVIDERS

Following are a number of questions that you, the student or trainee, should ask as part of your personal exploration. Many of these questions will help you search for college or graduate school opportunities. Others will aid in your selection of a training program that will prepare you for job entry or advancement. The list should not be viewed as exhaustive, and questions are not presented in any kind of priority order.

Program content, academic philosophy, and reputation

- Is the curriculum you wish to study or training program you wish to pursue available?
- What is the reputation of the institution in general and the program (i.e., journalism, engineering, culinary arts, etc.) in particular?
- Is the training program accepted in the field as a viable place to learn or enhance your career and occupational skills?
- Do graduates find good jobs, get promoted, advance into more challenging career areas, and are they admitted to graduate school or extended education pursuits?

- Will you be exposed to the latest tools and technology in your education experiences?
- What are the requirements for graduation or successful completion of the study program?
- Does the institution ascribe to a particular philosophy of teaching or learning that is consistent with your needs and personality?

Admission and eligibility requirements and competition

- How will your abilities, aptitudes, and previous achievements stack up against other applicants and enrolled students?
- How have students with your academic credentials fared in the admission process?
- What is the profile of the typical student or trainee?

Location and setting

- Are you interested in studying or training nearby, in the state or region, or anywhere in the United States or the world?
- How important is the education setting (e.g., open spaces versus high-rise buildings or a "hands-on" work environment)?
- If you are currently working, is the location of the institution or training program reasonably accessible?
- Are there distance learning or remote education vehicles that will serve your needs?

Institutional or training characteristics

- What percentage of admitted students graduate or complete the training program?
- How long does it take to earn a degree or certificate?
- Will the institution or training program meet your immediate and long-range academic and career needs?
- Does the institution offer internship, cooperative learning, or other practical education experiences?

- Will the education or training program requirements mesh with your personal, family, and work responsibilities?
- What is the typical class size?
- Will you be required to study full-time or are part-time programs available?
- Are distance learning options and remote education available and would you consider an online learning experience? How would online study or an online degree be regarded in your chosen career?
- Is the training timetable compatible with your personal and work schedule?

Accommodations

- Are the dormitories and living accommodations comfortable and well furnished?
- Will the food service respond to your dietary needs?
- Can your health, physical fitness, and recreational interests be satisfied?
- Does the institution or training program respond to the needs of commuting students?

Social, cultural, and extracurricular atmosphere

- What social, cultural, and leisure time opportunities are available?
- Do you have interests outside of the classroom (i.e., music, sports, drama, volunteerism, etc.) that you would like to maintain while you study? If so, will the institution, program, or community allow you to pursue those interests?
- Is there a church, synagogue, mosque, or other related congregation on campus or in the community that will satisfy your faith-based interests?

Special needs or considerations

- Can the institution or training program respond to tutorial, counseling, health, or any other needs that you might have?

- Does the campus and surrounding community present a secure living environment?

- If you have any type of disability, can the institution or program accommodate any special needs that require attention?

Cost

- What is the cost of tuition, room and board, enrollment, health benefits, and other fees?

- What financial aid opportunities and education assistance programs exist for which you are eligible?

- How much debt will you have to assume to achieve your education goals?

Many of the above questions look on the surface as the questions you might ask if you are a young adult embarking on your initial postsecondary education experience. Look again, as they are equally important if you're searching for an occupational training program, graduate school, or some other education experience that will occur later in adulthood.

STRAIGHT TALK ABOUT EDUCATION AND TRAINING

Choosing a place to study may be second only to your choice of a career in terms of importance. In truth, those examining college or graduate school opportunities will be choosing a place to live or inhabit over their study years. Whether a college or a training search, try to find an environment where you will feel comfortable as both a student and a citizen, a place that presents the social, cultural, and lifestyle characteristics that you desire.

Don't go looking for Utopia University or Perfect State College. Neither exists for many students. Look for the things you want and things you want to avoid. When you find the right balance in those elements, you probably have found institutions and training programs worthy of a closer look.

Infuse knowledge, skill, and competence that you experience into a lifelong learning scheme. Include in that scheme an occasional recreational learning experience like the study of jazz, knitting, cooking, or American literature. Learning diversions like this are good for your life–work balance.

Resolve that you will do everything within your power to follow the correct learning paths. That means looking at schools, colleges, graduate schools, apprenticeship programs, distance learning, as well as business/corporate and organization training. Once a thorough search has been conducted and a decision has been made, take whatever actions are necessary to enjoy a learning experience that will have a positive effect on your occupation or career.

CHAPTER 6

Challenge: Finding and Using Quality Information

We are drowning in information, but starving for knowledge.

—JOHN NAISBITT (1929–2021), AMERICAN FUTURIST AND
AUTHOR. HIS BOOK, *MEGATRENDS: TEN NEW DIRECTIONS
TRANSFORMING OUR LIVES*, WAS ON THE *NEW YORK TIMES* BEST
SELLER LIST FOR TWO YEARS.

A COMPREHENSIVE CAREER AND EDUCATION SEARCH BEGINS WITH knowing what questions to ask and culminates in collecting the answers and infusing the findings into the decisions that you must make. Before any of this can happen, however, you must identify the sources that will provide the information you need and learn how to use them.

It is possible that you think you know what you want to do in the future right now. You may be right, but that is all the more reason why a thorough examination of the larger list of occupations and careers should be something you should do. If the preferred occupation stands up to the added scrutiny, it will validate the career view you currently hold.

Information will serve as your mirror to the future. Is that you flying that plane, surveying that acreage as a potential building site, or owning that travel business? Are you willing to move to the West Coast or Pacific

Northwest where so many of the information technology and computer systems jobs are located? Does the pressure of meeting deadlines in a field like journalism really mesh well with your personality? Career information will help you in your discovery.

The more you know about careers coupled with what has been presented earlier about what you need to know about yourself will aid in determining options and making optimal choices. Information serves three functions.

By far the greatest use of information in career development is the question-answering function. As you learn about yourself, it is natural to inquire and connect that self-knowledge to careers and occupations. This

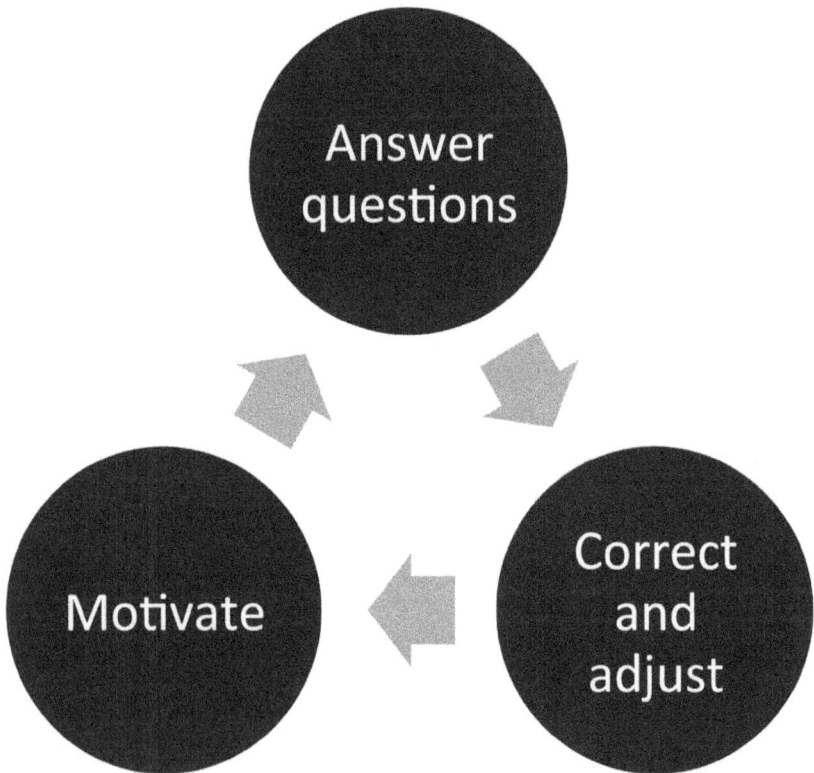

Figure 6.1 Functions of Information in Career Exploration and Decision-Making

requires the discipline of searching for answers from reliable sources and then using what is learned.

The corrective and adjustive function is a bit more complex. As you pass through life, you are exposed to an incredible amount of bad information. Some of it is outdated and no longer relevant. Some of it advances myths and misunderstandings commonly held by people. It wasn't too far back in U.S. history when gender and racial discrimination were omnipresent in the workplace and many occupations were considered "off limits" to women and people of color. Some of those biases and stereotypes linger in our society, and quality information plays a role in correcting and adjusting them.

Finally, information has a motivational function. The more you learn about the world of work, the more you will want to learn. Answers generate new and different questions.

INFORMATION CONTRIBUTES TO QUALITY EXPLORATION AND DECISION-MAKING

Career or occupational research is an essential part of the exploration process. It will take you from a casual understanding of the career to a more detailed and formal view of the work and the people doing it. Along the path to career discovery, you will learn or encounter things that resonate both positively and negatively. That's a sign that the information is teaching and helping.

There are a number of reliable information sources that have been used successfully to gain information that leads to greater career awareness. Regardless of your place in the career development process, any one or combination of the following sources can provide valuable information.

People

Individuals currently working in specific careers can be a source of information to one examining that occupation or cluster of occupations. Interaction with professors and teachers who have sent students off into the workforce can also yield answers to your questions.

Informational interviews and taking the opportunity to "shadow" people in their work settings are the best ways to tap this resource. If people in a given career are employed in different environments (e.g, nurses work in private practice, school, small clinic, laboratory, and large hospital settings), familiarize yourself with as many different variations of the occupation as possible.

Career literature

Guides, directories, and the larger career reference resources like the *Occupational Outlook Handbook* (comprehensive career directory) and the *Occupational Outlook Quarterly* (print and internet magazine) of the U.S. Department of Labor provide a wealth of information about many different careers. The *Occupational Outlook Handbook* was originally intended to help returning veterans after World War II make career and education decisions and has grown to be one of the most widely used career guidance tools in history.

These publications can be found in many school and community libraries or by visiting the Labor Department website (www.dol.gov). These same libraries will also have guides and directories from other publishers. Many popular print and electronic magazines (e.g., *Forbes, AARP Magazine, Inc.*, etc.) and newspapers (e.g., *USA Today, New York Times, Wall Street Journal*, etc.) provide their readers with regular stories about career trends and related matters on a regular basis. A list of some of the more popular career information publications and sources can be found in the appendix.

Internet and online sources

There are so many places on the internet where career explorers can find information to assist them in their personal career development that it would be a futile to try to list them all here. Looking at specific occupations or careers will turn up a wealth of online information. There are also a number of general self-help sites offered by the U.S. Department of Labor, state departments of labor, and other parties. Once you are ready for job entry, a number of developing job boards, often established around business and occupational schemes, represent sound gateways for job identification and application. A number of the more popular internet job boards will be identified in the appendix.

Many of the print sources mentioned above also offer their career stories via online blogs and exchanges. Ask counselors what websites they recommend for someone who is at your particular place in the career development process. In the appendix, the reader will find a list of websites offering a wealth of information.

Educational institutions and programs

Schools, colleges, and training programs provide information about careers they prepare people to enter. In addition, there will be many general school and college guides (e.g., Peterson's, Barron's, College Board, etc.) in your school or community library that present an array of educational options leading to career and work opportunities after graduation or completion of study requirements. The website of the U.S. Department of Education (www.ed.gov) offers a number of resources in varied formats to help prospective students access and use education information. A core list of educational guidance literature and media can be found in the appendix.

Major employers

Companies, businesses, and firms, especially those employing large numbers of people in a career cluster (e.g., United Airlines for pilots, flight attendants, and airline personnel; Microsoft for computer analysts, programmers, and information technology specialists; and Chrysler for automotive engineers and designers) provide both general information for career explorers and specific employment information for job seekers. Many large firms have a "Careers at ____" link on their website. Accessing the *Fortune* magazine annual list of the largest businesses (known as the Fortune 500) will connect you to the largest American and global employers.

Organizations of professional and skilled workers

Professional and trade associations, representing people in a specific career field or industry, have for many years been excellent sources of both occupational and educational information. Organizations like the National League of Nursing (nursing careers), National Association of

Broadcasters (television and radio careers), American Chemical Society (chemist and science careers), and many similar groups create and disseminate literature and media about careers in their areas of special interest. In the appendix, the reader will find a list, including general website addresses, of professional and trade organizations that produce educational and career information.

The *Encyclopedia of Associations* and *Directory of National Trade and Professional Associations* are excellent references to these groups, and one or guides are likely to be found in your community library. You can acquire the career and education resources of these organizations by contacting them via email or postcard. Each organization distributes career and educational information as a public service, and most of the time it is free.

Government agencies

The largest employer of people in the United States is the federal government. Add state and local government to the federal work numbers, and you have a significant number of people and positions. Because government employs such a large number of people, federal, state, and local agencies have generated career information resources describing the positions available and the qualifications they seek in candidates. State agencies are also sources of licensure and certification information.

The branches of the U.S. military represent an incredible number of opportunities for both educational and career experiences. You can learn about the opportunities available for both officers and enlisted personnel in each branch of military service by contacting the following websites:

- General military careers: http://www.bls.gov/ooh/Military/Military-Careers.htm
- Air Force—http://www.airforce.com
- Army—http://goarmy.com
- Coast Guard—http://www.gocoastguard.com
- Marine Corps—http://www.marines.com
- Navy—http://www.navy.com

One of the easiest ways to learn of government careers is to conduct an internet search using "Careers at the Department of (e.g., Health and Human Services)" in a popular search engine like www.google.com, www.ask.com, or www.yahoo.com.

PUT CAREER INFORMATION TO THE TEST

As an information consumer, you must evaluate what your research reveals to make certain it is accurate, current, and free of bias of any sort. The age of a piece of career information, along with the use of any numbers, can make it obsolete quickly. One simple practice that will help validate any questionable information is to obtain a backup or second source.

People actively working in the occupation, for example, or professional counselors can also serve as "sounding boards" when questions of accuracy arise. When you find career, occupation, education, or training information, the next step is to put that resource to a test to make certain it is of the highest quality.

An examination of the following criteria will assist in that determination:

- Source—Who is the creator and disseminator of the information and what is their motivation for making it available? The vast majority of career and education information sources are reputable and reliable, but one must be vigilant in checking both the content and the motivation of the source. Many information creators see this work as a public service. It is their way of ensuring consumers have an accurate and current depiction of the work performed in their career or field.

- Accuracy—Does the information depict the occupation or career in a comprehensive and correct manner? Many careers combine both positive (i.e., opportunity to travel) and not-so-positive (i.e., reporters for the Weather Channel report often from the midst of hurricanes, tornadoes, and other very dangerous weather situations, etc.) aspects. Does the information present opposing or contradictory views in a candid, realistic manner?

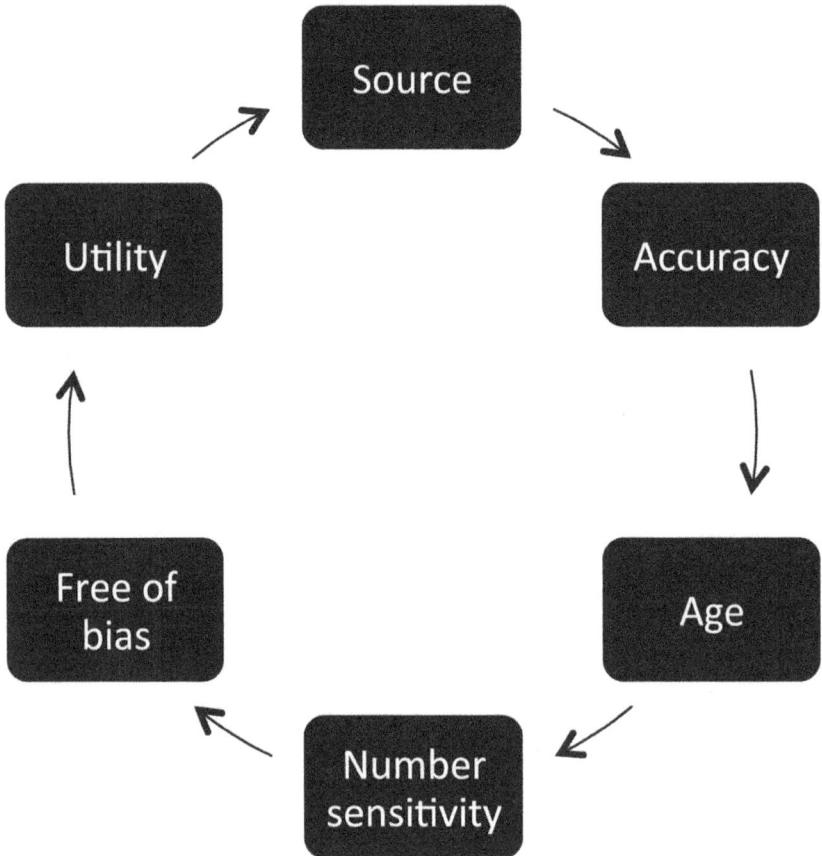

Figure 6.2 Career Information Evaluation Concerns

- Age—When was the information created? A piece of information that is five years old is considered an antique to most. Parts of some career information do not change with time, but others, like employment outlook data, can change dramatically in just a short period of time.
- Number sensitivity—Nothing will make a piece of career or educational information inaccurate more quickly than a number. Information like salaries, tuition costs, hours required for certification, and other similar data need to be "second sourced" to ensure their accuracy.

- Free of bias—Does the producer and disseminator of the information have any particular reason to shade the truth or distort the facts? Many for-profit career schools, for example, use their career information to recruit students and have been known to exaggerate data (i.e., job placements, etc.) in presenting an overly positive picture. If something appears "too good to be true," it is probably worth checking.

- Utility—What some will suggest is career and education information may be laden with statistics and terminology that make it far from user friendly. Some publications, blogs, and other information sources are nothing more than recruiting ads. Find and use information whose creator had you mind when the information was generated, and it will be more likely to pass the utility test.

All career and education information needs to be examined to ensure accuracy, relevance, and utility. When you question or doubt anything, including the information presented by people (human resources), don't fail to validate the information by using an alternative source.

IMPORTANCE OF STATISTICS IN CAREER STUDY

Many of the questions you will have about a specific career or the world of work in general can be answered by reputable statistics. It is important, however, to look to experienced providers and reliable sources (i.e., Bureau of Labor Statistics, etc.) for this information. Statistics are great at projecting demand and providing descriptive information, such as how much one can expect to earn in a particular occupation. For earnings and employment information by occupation, industry, and geographic area, check the BLS Occupational Employment Statistics survey, online at www.bls.gov/ncs. Several other good statistics sources include:

- National Compensation Survey—Information about wages and earnings. Online at www.bls.gov/ncs.

- Current Population Survey—Information about educational attainment, self-employment, and work hours. Online at www.bls .gov/cps.
- National Association of Colleges and Employers—Data on entry-level information for college graduates by major and industry. Online at www.naceweb.org.

STRAIGHT TALK ABOUT FINDING AND USING GOOD INFORMATION

When you have conducted a thorough career examination and received answers to all of your questions, a true picture of the career or occupation is likely to emerge. It will present a view of the career, how one gets to it, and what it will be like once there, and it will do this for as many occupations as you wish to examine. This knowledge is essential to quality career decision-making.

Career information surrounds you. What was once difficult to find and often suspect due to age and accuracy is today abundant and of much better quality. Today, the internet complements print and media resources in ways that would have been thought impossible just a decade or two ago. Quality decision-making requires that information users seek and find the most accurate and current information available at the time.

The only thing worse than not having good career information is to have it and not use it effectively. The quote by futurist John Naisbitt, at the beginning of this chapter, addresses the danger in finding information and then not turning it into knowledge. Whether you are at the beginning of your career development or the middle, don't move forward with any life-impacting decision without a full knowledge of where that choice will lead and the consequences it will generate.

CHAPTER 7

Challenge: Establishing Realistic Career Aspirations

Everyone in this world is dealt a different hand—some better, some worse than others—but what's more important is how you play that hand. This is what builds character. And with great character comes great reward.

—CHRISTINE HA, VIETNAMESE AMERICAN CHEF AND WRITER.
SHE WAS THE FIRST BLIND CONTESTANT AND THE WINNER OF
THE THIRD SEASON OF THE *MASTERCHEF* COMPETITION.

TO SAY YOU SHOULD MAKE THE MOST OF YOUR ABILITIES, APTITUDES, interests, and other career characteristics is an understatement. Aspirations, whether they be educational when you are young or career focused as you progress through adulthood should be a reflection of who you are and what you are capable of becoming.

Establishing and then fulfilling your aspirations resembles the archer aiming for the bull's-eye on the target ahead. You want to hit it square in the center or not be too far off. Aspirations must be built on a foundation of reality, which means you must engage in an assessment of the personal characteristics and the strengths that you bring to the education or career table.

Each of the steps in your career development will unearth aspirations and goals for you to work toward. Your aspirations are likely to be adjusted as you grow and change. As your personal characteristics evolve and you mature in different ways, a different you appears. When this occurs, reassessment of any previously constructed aspirations is required. What was once called the "midlife crisis" is, in reality, a natural occurrence.

People change and then must deal with that change. Your personal career satisfaction is dependent on your ability to make life modifications when they become necessary. You're not finished developing—a new edition of you is on the way. Sadly, however, you stand a reasonable chance of being the victim of faulty aspirations. You may overaspire, while others underaspire or misaspire. Let's dissect these behaviors.

OVERASPIRING BEHAVIOR

Overaspiring, in many instances, occurs when you attempt to do more than you are capable of doing. You get in over your head! It is evident on the athletic field where you attempt to play a position not suited for you or one that requires a skill or talent that you don't possess. It also occurs when you won't accept the reality of your qualifications for a particular occupation. The worst outcome of overaspiring is that it typically results in a failed or wasted career and education situation.

Consider the career explorers who aspire to be a medical doctor (MD) and eventually determine that they don't possess the intelligence, aptitude, or commitment to study long term that is required of this occupation. Instead of considering another career in health and medicine that may be well within reach, they often reject the entire field and wander off into something that may be equally outside the range of their abilities and true interests. If this is you, consider the range of careers within a particular career cluster before abandoning it altogether.

Others can overaspire differently in their educational pursuits. Education is a valued pursuit in our society, but often that value can become distorted or overblown. It is possible to aim for and achieve more education than you may need for entry and progression in some career and occupational roles. While too much education may not be a bad problem to have, it can divert you from the true educational path you should have been following.

Often, overaspiring can be traced to your lack of personal self-awareness or failure to comprehend what is required to achieve a specific education or career objective. It often has to do with action and time. If you want to travel forward two or three steps at a time, you're taking a risk and inviting the inevitable fall. Equally important is allowing for life events to occur and take hold before you abandon them. Don't rush success!

Take the student who, upon examining a grade of D in algebra on a report card, vows to get an A the next grading period. An A grade may be attainable, but it may be more realistic to shoot for a C or B as an intermediate target. The same occurs in the world of work. You set your eyes on a particular career as if it is the prize or the championship you seek to attain. You lose sight of reality and often refuse to admit that you may have simply erred or aimed too high.

Overaspiring can also occur when an external force (i.e., parent, spouse, partner, friend, etc.) pushes you in a particular direction that may appear reasonable to them but of limited interest to or unattainable by you personally. Using another education example, you are likely to know people who allowed too much external influence to affect their decision to matriculate to a particular college. The college required more of them than they were capable of giving, a common overaspiring example. Aspirations must be realistic and achievable. Those that are not are destined for disaster.

UNDERASPIRING BEHAVIOR

When underaspiring occurs, it means you set your sights too low and elected to follow education or occupational pursuits that did not challenge you. It can happen in the workplace or in school. Often, you set your sights too low because of the sphere of the experiences you have had and the information you are able to access. There is also "safety" in setting the bar low enough that you will leap over it with ease.

You can also underaspire because you have not conducted the degree of self-awareness needed to bring you to a complete understanding of your abilities, achievements, interests, and other characteristics. Let's confront reality again. Some people suffer from "ambition deficiency" and are constantly searching for the easy or expedient path to success. You see your studies and your work as a means to an end. You may not like where you are or what you're doing, but a steady paycheck permits you to get by and achieve most of your lifestyle preferences.

If you are an underaspirer, you're squandering intellect and ability and may need a generous dose of inspiration—a solid push from behind. The required jolt may come from you or from some external source (i.e., family member, boss, friend, etc.). When you fail to use the abilities and talents you possess, you are welcoming a career or education dilemma somewhere off in the future.

Other times, extraneous factors can influence your goal attainment. This happens, for example, when cost plays too influential a role in your consideration of college or graduate school and you don't determine if there are ways to make a particular education experience more affordable. If the cost of anything is ever a deterrent, your response should be to examine every financial alternative before accepting or settling for something that is not right for you or beyond your attainment.

Another characteristic of underaspirers is they allow the sting of failure or difficulty to hang around too long, for example, the college dropouts who never return to college after not succeeding. The fact that they were admitted to college is evidence that an institution saw them as able to do collegiate work. Maybe they were in the wrong college or studying the wrong thing, but to abandon college altogether is an overreaction that shouldn't linger as long as it often does.

MISASPIRING BEHAVIOR

Misaspiring can be associated with either over- or underaspiring. It simply means that you're doing something wrong that is causing you to be off the target in some regard. It can occur when you elect to pursue a work situation or learning experience that is consistent with your abilities and aptitudes but misses the target with respect to your interests and preferences. In the world of work, you might enjoy being an environmental engineer but not enjoy doing the work that you love for your current employer. In many situations, college students are enrolled in a place where they are able to compete academically—they just don't like where they are studying. Each is an example of an error, misstep, or omission you must address.

INFLUENCES ON ASPIRATIONS

Witness the following advertisement or business sign, the likes of which you have seen many times—Wilson & Sons, Electricians. Did Mr. Wilson's sons have a choice or were they predestined to be electricians before they ever left the maternity ward? America is rich in a tradition of work and occupations being pursued by generations of family members, and there is nothing wrong with that if following in the family footsteps is a choice the person makes and not an ultimatum dictated by parents and family tradition.

Also consider the toddler who is wearing a T-shirt with the name and seal of a college emblazoned on the front followed by the words—Class of 2038. The institution is probably the one that Mom or Dad attended. The college might possibly be the appropriate one for the toddler one day as long as that decision is one that they will make, devoid of any undue influence or pressure from the parents. Aspiring is about what you want to do—not what others want you to do.

Before leaving the subject of aspirations, don't ever allow someone or some institution to say you can't do something. "Be all that you can be" is a familiar slogan made popular by the U.S. Army a half century ago as a part of its recruitment efforts. Add to it "Be whatever you want to be." If you have the ability to prepare for and enter an occupation or career, don't allow anyone or anything to steer you away from it. In his first attempt at making his varsity high school basketball team, Michael Jordan failed. He dedicated himself to improving his court skills and succeeded the following year. The rest is basketball history.

Just a generation ago, girls and women were often told their career and education interests were for "men only" and shouldn't be pursued. Discrimination in many forms restricted the diversity and inclusion of role models. Girls didn't see women in a full range of STEM (science, technology, engineering, and mathematics) occupations. Young people of color didn't see minorities in a lot of occupational roles. Until the nation enacted laws against discrimination, girls and women, minorities, and the differently able were void of role models in many work environments and education settings.

It is only recently that American law schools have admitted an equal number or more women than men into studies that lead to careers in the law. Overt and subtle discrimination of any kind can have a telling effect on your aspirations. Resist it at all costs.

SENSING REALITY AND ACTING ACCORDINGLY

Managing aspirations demands that you plant them in a bed of reality. It doesn't mean that you will not change or the worlds of work and education will not change before, during, and after you achieve them. You may be challenged intellectually or skill-wise today, but that may not be the case in five, ten, or more years. Something that appears vague and not worthy of consideration today may move positively up your aspiration ladder over time. A number of careers and occupations may seem unrealistic or out of reach today, but that doesn't mean that it has to be that way forever. Call it "aspiration delay" if you want, but it simply means you are traveling at a different speed or taking a different route to your future career.

There is nothing wrong with aspirations that involve a little dreaming; in fact, it may be a "healthy" way for you to keep future doors open to a range of possibilities. Just don't allow "fantasy" to pervade your thinking and influence your behavior in ways that are not good for you. The adage "keep your feet on the ground . . . and reach for the stars" is probably a good way to proceed.

STRAIGHT TALK ABOUT DEALIING WITH AMBITION AND ASPIRATIONS

Successful career development requires that you develop a realistic plan—the architecture—of the career and education experiences you seek to attain. This plan is only implemented when you have engaged in an effective self-assessment and conducted a thorough search of all of the paths, short and long, you must follow to achieve your goals and aspirations. You must do everything to make certain your aspirations are yours and not those of others.

When learning or occupational experiences teach you things about yourself that are new or open doors of opportunity that didn't exist before, there is nothing wrong with establishing new or modified aspirations for yourself and new timetables for their accomplishment. More than one grandmother is seen each year walking on to a stage in her cap and gown to accept her college degree. Her achievement was never about ability; most likely it was about opportunity.

If you've overaspired, step back and take a long hard look at yourself and adjust your sights. If you've underaspired, engage in a similar examination, but do so with the objective of raising the bar higher than it has been until now. If you've simply misaspired, recycle back through the appropriate stages of the career development process in the hopes that continued self-assessment and exploration of options will help you get closer to the bull's-eye. The last thing you should do, however, is bail out or "throw in the towel" out of frustration. Getting it right is within your grasp.

Counselors are great at helping with aspiration checking, and the more they know you and your development, the better able they will be at helping you consider the realism of your aspirations. But remember, it's never the counselors' call; it's yours. Don't ask or expect counselors to tell you what to do. It's your life and your decision; you must "own" it from the moment you make it.

Counselors are skilled in the use and interpretation of assessment tools, and a session or two of effective reality checking may be just what you need to move forward. Similarly, a staffing professional who is skilled in the workings of employment transitions (i.e., job seeking, changing, etc.), the headhunter that was mentioned earlier, can be an excellent "sounding board" regarding the job search and placement process.

.

CHAPTER 8

Challenge: Utilizing Human Resources and Life Experiences as Career Teachers

We learn 10 percent of what we read, 20 percent of what we hear, 30 percent of what we see, 50 percent of what we see and hear, 70 percent of what we discuss with others, and 80 percent of what we experience.

—WILLIAM GLASSER (1925–2013), ACCOMPLISHED PSYCHIATRIST, EDUCATOR, AND COUNSELING THEORIST. DR. GLASSER IS THE DEVELOPER OF REALITY THERAPY AND CHOICE THEORY, WHICH FOCUS ON PERSONAL CHOICE, RESPONSIBILITY, AND TRANSFORMATION.

PEOPLE ARE ENGAGED IN CAREER AND EDUCATION EXPERIENCES ALL around you. Imagine the working people that you can reach out and touch. They are the teachers or professors in your classroom; the first responders protecting your safety; the health care providers in all of the various departments at the local hospital; and the managers, clerks, and service providers in all of the businesses and firms in the community.

Each has a story to tell about their work and the paths they followed in their career development. Each is living a career experience that you might like to know more about. For example, what could be more informative if you were considering going into business for yourself than to talk to and observe a business owner who has done it?

It is likely that you know someone who is currently in graduate school or has recently completed an industry-sponsored training program. Sitting down and "picking the brains" is a valuable way to gather information and answers. In fact, the interaction itself often leads you to ask questions you hadn't thought of before.

BEYOND THE TIP OF THE ICEBERG

Remember the iceberg phenomenon mentioned in chapter 3? The most visible workers (i.e., educators, health care professionals, sales representatives, etc.) that you encounter in your daily living are the easy ones with whom to interact. They represent just the tip of the iceberg. Your antenna doesn't need to work very hard for you to connect with them and allow you to see what they do.

Other workers, similar to the mass of an Antarctic iceberg, will be invisible. You know it's there—you just can't see it. The world of work is similar. You don't typically see the architects, but you see the homes, schools, office buildings, and other structures that they design. You don't see the journalists, but you read the newspaper or weekly news magazine that contains their writing. You don't see all the medical analysts who might study your tests and records, but your physicians depend on their work to diagnose and treat you.

Many witness workplace roles by viewing television, reading books, and observing their roles on the internet and in newspapers. Here, you must use caution, as fictional roles are often exaggerated or glamorized as a part of creating an entertaining plot or story. Every lawyer who enters a courtroom does not win as many cases as those often depicted in television dramas.

They and countless others are the "behind the scenes" professionals, skilled workers, technicians, and support personnel whose importance is major but whose visibility is either negligible or totally screened from public view. Still others, like CIA agents, will most likely be inaccessible to you, and what you learn about their work will have to come from other sources.

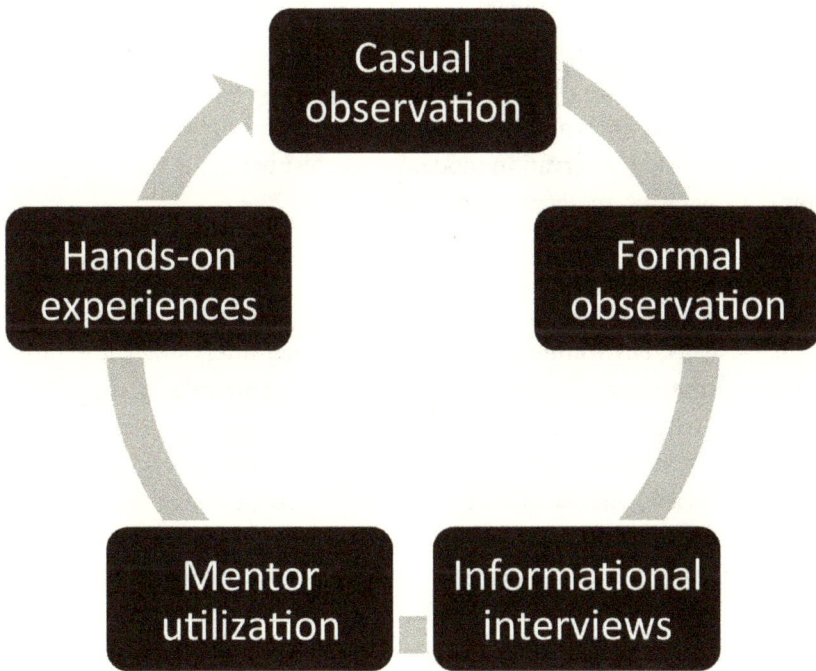

Figure 8.1 Using Life Experiences to Explore Careers

LIFE EXPERIENCES AS CAREER TEACHERS

There are a variety of ways in which you can learn about careers, including the following.

Casual observation

As a casual observer of people and what they do in the workplace, you are learning about careers and occupations. These informal observations can be packed full of good information, and the lessons learned will help guide you in choosing or changing your personal career one day. An occasional cup of coffee with a friend or family member—or better yet, someone from your occupational or career network—can yield valuable information you wouldn't access otherwise.

Formal observation
Known as "shadowing," this technique allows the explorer to get "up close and personal" in the observation of workers and work settings. Shadowing is usually informal with the explorer spending a half-day or day purely in a casual observation mode. Its greatest benefit is that you get an "insider's" view of an occupation.

Informational interviews
Another popular avenue for getting the inside perspective on an occupational or work environment is the informational interview. These information-gathering tools permit you to research a particular occupation or workplace with one or several people and get answers to predetermined questions about what they do. There are two ways to access an informational interview, one via the networks you've created over time and the other via cold calls. Expect network calls to be more productive.

With informational interviews, there is no expectation of employment by either you or the workplace, but the experience can result in motivated job seekers getting the attention of the firm or company, a tactic that could pay dividends in the future if you make a positive impression. Informational interviews have been known to result in internships, part-time temporary work, or volunteer opportunities where many additional things will be learned.

Mentor utilization
Most early and midcareer individuals have a former professor, an early boss, or a supervisor or a professional colleague with whom they connected, an individual of certain stature and one whose accomplishments and opinions they respect. They can be excellent mentors.

For every professional and trade, there is a corresponding organization comprising people who work in that occupation or career cluster and have followed the required education and training routes.

Membership in these organizations will allow you to "rub elbows" with the people who are doing the work that interests you or that you are studying. These individuals, and others like them, can be your mentors. Mentors are "sounding boards" with whom you can pose questions hypothetically and get a learned opinion. Mentors who are now doing what you hope to do someday can light the path that you must follow to get to the same or similar career position.

Hands-on experiences

The agreeability of particular educational or training experience can be determined by sitting in and auditing a class. Part-time and summer employment for the student still in school can produce similar results. Other hands-on experiences like volunteering or service learning (a contemporary term for volunteering by students) provides an excellent opportunity to touch and feel an occupation from the inside.

Volunteering or pro bono work while you are working can also be a valuable teacher. In addition to learning and performing relevant occupational tasks, the volunteer gains valuable insights as to people at work and the setting where the experience is occurring. A volunteer is able to get a sense of the knowledge possessed by the workforce, as well as the skills they display on a daily basis. Volunteers also learn about the atmosphere, politics, and culture of the workplace and how those characteristics resonate with them personally.

Internships and fellowships, paid and unpaid, are growing in popularity as teaching and orientation tools. As a part of your study, you may be required to engage in a formal work experience, under the supervision of a professional or skilled individual, for a defined period of time. Most interns move into their roles gradually, and eventually, their hands-on experiences have them performing all or most of the functions of a given occupation. If you are not currently engaged in an educational experience that offers internship or fellowship opportunities, approach a human resource officer of a firm or company that interests you and see if an individualized program can be created for you.

Before leaving the "learning by doing" concept, consider using temporary employment in a specific setting to use many of your senses to get a feel for occupations and the settings where you find them. As a "temp," you get to see, hear, and touch the occupations, presenting experiences you can only get from the inside. If you are interested in IT or engineering work, for example, identify a staffing firm that specializes in supplying temps or contract employees to this industry. And like summer and part-time employment while studying, you get paid to do this temporary work.

When you participate in a hands-on experience, become a "sponge" and soak up as much as you can about the careers displayed before you and the environment in which the work is conducted. You may not use it immediately, but this is valuable information for life.

THE VALUE OF THE TEST DRIVE

Before you buy a new car, you take it out for a test drive. You wouldn't spend a significant amount of money on a clothing purchase without going into the fitting room and trying the garment on. Why then would you venture off into a major educational or career experience without a similar test-drive or fit check? But many do—and live to regret it.

Opportunities to engage in this type of exploration will allow you to test-drive a career or education experience, and they can be both proactive and reactive. Proactive exploration is when you are moving developmentally through the various life stages and plan your future experiences in an orderly and progressive manner. The best part of proactive exploration is that it usually means you're in charge and going where you wish to go.

Reactive exploration occurs often when the work or education activity that you are experiencing takes a turn that requires immediate or corrective action. It involves problem solving, barrier removal, and other impediments that step in the path of normal or routine development. Many view proactive exploration as fire prevention and reactive exploration as putting out fires.

Proactive test-driving should be experienced when you are engaged in the following:

- Selecting a career
- Choosing a college or training program
- Selecting an initial job
- Attempting to exit a job or occupation you don't like

- Attempting to reenter a job or occupation after a planned leave of absence
- Making a move or change that will enhance your career development
- Electing to slow down or identify a second career or retirement options later in life

When you know options and decisions are in front of you or you aren't being pressured to act hastily, you can be proactive in your exploration. Other life and work situations do not allow the same degree of time and flexibility as these, but you should attempt to engage in whatever test-drive options will help you move forward.

REVELANCE OF WORK ENVIRONMENTS

Another consideration for some career explorers could be an examination of the environments where you might work. Individuals with specific occupational skills—-accounting, writing, information technology, management, research—can work in a variety of environments. Each environment is different in multiple ways (i.e., mission, occupation mix, size, etc.), all worthy of additional examination.

Following are examples of some of the settings where many different careers and occupations are performed:

- Banking and financial centers
- Government agencies and military installations
- Hospitals and health care facilities
- Manufacturing and industrial facilities
- Military bases and complexes
- Retail centers and outlets
- Schools and colleges

Other work environments have no walls, for example, the forest ranger working for the U.S. National Park Service. While a portion of this role may be performed in an office environment, it can also be extremely mobile—moving from work setting to work setting in a car or truck—and then working in the outdoors most of the time.

Construction engineers, managers, and inspectors, as well as many of the skilled craftspeople (i.e., carpenters, welders, plumbers, electricians, etc.) that work in the building industry work in settings that are changing all the time. Their projects have a beginning, middle, and end, and then they move on to the next setting and building project.

EVALUATION OF HUMAN RESOURCES AND INFORMATIONAL EXPERIENCES

Human resources and life experiences can be very influential in exploration. But like all informational tools, they have to be evaluated with respect to accuracy, timeliness, and relevancy. Individuals in a career position who haven't kept pace with the technology of their role and its impact on the workplace are as outdated as a ten-year-old book or video.

Experiences of this nature can be excellent sounding boards for the questions that emerge from your study of print and other sources and can offer the clarification or extended information the original source didn't offer, but only if they represent the best information available. Don't shy away from seeking a second opinion when the situation calls for one.

STRAIGHT TALK ABOUT EXPERIENTIAL LEARNING

You can visit all of the internet sites and read all of the career literature available and not get as much information as your interaction with members of the workforce and exposure to work environments can create. Whether your exposure is casual (i.e., shadowing, campus visit, etc.) or intense (i.e., informational interviews, part-time employment, etc.), you will walk away with more than you ever anticipated.

Trying on a career in some capacity before you invest ego, energy, time, and money is nothing more than "trying before buying." It's seeking the counsel of others and engaging in any number of learning experiences that will immerse you sufficiently to test your aptitudes, interests, and the other factors that have led you to place this career high on your aspiration list.

There are multiple ways to learn, but none more effective than experiences that employ your senses. You will observe, see, hear, and touch any number of careers and occupations over the course of your development. You may even find a work environment (i.e., bakery, restaurant, etc.) with a unique smell or taste. These experiences will be etched in your brain and retrieved at many decision-making times. In addition, the "try work on and see how it fits" approach—using internships, volunteering, and part-time employment—are all hands-on experiences that will enhance the career exploration process. Lastly, they can look extremely good on your resume.

Each experience will tell you if you like and are capable of doing something. They can also leave you with a "take it or leave it" attitude or response of indifference. And finally, they can tell you the things to avoid and steer away from. Nothing beats a real-world experience before or early, midway, or late in your career development. Every working individual with whom you interact and every life experience you have can be an extraordinary teacher.

CHAPTER 9

Challenge: Making Time and Calendar Your Career Allies

Time is what we want most, but what we use worst.

—WILLIAM PENN (1644–1718), QUAKER FOUNDER OF THE
COMMONWEALTH OF PENNSYLVANIA, WHICH WAS ONE OF THE
THIRTEEN ORIGINAL U.S. COLONIES. HE WAS AN INFLUENTIAL
SCHOLAR, A REAL ESTATE DEVELOPER, AND THE FIRST
GOVERNOR OF THE PROVINCE.

WILLIAM PENN HIT THE NAIL SQUARE ON THE HEAD MORE THAN 300
years ago. Time can be your best friend and your worst enemy, and how
it affects your career and education is largely up to you. Let's look at a
common myth about time right up front. You cannot manage time—it
is a constant. You can manage the things that you do with your time, but
365 days, twelve months, four weeks, seven days, twenty-four hours, and
sixty minutes are constants.

People who display good time behaviors, however, have an advantage, as their proactivity affords them the maximum amount of time to
consider options and take action. People who don't practice good time
behaviors find themselves challenged by getting things done and getting
them done on time.

TRANSITIONS TAKE TIME

Consider the number of interventions you might possibly experience and how time is important in achieving maximum satisfaction with these nine transitions:

- High school to college and or some other form of postsecondary education
- College to college or training program to training program
- Education to employment
- Employment situation to employment situation
- Within career or employment mobility
- Returning to employment after a planned (i.e., parenting, health matter, etc.) or unplanned (i.e., job loss, termination) leave
- Employment to additional education and/or training
- Full employment to telework, job sharing, part-time, or reduced employment
- Active employment to retirement

The financial risks and time commitment associated with any of these transitions will be substantial, and you must be sensitive about conducting each transition in an efficient manner. Otherwise, your return on investment (ROI) will be jeopardized.

High school to college or some other form of postsecondary education

Educational planning requires time for exploration, discovery, and consideration of the various options. Unfortunately, too many adolescent and young adults fail to allow for sufficient self-awareness and exploration of options that might lead them to a school, college, or training program and preparation for the work world. To maximize personal benefit in the school to college transition, you must create a calendar to complete all of the relevant tasks.

College to college or training program to training program

You don't want it to happen, but often you have found or will find yourself in the wrong place to study or mired in a subject (i.e., college major, etc.) that you have discovered isn't right for you. Transferring from one educational experience to another needs to be done better than the initial action, or similar consequences are likely. Following degree attainment, another planning period and time commitment must be made for those moving on to a graduate or professional school.

Education to employment

You've attained the knowledge, skills, and core competencies to perform a particular occupation, and now you must look the job search and acquisition process square in the eye. Employment doesn't come looking for you. You must go looking for it. There are a number of tasks that you need to initiate long before graduation, and you must allow sufficient time to consider all of the options open to you in order to land in a good location to begin your career.

Employment situation to employment situation

It is possible that you have outgrown or may outgrow your current situation and need to examine options elsewhere. The absence of growth and promotion opportunities or ability to achieve your full potential are most often cited as the reasons you might seek to find another employment situation. When you are faced with this situation, act deliberately and make certain you've allowed sufficient time to get you to an improved situation. And most importantly, don't quit your current employment situation until a new one has been contractually or formally secured or until you are confident you can survive a period of unemployment.

Within career or employment mobility

Career growth, mobility, and maintenance each present different challenges. Certainly, you will need to consider what educational experiences you will need to grow and move. Whether within your current employment situation or moving on to a new one, time is an essential ingredient in the developmental process. You will also discover the change—any change—results in more positive outcomes when it is planned and you are at the controls.

Returning to employment after a planned or unplanned leave

Stay-at-home moms have new counterparts in the contemporary culture—stay-at-home dads. Child-rearing, care of an elderly parent or relative, or taking health or medical leave are just a few examples of why you may interrupt your employment with a planned leave.

Job loss that is unexpected falls under the unplanned leave definition. Returning to employment from planned or unplanned leave, whether to your existing employer or a different one, requires some time use skills to ensure a quality transition. A portion of the time you are away from the workplace may have to be spent in meeting the continuing education requirements of your license or certificate.

Employment to additional education and/or training

Often, working individuals find they must mix additional education or training with their current employment situation, a situation that offers an array of challenges in order to implement. If you are working and trying to complete a degree, enrolling in graduate school on a part-time basis, or attempting to engage in new or supplemental training to upgrade your current occupational skills, you will need to not only use time to plan the transition but also to develop a work and study calendar that allows you to do both.

Full employment to telework, job sharing, part-time, or reduced employment

Workers today create any mixture of work schedules that will allow them to ease out of a full-time schedule and move into a different work mechanism. Employers that allow flexible schedules, remote/telework situations (i.e., working from home, etc.), job sharing (i.e., splitting one position between two employees, etc.) or reduced hours offer the best opportunity for you to modify or reduce your work commitment should that be desirable. Such circumstances don't occur overnight, and flexible time use is essential for these transitions to be successful.

Active employment to retirement

Possibly the transition requiring the largest commitment of time is when you are preparing for and transitioning from active employment to retirement. If you haven't prepared for the security of retirement, it may be delayed or prohibit you from retiring at all. From at least mid-career forward, you need to consider and begin to set retirement or exit goals that are accompanied with a calendar for implementation. Exiting the workplace will get more focused attention in part 4, but you must recognize early that poor time use in preparing to leave your career can produce chaotic and unintended results.

TRANSITIONS REQUIRE TIME

You have likely experienced one, two, or more of the above transitions. Hopefully, you gave yourself ample time to do all the things you needed to do. If you want to move through any of the remaining transitions or repeat any that have already occurred, there is an appropriate calendar of fixed tasks and strategies that you must follow in order to ensure success. Further, any fixed calendar must have the flexibility and leeway to allow for the "unexpected," something that may slow down or speed up the events. Catching the entire population totally without warning is a clear example of why backup and contingency plans should be factored into the individual's routine progression through the career development process.

PRINCIPLES OF TIME USE

If you are going to be the best broker of the time available, you must understand six principles of time use that will impact what you get done and how long it will take. Consider these principles.

Be able to prioritize

If you do not possess a sense of the life–work balance you desire, you will be impeded in your ability to set priorities. Aspiration achievement is dependent on these priorities, a simple understanding of where you wish to go, and the implementation of both behavioral and time strategies that will take you there. The opposite of being able to set priorities is the dreaded P word—procrastination. Procrastinators spin their wheels and get mired in the quicksand that results in missed opportunities.

Many management gurus suggest that planning is all about vision. Do you know who you are, what you want to go, and how to get there? Those that do are the best positioned to move flawlessly through the career development process. Ultimately this vision, or lack thereof, will influence your ability to prioritize, plan, and focus.

Create a workable plan and stick to it

Planning comes in many forms. The daily planner identifies the immediate and keeps you on track toward getting those things done. The weekly or monthly planner opens that window more and allows you to see tasks to be completed in a larger time period. The ideal situation would be for you to have a one-year, five-year, or longer plan. No matter the duration of the plan, it's incumbent for the individual to have alternatives and contingencies waiting in the wings should Plan A be unexpectedly interrupted or have to be aborted.

The ability to plan is also viewed by human resource management specialists as the single most important factor influencing performance and productivity. If the employing entities have figured that out, shouldn't you apply it to your personal performance and career direction?

Address change as an opportunity, not a threat

Yes, change can influence time use. When you accept change and "go with the flow" you are likely to attain the career and education goals that you set. When change is viewed as a threat, it throws you off course and can lead to procrastination as you sort out its impact. When your career jumps the track, it will need to be set back and maybe jump-started. Two things about change are certain—it's going to occur, and you must devote time to deal with it.

Know when and how to decide

In multiple places in this book, the importance of decision-making has been cited and stressed as critical to progress. Decisions are not time consuming—indecision is. After all of the facts have been gathered, all of the options identified, and all of the consequences determined, it is time to make a decision. Yes, decisions need to be evaluated, as actions are taken to implement them, but decision-making should never be allowed to become the action that brings any part of your career development to a screeching halt.

Often, the inability for decisions to be made or made efficiently lies within the organization within which we are situated. Effective time users have identified the faulty protocols, procedures, and systems that surround them. Correcting or eliminating these time slipups will give you additional time for more important things.

Identify and arrest your "time bandits"

Given the opportunity to identify them, everyone can name one or more things that steal their time. These "time bandits" must be arrested. The worst bandits need to be eliminated or removed from influencing your progress and development. Other bandits, those considered the inevitable, need to be controlled to the extent possible.

Procrastination and indecision are bandits that can be reduced or eliminated. Bad behaviors can be unlearned. New and improved behaviors can be learned. Try it—it really works.

Interruptions are a fact of life. These inevitable interruptions to even the best calendar or plan are the ones that need to be controlled. If you're spending too much time in unproductive meetings, for example, someone needs to examine the purpose of those meetings and find ways to make them more efficient. If you have "desk stress," maybe an occasional reorganization of your workspace and tools will save you time to address the more important things on your planner or calendar. As many supervisors have expounded—it's not about working harder . . . it's about working smarter.

Finally, good time users must master the practices of "intelligent neglect" and "urgency elimination." When your day, week, and month becomes cluttered with important things you must do, which of those can be moved to a lower level of priority in order for you to gain control again. Which can be assigned to another member of the team? Which don't really have to be done after all? You may do the things you enjoy the most first. Reverse that and do the things you like least at the beginning.

Stay healthy

Never underestimate the importance of diet, sleep, exercise, and relaxation. Good physical and mental health can influence the career development process in more ways than most realize. This means eating right, exercising appropriately, getting sufficient sleep, and learning to mix the complexities of your life with an appropriate taste of relaxation and enjoyment.

The more stressed and anxious you are, the more improved time use will be a challenge. Many counselors and human resource professionals suggest these are the types of unhealthy conditions that can lead to burnout among workers. Occasionally, a complete exit from the daily routine (i.e., unplanned day away, long weekend, vacation, etc.) is good for your mental wellness.

DIFFERENT PERSONALITIES USE TIME DIFFERENTLY

Are you the quick-acting, multitasker or a deliberate, focused, see-one-thing-through-to-completion kind of person—or someone else—dramatically different from each of these examples? Do you know your "prime times"? Are you a morning person, after-lunch go-getter, or late afternoon dynamo? When it comes to getting things done—from searching websites for employment opportunities to completing applications to study—whoever you are—you need to operate from a position of power. Time will give you that power.

Your personality and knowledge of self can be influential in how you use time and in your ability to exert your personal power as a time user. Experts in time use and management will be the first to tell you that there is no one-size-fits-all model for becoming a better time user.

You have to relate what you know about you to an understanding of the tasks that need to be performed. Most certainly, this is a daily thing, but it can also be viewed from a weekly and/or monthly perspective. Are Fridays crunch days for some reason? Do you have reports due at the beginning of each month that are extra time demanding? Experiment with the behaviors that will result in their achievement.

A DOZEN SOUND TIME BEHAVIORS

Consider the following twelve behaviors as you set about to choose, prepare for, enter, progress in, reenter, or leave the workplace. They will place the power in your hands, not the hands of others.

1. Control what you need to do—don't let it control you.

2. Avoid doing the easiest, friendliest, enjoyable things first.

3. Exert schedule "power" and set time aside specifically for you and your career needs.

4. Get past the "getting started" barrier.

5. Maintain a calendar—know when you have time to be casual and exploratory but also when things must be finished and submitted.

6. Know the difference between doing quality work and having an obsession for perfection. Push back from the keyboard, end the task, and seal the deal.

7. Eliminate "desk stress" and make certain you have quality tools and resources to do what you need to do.

8. Identify milestones at which progress will be measured and reward yourself at the end of the journey (if nothing more than a piece of fruit or a chocolate bar).

9. Arrange all tasks in a logical, doable order and create a workable to-do list.

10. Start everything at the right place and follow the most productive route to accomplishment.

11. Allocate time, pace yourself, and diversify the tasks.

12. Accept the fact that being late is likely to result in a missed opportunity, a chance that may or may not ever pass your way again.

The words of Warren Bennis, emphasized in the preface, are worthy of reexamination. In everything about your career and education, you must concentrate on doing the right thing and equally on doing things right. Doing the right thing is effectiveness, efficiency, and the foundation for competency. Once the right thing is the target, concentrate on proficiency—doing it right.

STRAIGHT TALK ABOUT ENGAGING IN GOOD TIME BEHAVIORS

Those with a history of poor time use have to change, and this change is only going to occur through discipline. Eliminate the behaviors that cause you not to get done what needs to be completed. This happens through planning, priority setting, and being able to be either proactive or reactive when necessary. Stated differently, if you know your destination, give yourself sufficient time to travel there. Accelerate or decelerate as time permits and only take any shortcuts that are regarded as acceptable.

The identification and elimination of your personal "time bandits" will result in positive things. Again, doing things differently than you have done them for most of your life will require a heavy dose of discipline. You will have to "suck it up" and employ new behaviors.

Modern technology has changed the way people look for opportunities (i.e., virtual colleges tours, job boards, etc.) and apply for admission or positions (i.e., internet application tools, electronic interviews, etc.), and users must set aside some time to learn and practice these new tools and protocols.

Finally, sustain a healthy life–work balance. Healthy and satisfied people are the best users and consumers of their time. And they achieve career success before most.

CHAPTER 10

Challenge: Engaging Professional Counselors

No matter what achievements you make, somebody helps you.

—ALTHEA GIBSON (1927–2003), FAMOUS AMERICAN AND
INTERNATIONAL TENNIS CHAMPION. SHE WAS THE FIRST
PERSON OF COLOR TO WIN THE GRAND SLAM TITLE, WHICH
INCLUDES THE FRENCH OPEN, WIMBLEDON, AND THE U.S.
OPEN TOURNAMENTS.

SELF-MADE WOMEN AND MEN, WHILE THEY DO EXIST, ARE FEW AND FAR
between. Most successful people have been guided in some way, formally
or informally, by others. Even those individuals known as pioneers or
persons who rose to become influential voices of their profession (e.g.,
Walt Disney, Rachel Carson, Thurgood Marshall, Ernest Hemingway,
Margaret Mead, Louis Armstrong, and Sandra Day O'Connor) had relationships with people in their personal career development that resulted
in their being able to achieve more than they thought possible and move
more efficiently through the process.

THE EFFECTIVE USE OF COUNSELORS AND COUNSELING

Prominent among the individuals who can have an impact on your career and education development are the professional counselors that you are likely to encounter in school, college, private practice, community agencies, and other counseling settings. Professional counseling is defined by the American Counseling Association (ACA) and twenty-eight related counseling organizations as follows:

> *Counseling is a professional relationship that empowers diverse individuals, families and groups to accomplish mental health, wellness, education and career goals. (ACA 20/20 Initiative)*

In their quest to honor the integrity and meaning of this definition, counselors exist to help you in a variety of ways. Properly utilized, counselors can become one of your strongest career development allies, especially if given the opportunity to play the "path lighter" role suggested multiple times in this book.

To use counselors effectively, it is important to recognize what counselors in varying settings do and how each may address one or more parts of the exploration and decision-making process and then be available to help you enter, succeed, and grow in the career field you have chosen. To not use them in these ways is to squander an incredible human resource.

The National Career Development Association, one of ACA's founding divisions, is the recognized leader in developing standards for the career development profession, for the provision of career counseling programs and services, and for the evaluation of career information materials. Seek the counseling assistance of those affiliated with this long-standing professional organization.

Private practice ➡ Agencies and organizations ➡ Workplace ➡ Schools and colleges

Figure 10.1 Counseling Settings

COUNSELORS IN PRIVATE PRACTICE, AGENCY, ORGANIZATION, AND WORKPLACE ENVIRONMENTS

Throughout the time you are studying and again after you have entered the working world, a number of different counselors in community agency and organization, private practice, and workplace settings will be available to offer their professional services in support of the decisions you have made and the transitions you are experiencing.

The private practice counselors that specialize in career counseling help their clients assess and improve their career situations, especially circumstances where individuals believe they may have chosen poorly or are experiencing personal growth and development changes that necessitate revisiting all or a portion of the career development tasks previously completed.

Private practice counselors also deal with a range of workplace adjustment issues (i.e., peer relationships, manager/employee relationships, work-related stress, etc.) that can often be a source of difficulty to people's mental health, impede their performance and productivity at work, and ultimately inhibit their ability to enjoy career success.

In every community, some individuals needing assistance with career development and human growth and development concerns will find nonprofit organizations and services that offer an array of counseling programs. Such sponsors can range from local faith-based religious organizations (i.e., Catholic Charities, B'nai B'rith, etc.) to a cluster of retired business leaders (i.e., SCORE/Senior Corps of Retired Executives). Often, these community groups focus their attention to specific needs of target groups (i.e., homeless, ex-offenders, veterans, seniors, etc.) but find that their clients need help with career or work concerns. When sufficiently publicly or privately supported, these community organizations are typically staffed by professional counselors and volunteers who specialize in the transitions being experienced by the clients they serve.

Other counselors working in state and municipal government settings typically help unemployed and underemployed individuals with job placement. All of these counselors deal with clients in stressful situations and have mastered the techniques associated with responding to the clients' situation in a positive and constructive manner.

Counselors are becoming increasingly visible in the contemporary workplace through the employee assistance programs (EAPs) offered by employers to help individuals deal with adjustment, mobility, and work-related issues; people-oriented matters; and other issues that need to be addressed if the individuals are to realize their full potential. EAPS can vary from in-house services to contract services with an external counseling entity. Often, employers extend these counseling services beyond just career issues to target personal and mental health issues that affect employee performance or productivity.

COUNSELORS IN EDUCATION ENVIRONMENTS

Throughout the school, college, and training experience, counselors function in various ways to facilitate your personal career and education development. They are known by various titles, including school counselors, career counselors, admission counselors, and financial aid counselors, each performing a specific role in support of the clients they serve. They offer an array of personal services, including individual and group counseling that helps you:

- Identify and refine career and education goals and objectives.
- Identify personal characteristics and traits that may be relevant to your future career development.
- Understand the workplace and the many careers that are performed within it.
- Examine the various education paths to careers.
- Examine careers that are compatible with the information you are learning about yourself.
- Review and interpret findings of standardized tests, interest inventories, and related assessments and their implications for your career and education objectives. A list of the more popular career-oriented assessment tools can be found in the appendix.

- Help you relate current experiences (educational and occupational) to potential success later in a career.
- Evaluate information, develop career and education plans, and make tentative decisions.
- Assist you in taking the steps necessary to realize your career and education plans once you have made a quality decision.

The work of the counselors in education settings often goes far beyond the actual counseling function. They also:

- Refer you to information sources (e.g., publications, internet sites, DVDs, etc.) about career and postsecondary opportunities and options and/or specific information tailored to your personal career goals and objectives.
- Provide special programs such as career and college fairs, job placement, career shadowing experiences, and exposures to human career resources.
- Offer transition services aimed at helping you apply to schools, colleges, and training programs that will help you achieve your tentative and long-range decisions.
- Assist you in identifying and acquiring financial assistance in the pursuit of your goals.
- Guide you toward internship, cooperative education, and employment experiences where you will experience the work world.
- Help you apply for employment or graduate school following your initial postsecondary education or training experience.

It is important to note that many education institutions extend the use of their counselor services to former students and alumni. Even if you have been separated by time from the school or college, these services represent a good reason to reconnect.

FIRST-RATE COUNSELORS MAKE A DIFFERENCE

Quality counselors and counseling services are available to you throughout your personal career development. Counselors can connect explorers and decision-makers to information that will result in a better understanding of options and opportunities. They can administer and interpret a variety of assessments and interest inventories that help answer the "Who am I?" question. Counselors also serve as excellent sounding boards for evolving decisions being considered by clients and provide support during the various transitional periods.

The identification of competent and qualified counselors, however, is something that requires your ongoing attention. Care should be exercised to use professional counselors, individuals whose preparation is strong and who practice according to the highest professional and ethical standards. Determine if the counselor possesses the appropriate professional credentials, including a license issued by the state and/or a credential conferred by a national certification body. Those affiliated with the American Counseling Association (ACA), the National Board for Certified Counselors (NBCC), the National Career Development Association (NCDA), and the National Employment Counselors Association (NECA) and pledged to uphold the professional and ethical standards of those groups represent a good place to start any credentials check.

All fifty states, the District of Columbia, and other jurisdictions have licensure laws that are designed to ensure that professionals working in counseling settings have met established standards. If you wouldn't turn your annual taxes over to anyone other than a Certified Public Accountant (CPA), why would you turn your career development over to anyone other than a licensed or certified counselor?

Be wary of individuals calling themselves career coaches, lifestyle consultants, and other self-aggrandizing titles. Using coaches and consultants lacking professional certification and evading licensure and credentialing laws can be a waste of your time and money.

In part 2, you will find references to the specialists who are skilled at guiding candidates for employment through the school-to-work and occupation-to-occupation transitions. Known as search and staffing professionals, these direct-hire helpers are in the business of placing the "right" candidate in the "right" position, an action that should please both you and your eventual employer.

STRAIGHT TALK ABOUT USING PROFESSIONAL COUNSELORS AND OTHER HELPERS

Don't avoid counselors and others who can aid you in the pursuit of career satisfaction and success. Engage them. Survey the institution, government, community agency, private practice, and workplace environments, as well as schools, colleges, and training programs to identify these unique professionals. When found, allow the competent counselor to assist you in your career and education development.

Counselors and other career helpers likely temper the advice they give, and you should never pressure them to make the decisions that you need to make for yourself. "Tell me what to do" is a statement you should never expect a counselor or helper to respond to. Counselors are in the business of helping you consider and light personal paths to your future. Rightfully, they will resist telling you what to do because it's your life and your career and it has to grow from your decisions.

PART 2

THE INITIAL STEPS

FINDING, ACQUIRING, AND MOVING INTO THE FIRST OR ANY JOB

Note: Rather than repeat messages, this and future sections of the book will reference information and solutions that were presented in in part 1. Self-awareness, exploration, decision-making, and other tasks are repeated at various life and career stages. Once you have mastered these techniques, they will have many application points.

CHAPTER 11

Challenge: Adapting to Work, Worker, and Workplace Change

It is not the strongest of the species that survives. It is the one that is the most adaptable to change.

—CHARLES DARWIN (1809–1882), ENGLISH SCIENTIST
AND STUDENT OF NATURAL HISTORY BEST KNOWN FOR HIS
CONTRIBUTIONS TO THE SCIENCE OF EVOLUTION, WHICH HE
PUBLISHED IN HIS BOOK, *ON THE ORIGIN OF SPECIES*

INDIVIDUALS SEEKING TO ENTER OR REENTER THEIR RESPECTIVE careers are finding an American workplace today that is somewhat different from the recent past and light years dissimilar from the one their parents entered and functioned in just a generation ago. To be certain, many occupations cling to methods and routines established over time, but even those established approaches are performed today within a workplace culture that Dad and Mom would hardly recognize. Further, the pace with which change is being introduced in how America works requires vigilance by those who wish to grow and prosper in their chosen career.

The first part of this chapter will speak to the changes that individuals entering and reentering the workplace will find different. Then the discussion will move on to an examination of the expectations that a changing workplace has for future workers. Later in this book, the reader will find two chapters devoted entirely to future work, workers, and workplaces.

Success at entry and reentry in the workforce will be as dependent on a "fitness for change" as much as on the knowledge and the skill set possessed by the candidate. Those capable of adapting to these changes will succeed. Others will struggle.

WORKPLACE CHANGES THAT REQUIRE ATTENTION

How is the contemporary workplace different from the one workforce members entered just a generation or two ago? What do employers expect today that they didn't ask of your parents and grandparents. How has the manner in which America works changed? Consider the following.

Maintenance of requisite career knowledge and skill set

It goes without saying that almost every career field has undergone a "knowledge explosion" that successful careerists must master and convert into a productive, efficient skill set. There are no signs that this explosion will slow, and those who do not keep pace will be left in the dust. Employees who thought they would report for work with a diploma, certificate, or degree in hand and work forever now find that continuing education and skill renewal are essential to career survival.

Adaptability to a diverse community of workers

Diversity in all of its forms (i.e., gender, race, age, national origin, LGBT, the differently abled, etc.) has made the composition of the American workforce considerably different from yesteryear. According to the Center for American Progress, the workforce in 2010 was comprised of 154 million workers, 36 percent of whom were people of color. The population that will replace the aging baby boomers, however, will be comprised significantly of Hispanics, African Americans, Asian Americans, Pacific Islanders, and Native Americans.

One need only look at Bureau of Labor Statistics demographic studies to see the upward spiral of working women (including those in ownership/leadership/management roles) to grasp another element of change in the contemporary workforce. Additionally, because of factors like life-expectancy adjustments, improved health care, and the opportunity to work modified schedules, many older workers want to extend their careers. These and other people analytics portend a different diversity from the present.

Ability to use new tools and technologies
Over time, the tools and technology of many professions and trades have remained constant or changed gradually. That is no longer the case. Across multiple fields and industries, tools have become obsolete or outdated only to be replaced by newer versions that are likely to face a limited shelf life. The manner in which information is collected, stored, and communicated is in a constant state of flux, and staying relevant means becoming a virtual student of emerging tools and technologies.

Capacity for addressing accountability and quality
Success for any firm, business, organization, or agency is dependent on the identification of the strongest individuals to carry out the mission of that entity. Individually and collectively, each step that is made by the workforce contributes to that end. It is little wonder then that accountability and quality control have become paramount objectives in the contemporary workplace and employers are being conditioned to establish "evidence-based" systems that ensure their targeted goals are being achieved. The return on investment (ROI) yardstick is present throughout the workplace, one characterized by an emphasis on "what works" and "who makes it happen."

Adaptability to emerging work styles and structures
Employers continue to experiment with new structures, systems, and protocols for achieving desired outcomes. Remote work, telecommuting, flex schedules, distance learning, teleconferencing, and job sharing are examples that immediately come to mind. Advances in technology and

communication, for example, have made many of these changes viable and often at a lower cost and with no change in employee performance and production.

It goes without saying that the coronavirus pandemic forced employers to alter the style and structure of how they went about conducting their business. As a result, a "new normal" entered the picture as countless businesses, firms, agencies, and other work entities redefined work roles and the characteristics they wanted in the individuals who performed them. The result, in many instances, was a new or different staff member. Left to fend for their survival were employees not able to cope with or adjust to these new requirements and a different way of working. Concurrently, many employers set "return to work" rules that called for similar employee adjustments, as well as refresher training to combat any "learning loss" that may have been caused by work interruption.

Workers not only had to possess the knowledge and skill set required to complete their tasks; they had to adapt and fit into the new styles and structure their employers were creating. Workers not able to meet these style and structure challenges found themselves seeking job changes and relocations or being out of work because of their failure to comply.

Ability to achieve life–work balance and sustain self-care
Studies consistently recognize life–work balance and employee engagement as highly sought-after working conditions. This suggests that more individuals are approaching their work from a career development perspective, one that includes performing their occupational roles in a satisfying and agreeable workplace culture. Worker-friendly programs and rules (i.e., casual dress, flex days and hours, childcare and other support services, EAP programs, etc.) are welcomed and have been shown to influence productivity, loyalty, and retention. Correspondingly, the contemporary worker is placing greater emphasis on personal self-care and the avoidance of stress and anxiety as conditions that must be present in the career growth, mobility, and maintenance stages of the career development process.

EXPECTATIONS OF THE EMERGING AMERICAN WORKER

Now that you've been given a dose of how the workplace has changed and is changing, it's time to put the spotlight on any essential requirements for future entry and success in the fields of employment they represent. Knowing what will be expected of the next generation of individuals in a career field (i.e., health and medicine, hospitality, STEM, business and finance, etc.) is an indispensable ingredient to success in the placement world, a task made more difficult by the emergence of new occupations, representing fresh or heretofore unknown bodies of knowledge and skill sets.

Futurists take pleasure in telling us that many of the occupations in the contemporary workplace didn't exist the day the current workforce started kindergarten, a trend that continues at an accelerated pace today. Even the jobs that have been around for generations look dramatically different from when they were performed by our parents and grandparents. While these jobs were changing and evolving, hundreds of other occupations were becoming obsolete and disappearing.

A LOOK INTO THE CAREER CRYSTAL BALL

Few analysts can predict with perfect certainty the identities of the jobs of the future. Less difficult, however, may be the identification of basic skills that when present, would be desirable across the entire world of work. A look into our various career crystal balls could possibly yield the answers.

Criticized roundly in recent times for not preparing students who are equipped to succeed, schools and colleges appear to be willing today to address this deficiency. The addition of "career readiness" to "career capability" represents a theme that is currently gaining attention in both the education and employment sectors. Career capability, in this instance, represents the body of knowledge and skill sets required to practice a particular occupation (i.e., nurse, engineer, lawyer, accountant, etc.). Career readiness, on the other hand, represents a more refined set of abilities and talents that enhance one's employability and effectiveness after workplace entry.

DESIRED CAREER READINESS SKILLS OF THE FUTURE

Once cultivated in the classrooms of our schools and colleges, futurists project the five career readiness skills identified below would enhance the employability of their graduates. Each would be welcomed by employers as competencies they could nurture and develop through on-the-job engagement within the employment setting. While preferred by employers of the past and present, these skills are considered likely to be the subject of greater scrutiny in the future.

- Learning skills beyond just the knowledge and functions of a particular occupation that embrace an appreciation for learning, acceptance of its career-long presence, and a mastery of the technologies that support and extend our occupational capabilities

- Planning and management skills, embracing such structural characteristics as the ability to set and monitor goals, establish time and performance milestones, and evaluate outcomes in an organized and cost-efficient manner

- Communication skills, including listening; speaking; writing; networking; and when required, the ability to teach and persuade others

- Problem-solving and decision-making skills that can be applied easily to address workplace issues resulting in effective protocols and strategies

- Adaptability and flexibility skills beginning with a capacity for working both independently and as a team member and extending to interacting with diverse groups assigned to common tasks

Education has a formidable challenge, as most of these five skills emanate most successfully when they are included in experiential learning, laboratory, internship, and other hands-on activities. The best way to learn some of these skills is through engagement in doing them and learning from trial and error.

Individuals possessing these illusive abilities, along with the specific knowledge, skill sets, and experience deemed essential to the practice of the chosen career, will indeed be the most desirable candidates for employment. They will also be the best candidates for any lifelong learning and continuing education that will be forever present in their employment. Time will test how rapidly, efficiently, and effectively existing educational structures can be modified to ensure inclusion.

STRAIGHT TALK ABOUT ADAPTING TO CHANGE

Full achievement of one's career potential may be illusive for those unwilling or incapable of managing change in their careers, as well as the workplace culture that emanates from that change. Change is inevitable, and handling it is a skill that can be learned. It calls upon all members of the workforce to be change agents, individuals who can adapt to the ongoing changes described herein, as well as to be able to deal with the unexpected and the uncontrollable adjustments when they arise in the future.

CHAPTER 12

Challenge: Mounting an Efficient and Successful Job Search

Find a job you like and you add five days to every week.

—H. JACKSON BROWN, JR. (1940–2021), AMERICAN WRITER
BEST KNOWN FOR HIS INSPIRATIONAL BOOK, *LIFE'S LITTLE
INSTRUCTION BOOK*, WHICH BECAME A *NEW YORK TIMES* BEST
SELLER

IT IS OUT THERE SOMEWHERE—A GOOD JOB WHERE YOU CAN USE YOUR education, training, and work experience. Maybe three, four, or more job opportunities will appear as you enter, reenter, or move about the workforce. Having to choose from a number of job offers is a nice challenge to have to face.

Job search skills are different, more specific and exact, from career search skills. You conduct a job search. You go for a job interview. You consider a job offer. The term *job* will be used here for *occupation* and *career*.

A JOB COMES LOOKING FOR YOU

On that rare or extraordinary occasion, you may not have to look for a job. A job or group of jobs will come looking for you. Your status or reputation in school or in an internship afterward could result in an offer of employment before you ever thought to ask. Often, participation in a network will expose you to managers, owners, or supervisors who will encourage you to join their firm, organization, or agency.

Strong performance in one part of the workplace can expose you to others and often results in opportunities to move and grow. The more exposures you can create for yourself, the greater the likelihood that you and a vacant position will bump into each other.

For most, however, finding employment or reemployment involves a serious search and considerable information gathering. Unlike some of the earlier searches, your exploration this time is more precise and refined because where you land will be an important factor in your long-term career development. And if you're in the job market because you don't like your current position, you certainly want to get this transition right.

FACTORS BEYOND YOUR CONTROL

There are good economic times, and there are recessions and economic downturns. The workplace is expanding, or it's retracting. Job opportunities are plentiful, or they are scarce. The educational pipeline is preparing an adequate number of prospective workers, or the supply of certain graduates is inadequate. Some businesses and industries are experiencing growth and prosperity while others are simply offering replacement positions. The best opportunities may also have geographic constraints and require the job seeker to relocate.

Thriving industries cease or slow when multinational firms take jobs "offshore" to another global location. Often, employment opportunities are tied to demographic trends like the number of people coming out of school in a given year or those retiring from active employment at the other end of the pipeline. The one thing all of the above have in common is they are factors that are totally beyond your control. You can't stop them from happening, but you can possibly minimize their impact.

The structure and shape of the future workplace is something job seekers need to address. As baby boomers leave the workforce and millennials enter, the workplace is witnessing engagement changes. Baby boomers looked for full-time, ongoing employment. Millennials, in many situations, are looking at both direct-hire employment and contract staffing opportunities. The contract employee is an individual either performing a defined role or engaged in a particular project with the employer. The terms of employment (i.e., compensation, benefits, etc.) are set forth in the contract, which can be between either the employee and the employer or a staffing firm and the employer.

Each of the above represents something that may influence your job search, but one about which you have little or no control. They are business, economic, and societal issues that will influence how and where you look. Your ability to do good research and take the pulse of the occupation you want to enter will dictate how you conduct yourself as an applicant, meaning these factors will influence what, when, and why you will do certain things.

Never assume that a position you apply for and obtain is a permanent position or that you are a permanent employee. Unless you sign a contract to work for the employers for the rest of your life, you are an at will employee working at the pleasure of the firm, organization, or agency. In defining "at will," Wikipedia, the online encyclopedia, states: "the employer is free to discharge individuals 'for good cause, or bad cause, or no cause at all,' and the employee is equally free to quit, strike, or otherwise cease work."

One thing you can control is how hard you work at finding a job. Searching for work is work—hard work. Accept that fact from day one, and if you want the best results, launch an organized, articulated, and systematic assault on the world of work. The same energy and attention that you devoted to choosing a career must now be directed to choosing the job that will take you to it.

IT BEGINS WITH GENERAL RESEARCH

A major portion of the search process begins long before any interview occurs, and it has to be completed for you to get the "big picture" of opportunities in your chosen occupation. It's a part of the hard work you will need to perform. Methods for researching careers include:

- Monitoring job trends, compensation, qualifications, and credentials needed and employment locations or settings, including regular reading of the business pages of one or more print or digital newspapers
- Keeping abreast of the occupational world by participating in professional and trade events, attending conferences, reading work-related journals and magazines, and tracking your field on social media sites like LinkedIn
- Monitoring job-specific websites, including those sponsored by professional and trade organizations, as well as those of major employers of the occupation you wish to enter or reenter
- Attending job fairs, professional and trade shows, and other events where employers may be found
- Volunteering, working part-time, or performing temporary work in settings that appeal to you

Each of the above can send you a signal about openings and opportunities that you might not consider otherwise.

NEXT, YOU ARE THE RESEARCH SUBJECT

Any research that you conduct and the findings generated by it must be considered against a set of criteria that you must create for determining if a particular job is one you want to pursue. In other words, you have to identify the kind of job, compensation, location, and other elements that are needed to spark your interest. After you specify these parameters, you have to make certain you will know it when you see it.

Following are six criteria most job seekers use to filter options:

1. Position and responsibilities—What is the employer looking for? Do you possess the basic education and work experiences that qualify you to go after this job? Will you be successful if hired?

2. Salary and benefits—Does the position pay a competitive salary and appropriate benefits?

3. Culture—Is the position situated in an environment whose culture (i.e., operating mechanisms, setting, style, size, politics, etc.) appeals to you?

4. Location—Is the position situated near you or in a place where you'd be willing to relocate to?

5. Growth opportunities—Is the actual job position in a business hierarchy that will allow you to make both vertical and horizontal transitions that promote your occupational needs and career potential?

6. Life–work balance—Will the work and the employer afford you the life–work balance that you desire, as well as offer the preferences (i.e., schedule flexibility, remote work, opportunity for travel, etc.) that make the position even more desirable?

When you have completed this personal research project, make a list of the "must haves" and "would like to haves," which you can use as a point of reference or filter throughout the job search. In the final analysis, just as the employer is going to look at you, you are going to look at the position and the employer. What's it going to take for you to accept an offer? What will an employer have to present for you to consider changing your work setting? If your research of specific employment options doesn't give you great answers to most or all of these questions, it is probably an opportunity you should remove from consideration.

NOW, THE RESEARCH TURNS INTO ACTUAL JOB OPPORTUNITIES

Regardless of the economic climate or the number of positions that may be available at any given time, entry-level job seekers and seasoned job changers will have to tap into a variety of resources, both formal and informal, to learn of the postings that might interest them. Saying you don't know where to look is a lame excuse. These are the places.

Word of mouth

Human resource officers are quick to point out that a significant number of people (i.e., half or more) learn of vacant positions from family, friends, professional colleagues, or someone with whom they have ongoing contact. Part of hearing about jobs is making it known that you are looking—whether it is your first job after school or a second or third position once you have ventured into the workplace.

One should never underestimate the power of casual communication. Too many people have learned about the job they are currently in by learning about it this way. One final thought, never underestimate the power of "who you know." Far too many successful people are helped by someone close to them for this search element to be minimized.

Your informal connections, as well as the formal networks that are explained next, can give you a view of the job, the hiring process, and the workplace culture that you might otherwise not discover. In some instances, they can make recommendations or be the "push" that sees that your resume gets a thorough look or gets you the all-important interview.

Formal networks

You've likely heard the expression "It's not what you know that matters—it's who you know." Recognizing that employers are first looking for knowledgeable, skilled, and competent workers, there is a certain amount of truth in that statement.

The people you interact with in your occupation or craft can be a valuable source of job postings, many of which never find their way to an advertisement or electronic job board. This interaction may be informal (i.e., you and your fellow engineers have a team in a local coed softball league) or formal (i.e., you become a member of professional organizations, attend industry-related seminars and conferences, read work-related newsletters and blogs, etc.).

In all people connections, never underestimate the power of your voice; let it be known that you are looking for a job, and don't be shy about seeking out people for help. It may be the link that gets you the job you want.

Informational interviewing

The opportunity to sit and talk with someone doing the work you want to do or to "shadow" them for a half-day in their work environment can be a very effective research experience. These experiences should be viewed as purely informational, meaning no position is open and no promise of employment is expected or offered. Whether early in the career exploration process or now when you are looking for a job, the informational interview can be extremely influential.

In informational interviews, roles are reversed. You are the interviewer, not the one being interviewed. They do, however, offer the interviewee the opportunity to look at you, a factor that can prove beneficial if a vacancy for which you are qualified should ever open.

Social media

Social media sites, such as Facebook, Twitter, Instagram, Pinterest, LinkedIn, or others, have become popular vehicles for how Americans learn what is happening in the world and how we communicate with others. A recent survey by the Pew Research Center Internet and American Life Project discovered that eight in ten internet-using Americans were subscribers to Facebook or some other form of social media. With that level of exposure, it is little wonder this burgeoning medium is being used to identify jobs and communicate the availability of prospective employees.

Social media is also used by employers. A recent CareerBuilder. com posting conveyed that 37 percent of employers surveyed used social networks to screen candidates. How influential those findings are in determining how many job offers are being made may be impossible to determine—but the greater the use—the greater their influence. When queried by CareerBuilder as to the motivation of screening candidates via social media, the responses ranged from wanting to see people in their lifestyle and work culture to a desire to learn more about work experiences and qualifications to the very frank response of looking for reasons "not to hire."

Over the period that social media has been used to facilitate job finding and changing, a number of "rules of the road" have surfaced that require consideration by the job seeker. They include the following:

- Ensure that one's personal profile is both professional and private
- Make certain that any career information is accurate and consistent with printed and shared resumes
- Update career and work-related information as experiences warrant
- Make certain that postings are free of opinions, and biases, especially regarding present and past employers
- Establish a presence in the career and occupational networks (i.e., professional organizations) that will benefit your career
- Avoid communications and connections that can be misinterpreted or interpreted negatively by an employer conducting a background check
- View internet exposures as intersections where the candidate and employer are going to meet and capitalize on those interfaces
- Communicate a clear and compelling message in a scholarly (i.e., grammar, spelling, etc.) manner
- Use considerable forethought, discretion, and caution in determining what personal information is to be shared via any social media site

CareerBuilder offers these three important tips about the use of social media sites: be careful, be discreet, and be prepared. Further, the employment website adds that nothing you post on a social media site is absolutely private and something you think innocent may be used to filter you out of consideration for a job. Using the limited access or privacy features of the social media site allows you to provide access only to those of your choosing. Finally, anything that you post on your social media page, regardless of privacy settings, should be something you wouldn't mind have on the front page of your local newspaper or e-blasted as a part of your alumni news.

Job seekers are also encouraged to reverse positions and use the employer's social media presence to learn more about firms, organizations, or businesses. Just as employers may wish to screen applicants using social media, candidates can utilize a similar strategy to determine if the prospective job or setting would be a good fit.

Job boards

The growing capability of the internet and its popularity with users has resulted in the development of a number of large job boards that job seekers can use to identify positions, obtain assistance, and even apply online. The Pew Research Center American Trends unit reported recently that 40 percent of all library internet users went online to look for a job or use or access other employment information.

The job board technology at employment candidate's disposal today has had a two-edged impact on the job search process. From your desk, or anywhere else for that matter, the internet allows you to search for jobs anywhere in the United States or the world. Online visitors can sort opportunities by occupation, cluster, employer, setting, location, and any number of other classifications. That's the good news.

The bad news is you have to sort through the glut of listings to identify those that are relevant to your specific search. Sounds hard to believe, but in some occupations in some industries, the overload of information can be bewildering.

Job boards and job search engines come in several varieties. First, there are the large, national boards representing every occupation under the sun. There are also a large number of niche boards that focus on jobs in a particular occupational area (i.e., sales and marketing, information technology, etc.), level (i.e., executive, manager, supervisor, etc.), setting (i.e., government, health care, etc.), or location.

Similarly, many professional and trade organizations have a job board capability, which they extend as a service to members. Finally, a number of websites offer topical news for a professional group (i.e., educators, engineers, nurses, etc.) and have incorporated their former

"Help Wanted" databases into a job board link. A thorough search should include all types, and a list of the more popular general and niche job boards can be found in the appendix.

Internet business, firm, or organization websites

Employers use the "Employment at _____" or "Jobs at _____" link on their business, firm, or organization website to inform job seekers of current openings and how to make an application. For example, a nurse interested in working in Atlanta, Georgia, would find valuable information by visiting EmoryHealthcare.com, a unit with ties to Emory University Hospital. The job seeker will find EmoryHealthcare.com is connected to nine clinics, hospitals, partners, and related health care providers, each representing nursing and other job opportunities.

Similarly, many professional and trade associations provide services to their members using the internet and publications and by offering career service activities to members attending meetings and conferences. The American Counseling Association (ACA), for example, aids members to find counseling jobs through internet postings, employment opportunity ads in *Counseling Today* magazine, and a face-to-face (employer and applicant) activity at the ACA annual conference. ACA and other professional and trade associations often see these services as a "value added" aspect of membership, and access is typically restricted.

Human resource officers use their business, firm, or organization website to post everything from vacant full-time positions to temporary positions and internship possibilities.

Search and staffing firms

Recruiters, often referred to casually as "headhunters" at many of the nation's search and staffing firms, connect people and jobs for a living. Their placements range from full-time direct-hire listing to the ever growing and popular world of contract staffing. Contract staffing involves a relationship between the individual and the employer for a set period of time and in accordance with defined contract terms. They are independent contractors and not official employees of the firm or business.

Often, contract employees are hired as full-time staff members at the end of their contract.

Many recruiters and the search and staffing firms they represent specialize in specific occupational and work-setting placements (IT and engineering, health and medicine, or sales), while others represent a broad range of positions and opportunities. They place people on the basis of a fee paid to them by the employer and work diligently to help their clients make "good hires." Recruiters post their positions on their own websites, as well as many of the social media sites and popular job boards.

If you've had a good experience with a recruiter and are now looking at a future change relocation, don't hesitate to use that contact again. Staffing professionals, especially if they work with a niche group of occupations (i.e., health care, engineering, hospitality, etc.), may have what you're looking for or something similar.

Newspapers and periodicals

One of the longest running places where job seekers will learn of jobs is in the "help wanted" postings that appear regularly in the classified section of most newspapers and other periodicals. These daily and Sunday (usually larger number of positions) editions cover everything from accountant to zoologist. With the decline in the number of readers, many offer their advertisers the additional posting of their vacancies on the newspaper website, and some of these sites are fairly large in both the range and number of positions they post. Another feature of newspaper advertising is the occasional special-focus (i.e., Technology Careers, Health Careers) edition.

Niche periodicals like the *Chronicle of Higher Education* post listings of the breadth of positions that colleges and universities are attempting to fill.

Federal, state, and local government agency employment services

The federal government and most state and local government agencies have created structures to help individuals identify openings and secure employment. The federal government is the largest employer of people in the United States and as such, has a considerable number of positions for people with varied occupational and educational characteristics. The USAJobs.gov website is the largest repository of federal positions and a good place to begin your search.

Agencies within the federal government also post vacancies. For example, if you wanted to learn how to become a special agent with the Federal Bureau of Investigation (FBI), you'd go online at https://www .fbijobs.gov/index.asp. The same would be true with all federal agencies. States and local government units can also be a source of employment for qualified job seekers. These positions represent everything from law enforcement officials to emergency medical service providers to tax assessors, to name a few. In addition, many state and local governments provide services, often local units of the state-level Department of Labor, that exist to aid unemployed and underemployed people find work. A tour of the main state website would help you identify the location of these services, where professional employment counselors are positioned to help you.

One note about government careers that applicants need to consider is the influence that budgetary and economic circumstances have on job placements and replacements. When the federal, state, or local governments are experiencing difficult times, those difficulties are usually felt by existing employees and those seeking employment.

College and university career placement offices
Job seekers currently in school will find the career services component of their student services program a valuable source of job information following graduation. This service can also provide support and information about graduate school and additional training considerations.

Career services programs regularly invite employers to their campuses to meet with students and engage in active recruiting. Most colleges and universities extend their career assistance and job placement work as a lifelong service to graduates, and many have created career networks that allow students and graduates to make future employment connections.

Career fairs, trade and business shows

Career fairs, along with trade and business shows, afford job seekers the opportunity to engage workplace recruiters "up close and personal." Armed with a sheath of resumes, the job seeker can move from booth to booth and learn about employment opportunities, both current and projected.

LUCK IN THE JOB SEARCH EQUATION

There are times when luck will affect the career development process, and it often occurs during the job-seeking phase. You may be the beneficiary of good luck or the victim of bad luck. In discussing the impact of luck in life, Oprah Winfrey, famed television host, once said: "Luck is a matter of preparation meeting opportunity." Ms. Winfrey was saying several things. First, opportunity for one may not be opportunity for another, and you must be prepared to enjoy luck or chance when it pops up in your life. What affects you positively may pass right by your friend or colleague.

There may be a modicum of truth in the "It's not what you know; it's who you know" or the "Being at the right place at the right time" axioms. However, luck or chance is defined an experience beyond your control that typically results in your personal good fortune. You can have the greatest network of prospective work contacts and not be ready for the opportunity that comes your way.

Career paths are seldom slick, well-lit, and paved superhighways to a better place. Often, they are beset with turns and hills that must be negotiated and the occasional obstacle (i.e., pothole) that requires special attention by the candidates for their goal to be achieved. Tom Freston, veteran media executive at such firms as MTV Networks and Viacom, hit the nail on the head when he offered the thought that career pathways are "almost always a clumsy balance between you attempting to make things happen and the things that are happening to you."

STRAIGHT TALK ABOUT THE IMPORTANCE OF GOOD JOB SEARCH PRACTICES

Job search and identification nightmares are avoidable but not without engaging in a measure of personal research. When you have identified the specific kind of work you want to perform and the setting or location where you want to do it, you're ready to step up your research and begin to scour the job postings and listings. Critical to the job search process is a solid understanding of the qualifications you possess and your understanding of the qualifications desired by each employer. Get this part right, and look into as many sources of job listings as you can unearth. Soon you'll be sending your resume to a stream of appropriate employers.

The approaches you use to identify employment opportunities must be varied. While your family, friends, and networks are an excellent source of information and a great sounding board for your job search ideas, don't let them be the only vehicle. Job identification has changed, really changed. If you don't include contemporary practices (i.e., internet, job boards, social media sites, etc.) in your search, good opportunities will remain invisible and never be considered.

Consider any job search skills you master to be skills for life. Rare today are the women or men who start and end their careers in the same location. Often, people elect to move or change either their work or their employer. In other situations, the circumstances of employment change (i.e., layoffs, cutbacks, etc.), and people find themselves seeking employment.

Good jobs don't go to the people who make the most contacts and send out the largest number of resumes. You will find a good job if the first part of your search process deals with the array of research tasks presented herein. That research will serve as the foundation for the formal job-seeking strategies that appear on the following pages.

CHAPTER 13

Challenge: Constructing a Winning Resume

Give me six hours to chop down a tree and I will spend the first four sharpening the axe.

—ABRAHAM LINCOLN (1809–1865), PRAIRIE LAWYER, MEMBER OF CONGRESS, AND 16TH PRESIDENT OF THE UNITED STATES

LINCOLN WANTED TO WORK WITH THE BEST TOOLS AT HIS DISPOSAL— in this case, a sharp axe. Job seekers need to work with the best tools as well. Whether it is a resume, job application, interview strategy, or inquiry letter, your tools have to be the sharpest you can create, and each must be honed like Abe's axe.

Over the next several chapters, the various tools that are used in the job application process are going to be examined in detail, and the common mistakes that applicants make regarding them will be exposed. Think of them as instruments in a toolbox that you will utilize to present yourself. You'll want a complete set of tools, and you'll want each to be in the best working order.

Your purpose is to find a job. First job or fifth job—it really doesn't matter. Fill your toolbox with quality tools; replenish or refurbish them when necessary, and you'll be prepared for the challenges of the job acquisition process.

The first tool to be examined will be the resume. No position has been taken regarding which resumes are the best, and no sample resumes are included here. This extends the belief that resumes should not be viewed from a one-size-fits-all perspective. There are any number of internet sites, including those established and supported by the U.S. Department of Labor, that offer sample resumes and templates for job applicants. What follows are insights into what job applicants do wrong with their resumes, addressing purpose, structure, and content (included and excluded) and ending with how resumes are misused in the job finding process.

Everyone would like to have a "killer" resume, killer in this instance being one that bowls over the competition and gets you interview after interview. If anything derails your job search process, it is a faulty resume that can make you the deceased. To avoid this happening, you can't settle for a good resume—you need a great resume.

THE RESUME: THE FACE THE EMPLOYER SEES BEFORE MEETING YOU

Resumes are first impressions. They are your face in the hands of a human resource officer or staffing professional. Yours has to be strong enough to make the first, second, and whatever number of reviews that will result in your being invited to interview. Employment managers often get hundreds of resumes. Only a handful move from the resume to the interview. Yours must be a cut above the rest.

Stories have circulated over time as to how long your resume will actually be scrutinized. Studies completed by human resource organizations and staffing firms suggest the time resumes are examined by influential reviewers is diminishing consistently. A few years ago, experts thought that review might be limited to a few minutes. Some recent reports, however, suggest today that it may be mere seconds. Why? Because the women and men doing the hiring are looking for certain things, and like speed readers, they have become speed scanners. In addition, resume reviewers often look for something unique or specific (i.e., career progression, professional credentials, etc.). Once discovered, your resume is put aside for additional study or discarded. If the specific content the reviewer is seeking is not found, your resume will likely find the recycle bin.

STRATEGIES IN RESUME CONSTRUCTION AND RECONSTRUCTION

There are a series of strategies that resume creators need to know and implement as they create the document that will precede them into the job acquisition process. First, the resume is a living document. It is your face before you ever appear in person, and an accurate, complete, and "reader-friendly" document must be your goal. It has to convey a "can-do" spirit but not appear overblown and exaggerated. Your resume should present the "what's in it for them" (WIIFT) rather than the "what's in it for me" (WIIFM) perspective.

The resume must grow and improve with age. If you are still a student, you should construct a first-class resume; one will always be "under development" and open to revisions and upgrades as your life, school, and work experiences unfold. If you are working, you need to engage in continuous reconstruction of your resume to make certain it helps you achieve your career goals and ambitions. Like shrubbery and trees, resumes need regular pruning. A number of strategies will achieve this purpose.

Different resumes for different positions

A one-size-fits-all resume is not desirable and likely to take you nowhere. Determine in advance—to the extent possible—what the employer will be specifically looking for and include those elements by selecting the right format or type of resume to use. Often, that information is available in advance, and you should give them exactly what they want.

You need to factor into your resume construction the fact that different elements or sections in your resume are going to get more attention than others. Given the short time reviewers typically take examining resumes, you will want to make certain yours contains the basic information and then adds what you believe the position you are applying for demands. If you think of the resume as a snapshot, it should entice the reader to request an interview where the snapshot becomes a full portrait.

Solicit the evaluation and input of others

Resumes that are designed, written, and reviewed in isolation may be destined for difficulty. Every resume can benefit from objective, second-party input. Pass it by the eyes of colleagues, professors/former professors, fellow students, family members, or a career counselor and solicit their comments. Add, revise, and delete as necessary. The best resumes are crafted by the person they represent because no one knows you better than you. Then seek the assistance of others, concentrating on individuals who know you and will be candid in their review.

Appearance and organization are vital

Resumes need to be attractive, organized, and laid out with the reader in mind. Be economical with the number of words that you use. Long paragraphs filled with bloated information are an immediate turnoff. Break up your message and put some space between passages that allow the reviewer to breathe.

Use the Times New Roman, Arial, or Calibri fonts, as they are considered the easiest to read, and don't mix the fonts or font sizes within the resume. Avoid color, bold type, italics, bullets, underlined passages, etc., all of which are a distraction, not an attraction. Resumes, especially the first time through, are scanned. Can yours pass the scan test?

Boast but don't brag

Make certain your achievements and accomplishments go beyond a mere listing of job duties. A little boasting is absolutely acceptable. And go beyond titles—point out the things that you did in each position. Add details about the things you are most proud of and how they contributed to your personal success and that of your employer. Don't forget volunteerism and service learning. Be honest and positive and come across as assertive but not aggressive. Exaggerating or lying on your resume or a job application can be quite tempting but must be avoided at all costs.

Deception will likely get you fired or result in other unpleasant consequences at some point in the future.

Stress your achievements

Design a resume that points to your achievements and accomplishments. Employers want to see what you have done, not necessarily what you think you can do. The closer you can connect these achievements to the types of experiences the employer understands, the better these attainments will be viewed favorably. This is the part of the resume where you get to take a "victory lap."

Convey action and clarity and be selective

Use action words like *designed, evaluated, led, organized, generated, increased,* and *eliminated.* Passages that use the "responsible for" or "participation in" leads tell the reader nothing about what you accomplished. Avoid jargon and repetition, use the right words, and explain any that are not universally known. For example, instead of stating that you're a CFP or a CMA, state that you are a Certified Financial Planner or a Certified Medical Assistant.

Omit personal information (i.e., sex, ethnicity/race, religion, height, weight, marital status, and health information) or reasons for leaving previous positions. Sometimes, this information is used to discriminate against applicants and is addressed in various federal laws such as the Civil Rights Act, the Age Discrimination in Employment Act (ADEA), and the Americans with Disabilities Act (ADA) among others.

Be careful of numbers

Use numbers cautiously. Include information like the number of individuals you supervised, the growth in revenues your work generated, and the number of projects you managed. Refrain from using dates (i.e., dates diplomas or degrees are conferred, etc.) and other information that will tell the reviewers how old you are and allow them to consider age (and possibly discriminate against you) on the basis of how old you are.

The experience dilemma

It is true that many employers prefer experience in prospective employees and will stress performance and productivity throughout the hiring process. There are others, however, who will place potential ahead of experience. This is especially true of employers who have positions involving a preplacement orientation or training experience. This employer is placing greater emphasis on personal characteristics, traits, and potential than on past experience and performance.

How do you handle the experience issue on your resume? Be candid regarding the experiences you had as a part of your education, internships, or summer or temporary work experiences and be prepared to expand on those activities should the opportunity to interview present itself. If you're in the midst of a job change, try to relate the experience concerns of the prospective employer to the work experiences you have had or are now having. This is called "bridging" and often generates positive results.

The references question

Human resource officers are divided on whether references should be included on your resume, and the use of the expression, "References provided upon request" is considered optional by many. You will likely, however, be required to provide references if you are the subject of further scrutiny. Be aware that the federal Fair Credit Reporting Act has guidelines for employers to use in conducting background and other checks that are designed to protect you and keep you fully informed.

Tell the world

Get the resume out using all of the networks and communication channels at your disposal. You will mail some and email more. Resumes can be posted on or made a part of your social media (i.e., LinkedIn, Facebook, etc.) profile. Send a few resumes to associates and friends who are in a position to put them before employers who may be looking for someone with your experience, knowledge, or skills. Create enough to hand out at career fairs and expos when you attend them.

Following the guidance in the above list of dos and don'ts will result in an accurate, sharp instrument to take with you in the next phase of the job acquisition process. The next section will describe the different types of resumes that you may consider in the construction or reconstruction process.

A RESUME TAILORED TO THE JOB OPPORTUNITY

Following on the theme that different job-seeking situations may require a special resume; some employers will specify the type of resume they would like to see. Others will allow you the freedom to select the tool that works best for you.

Following are the types of resumes you may have to create for different situations.

Chronological resume

This resume is basically a presentation of your employment history in succeeding order with your current or most recent position up front. Then other positions follow. Many human resource officers and staffing professionals prefer this type of resume because their eye can quickly examine your work roles and experiences. This is a good resume for those with a rich, evolving set of career experiences.

Chronological resume	Functional resume	Combination resume
Resume with profile	Targeted resume	Mini resume
Portfolio, website, and video resume	Curriculum vitae	Letter resume

Figure 13.1 Types of Resumes

Functional resume

This resume puts your knowledge, skills, and experiences front and center, rather than your employment history. It permits you to showcase and emphasize your talents and is often used by those attempting to change positions or those with "gaps" in their career history.

Combination resume

A combination resume places your knowledge, skills, and experience first and then goes on to depict your work history. It allows you to equally emphasize your occupational qualifications and work history.

Resume with profile

This resume amplifies the applicant's skills experience with brief profile statements to stress specific items.

Targeted resume

There will be occasions when the applicant will need to 'tailor" or customize the resume in order to respond to unique qualifications and experiences specifically called for by the employer. Targeted resumes become focused or individual tools and require more work by the applicant. When successful, the targeted resume matches the applicant effectively to the requirements of the employer.

Mini resume

This resume, typically one page in length, briefly highlights the career qualifications and experiences the applicant is presenting to the employer, and it often leads to a request for an expanded resume later in the process. The mini resume is also effective in communicating personal information to any individuals or networks where it can be shared and passed along. Never send the mini resume or snapshot to the employer who wants to see the full portrait.

Portfolios, websites, video resumes, and nontraditional tools

Artists, photographers, writers, and others are often called upon to submit samples of their creations and/or work samples that reflect the breadth, depth, and quality of their experiences. Writing samples and other creations may have to be submitted in advance, while more extensive art and photography portfolios are typically presented at the time of the interview. Applicants for a television field reporter position, for example, are usually called upon to submit a videotape of their news reporting.

Applicants for these types of presentations often prepare print or internet presentations that reflect their best work or a sampling of their varied products. However, the technologies today allow job seekers to create personal websites that become video resumes of sorts. There is some evidence, for example, that recruiters are looking at social media (i.e., LinkedIn, Facebook, etc.) sites as a first means of identifying prospective applicants for positions they represent.

A video resume is a way for job seekers to showcase their abilities beyond the capabilities of a traditional paper resume. The video resume allows prospective employers to see and hear applicants to get a feel for how applicants present themselves. Video resumes should have a beginning (where you introduce yourself), a middle (where you talk about your knowledge, skills, and experiences), and an end (where you speak briefly to your career goals and thank the viewer for considering your candidacy). Like your print resume, the video resume should be examined and evaluated by a colleague, friend, or family member.

Like the preparation for a live interview, you must dress appropriately, look directly into the camera, speak clearly and deliberately, and limit the length of the presentation. Even though you're an amateur video creator, do all within your power (i.e., record in an appealing environment, control extraneous noises, etc.) to create a first-rate video. This is often a situation where "practice makes perfect" and you may have to have several "takes" before you get the product you want.

Once you have created the video resume you feel represents you effectively, post it on one of the internet career networking sites (i.e., CareerBuilder, etc.) as a part of your profile. Be certain to include links to your website if you have one and include a link on your paper or online resume to the video. Share it with the members of your network who can connect you to job sources.

Finally, don't expect a website or video resume to be your only resume. The traditional print or online resume will likely reach far greater numbers of prospective employers.

Curriculum vitae

This tool is used in place of the resume in academic and scientific circles and allows you to complement your education and work history with in-depth information about your scholarly and research pursuits. Like the resume, the curriculum vitae follows an outline format that offers an overview of the basic experiences and then becomes lengthier, depending on the number of scholarly and professional details (i.e., articles published, professional presentations, etc.) that are added. Applicants for positions in higher education or scientific settings are most likely to be called upon to present curriculum vitae.

Letter resume

Increasingly career counselors and staffing professionals are recommending that applicants use a letter resume to respond to and apply for specific positions. They are most often used when you're expressing your interest in general employment and not necessarily applying for a specific position.

Whether presented via a letter or an email, three basic rules apply when developing a letter resume. First, begin your letter in a normal manner by introducing yourself and stating your reason for writing. Next, use bullet points to insert a summary of your basic resume points in the body of your letter. Finally, close by thanking the addressee and provide information for follow-up.

The job applicant has multiple resume formats to consider when stepping into or moving about the work world. Study them all and determine which ones will work best for you.

MISUSES OF THE RESUME

Resumes can be an effective tool in advancing your candidacy forward for a job, or they can stop it dead in its tracks. Following are seven ways in which applicants err in the creation or dissemination of their resume:

1. Develop a single resume and distribute it for every position you are considering. Even worse, you send it to firms, organizations, agencies, and institutions that haven't even posted vacancies.

2. Insert extraneous or irrelevant "stuff" in their resume. Resumes should be concise, lean, and friendly. They should not be full of padding and fluff.

3. Create a resume that is too short or too long. That is the reason you should tailor your resume for the position you want to obtain. Consider the words to be paint and give the subject (you) one good coat.

4. Come across as unprofessional in either their print or video resume. Examples are failure to proofread, use of incorrect or outdated terms and names, and the inclusion of inappropriate photos (i.e., party scenes that are accessible online where your video resume is posted).

5. Use terms like "results-oriented professional," "bottom-line-conscious individual," and "team player," instead of presenting an actual record of accomplishments that provide evidence of results, objectives, achievements, and traits. Many others falter in their lack of action verbs (i.e., completed, evaluated, managed, etc.) to depict their experiences.

6. Contain inaccurate or misleading information. For example, if you are not accomplished in the use of a particular tool (i.e., Microsoft Excel or Adobe Photoshop), don't list it as one of your competencies or skills. More importantly, don't present anything that isn't true. It will catch up with you later.

7. Avoid including information that is obvious. For example, once it would have been novel to say that one was competent in Microsoft Office. Today, it is expected that all applicants for certain positions have this capability.

8. Speak the correct and commonly used language. Refrain from using terms that are not universally comprehended across the career field

or acronyms that are not generally known and understood. Similarly, the use of slang, internet acronyms, and emojis in resumes or any form of work-related communications can produce negative results.

Follow the general guidance presented throughout this chapter and be mindful of these listed misuses and a great resume will soon be in your files.

STRAIGHT TALK ABOUT RESUME CONSTRUCTION AND RECONSTRUCTION

The primary objective of resume construction and reconstruction is to get from the big stack to the little stack and be invited for an interview. It should be your creation, and you should do everything you can to make yours "reader friendly" and cause it to stand out from the rest in the stack.

No attempt has been made here to recommend or offer the perfect resume. To do so would contradict the one-size-does-not-fit-all message that's being conveyed to you. Any number of internet sources will help you identify formats and provide templates where all you need to do is fill in the blanks. In reviewing these sites, you'll get to see the variety. Be wary, however, of following any one format just the way it's presented. You may look exactly like the last job applicant that used that template.

Don't allow your resume to get too old or stale. Revise it regularly and keep handy for that unexpected time when you might learn of a new and attractive job opportunity. Revisit periodically and keep current.

When you believe you have a quality resume, put it in the hands of anyone who can assist you in your job acquisition. Don't be shy!

CHAPTER 14

Challenge: Mastering the Job Interview

A good laugh makes any interview, or any conversation, so much better.

—BARBARA WALTERS, FORMER TELEVISION NETWORK NEWS ANCHOR, TALK SHOW HOST, AND REPORTER

SHOULD YOUR RESUME OR APPLICATION PASS THROUGH THE RIGORS OF the screening process, you'll likely be invited to interview for the position that interests you. You've passed the initial review test, and now you can consider yourself a serious candidate for the job. This is where the interview comes into play and your skills at interviewing are going to be scrutinized. Now, you get a chance to put a true face on what to this point has been just paper or an electronic document.

Unfortunately, this is the part of the job-seeking process where many fail. Job seeking requires the same diligence and dedication, along with a measure of confidence, that produce positive results up until this point. You got the interview and that's a positive. Now, you need to talk the interviewer or interview team into giving you the job. Don't talk yourself out of the job. Talk yourself into it.

STRATEGIES THAT IMPACT JOB INTERVIEWING

Job interviewing is all about behavior and how you present yourself. Consider the following strategies as you move into that important chair where your future job hangs in the balance.

Concentrate on presentation

Image conveyance is a critical part of the interview process. The person or persons sitting across from you are visualizing working with you on a project or imagining how you might be to manage. Some recruiters suggest one in four job seekers fail by not coming across with the right image, not looking or speaking the part. You have to look as good in person as you did on paper.

Be yourself

A host of articles and blogs will suggest all the things you should do or say in an interview. The path to success is for you to convince the employer about what you know, what you can do, what you are capable of learning, and how you will be the best "hire" that can be made. Sounds simple, but it's not.

Perfect answers to interview questions cannot be rehearsed. Prospective employers don't want to see how you are like all of the other candidates. They want to see how you are different. Don't try to be someone you aren't.

Prepare, prepare, prepare

Preparing for each interview will help you to understand better what the employer is looking for and allow you to tailor your presentation to fit those needs. The pre-interview period should be spent studying the employer and doing as much research as you can about the work it does and the position you are applying for. Your earlier research was about where the jobs are and whether they appeal to you or not. Now, your research has to become more specific.

Practice or mock interviews will allow you to "role-play." Better yet, videotape or audiotape those practice interviews and play them back. Would you hire you? What did you do right? Where could you have improved? Career service centers at colleges and universities often offer practice interviewing and critiquing as one of their many services.

Learn as much as you can about the workplace culture

Every workplace has a culture. Find out as much as you can about that culture in advance and display that understanding as you proceed through the interview, as it will signal your interest and motivation to become a part of the culture. A simple statement like, "I read where XYZ was ranked as one of the twenty-five fast growing firms in the region" is a great thing to insert over the course of an interview. The more you know about the way a firm or business functions, the better able you will be to personalize your interview responses directly to real situations.

The candidate that fails to research the employer and then interject that knowledge during the interview is inviting difficulty. These questions and the answers you create for them become a vital part of your preparation for the interview. Fill in any blanks regarding workplace culture when given the opportunity to ask questions during the interview.

Determine what employers want

Review the job description until you are certain you know what the employer wants and be able to connect yourself to this position. Know it inside, out, and sideways. Generally, employers want to provide quality goods and services, address issues and problems, operate efficiently, extend their reach, make money, or a combination of these and other goals. Tell the interviewer how you can contribute.

Is the employer changing direction, adding new products and services, or in a growth mode? Each could be relevant to why there is a vacancy. Others may have a specific or unique mission within which your role would be situated.

Be flexible and able to handle different situations

Interviews are seldom identical. The jobs, while they may be in your career field, are being offered in different settings by firms, agencies, and organizations that are likely to be distinctively different from each other.

Interviewers are also different and employ their personal style in taking you over all of the hurdles that each will want to see you jump.

A common tactic among interviewers is to ask you something or pose a situation that they hope will knock you off your stride. Should this occur, refrain from being defensive or argumentative. Remember that the interviewers are attempting to see how you will deal with a certain situation. They probably have a full complement of "yes" women and men and are looking to see if you are different. Pause, take a breath, and come back positively and forcefully.

There may be some positions (i.e., graphic artist, photographer, etc.) when the interviewer will ask you to present samples of your work in advance or at the time of the interview. Finally, if mastery of certain job functions is essential to employment, some employers may wish to use a portion of the interview time to administer a skills test; for example, an applicant for an editorial position may be handed a manuscript and asked to edit it. You will likely be informed in advance if performing a work task will be required.

Finally, be ready for everything from being invited to a team lunch or afforded the opportunity to take a workplace tour. Anything is possible, especially if the employer wants to learn more about you or see you in different positions.

Take risks—reasonable risks

Take risks if you're comfortable taking them and they don't appear radical or crazy. Most employers are not looking for radical or crazy. Offering innovative solutions with fresh ideas is usually fine—but recognize that every time you offer an "outside the box" response that works, a significant number will not. If your research identified a problem needing correction or something you see yourself fixing or changing, go forward in the interview with a plan for doing that. This shows assertiveness on your part and the forethought to offer a solution.

Before departing from the "risk taking" discussion, accept the reality that many employers are turned off and will even hold certain characteristics against you. Federal laws protect you from being discriminated against or treated differently because of your race, sex, religion, national origin, and age, and some states add others to the protected classes. However, it is not beyond the realm of reality that an employer may not like the obvious tattoos or body piercings that you exhibit or the flamboyant behavior you display. The reality is that most owners, managers, and supervisors tend to be older and not necessarily "tuned in" to the ways of the younger generation. Be sensitive enough to know where the line may be drawn.

Look, appear, and sound good

Don't underestimate the body language aspects (i.e., enthusiastic smile and firm handshake vs. cautious grin and wet noodle handshake) of the interview. What will be the interviewer's first impression of you and how will your presence be interpreted during the exchange? Are you dressed appropriately?

As you interact with the interviewer, refrain from using slang, jargon, street talk, or terminology that may not be understood. The internet has created a whole new world of "shorthand," which may or may not be understood in interview situations. Slang and street talk are seen by some as unprofessional and immature and should be avoided.

And most importantly, turn off your cell phone fifteen minutes before the interview and leave it turned off. A phone interruption tells the interviewers you aren't prepared to devote your full attention and energy to the interview. Finally, arrive on time or a bit early, even if it means taking a test run to the place where the interview is to be held. The late Jane Doe could easily become the "late" Jane Doe.

Your appearance (i.e., dress, grooming, hygiene, etc.) and conduct speak to your self-worth and character, and you want to project nothing but the positive.

Differentiate yourself

Your network participation and research should allow you to paint a profile of the candidates that you are competing with. You may even know some of them. This can certainly be the case when you are competing with others on staff for a promotion or growth position.

It is unlikely that you will be the only applicant with good grades and a set of relevant work experiences. How are you different? How do you stand out? That's what the interviewer wants to discover. Be wary of anyone saying they can "package" you for career success or websites that suggest the perfect phrases to use or the perfect answers to the interviewer's questions.

Answer each question honestly, enthusiastically, allowing your personality, values, interests—even your idiosyncrasies—to pour forth. These are the things that make you different. If you pretend to be someone you aren't and they hire you, who's going to show up for work—not the character you were coached to assume or the person with the padded set of answers.

Focus and know when to shut up

Stay on point and know when to close your mouth. The interviewer is probably not interested in your workout schedule or your passion for Labrador retrievers. Brevity beats overkill, and a good interviewer who wants to know more will ask or probe deeper into an answer you've given previously.

If you think you've been talking too much, you are probably correct and corrective behavior is in order. Avoid repetition, even when asked to offer a more intense answer to a previously asked question.

Concentrate on the now and the future

Refer to the past when it is appropriate. Yes, you'll likely get the chance to talk about your education or your current job but only use those experiences (i.e., opportunity for career growth and development, take on greater challenges, etc.) that will leverage the interview in your favor.

Don't dwell on yesterday unless asked to. Most interviewers want to see you address the "here and now" and the future. And avoid the "I've always done it this way" answer, as it suggests that you're rigid and either unwilling or incapable of change.

Showcase your desirable qualities and relevant experiences

Let the interviewer know about your leadership and problem-solving skills if the position calls for them. Stress your strengths, but do so via the depiction of experiences you have had. Send a signal to interviewers regarding how "coachable" you are and how you deal with constructive feedback and criticism if you get it. Beyond the knowledge and skill set you offer interviewers, they may want to determine how receptive you will be to the evaluation of your performance.

Avoid mind wandering and being negative, and control your emotions

During each interview, your mindfulness is being tested. Are you focusing on what the interviewer is asking you or on the answer you intend to present? Both are important, but if you don't practice good mindfulness, you may be creating an answer to a question you aren't being asked.

Never speak in derogatory terms about your education and training experiences or a previous employer or employment situation. Negativism can be translated as whining, and you become a whiner. It is not the image you want to project.

It is equally important to control your emotions. The job search process, as stated earlier, can be a time-consuming, frustrating, and, sometimes, stress-generating experience. Being unemployed or furloughed, in addition, can result in greater tension and anxiety. Don't allow emotional factors to enter the interview room with you and affect you negatively. Avoid emotional and mood extremes and navigate a more central path throughout the interview. Finally, never appear desperate or willing to take any job under any conditions.

Get answers to your questions

Asking questions during an interview serves two purposes. First, you get to learn what you didn't know or couldn't discover in your research about the job or the employer. Just as importantly, your questions tell the interviewer something about your knowledge and understanding.

Following is a list of suggested questions:

- What is the potential for career growth in this firm, organization, or agency?
- What are the opportunities for training and development?
- How would you describe the culture of the organization?
- In examining the responsibilities, I would like to know more about _____.
- What is your personal management style (if being interviewed by a future manager/supervisor)?
- From your personal perspective, what makes this a good place to work?
- What are the current challenges, and what is the philosophy of the firm, organization, or agency when addressing changes and challenges of the future?
- What is your timetable for making a decision and filling this position?

Don't consider the above list an exhaustive one. Your personal concerns should dictate what questions you ask. Just don't ask questions for which you already know the answer or for which the answers are evident and obvious.

Also, take notes about important issues or matters and jot down the answers to the questions you ask. But don't let the note taking distract from devoting attention to the interviewer's questions.

Expect to be tested

There could be situations during the hiring process, often in conjunction with the interview, when you may be asked to sit for an examination of some sort. Some employers believe these tools measure things they associate with successful performance on the job. Employers have been known to use the Wonderlic Cognitive Ability Test (measures intelligence, capacity for learning, and problem solving), the Myers-Briggs Type Indicator (measures psychological preferences in the manner in which people see the world and make decisions), and the Minnesota

Multiphasic Personality Inventory (measures personality structure and its relationship to occupational situations).

These are just three examples of how assessment tools might be used by employers in the screening process leading up to hiring. Some employers have developed instruments of their own that they will use to screen candidates and measure desirable knowledge, skills, characteristics, or traits.

Prepare for the dreaded salary discussion

It would be great if all employers posted salary information as a part of the ad or posting, but in reality, more don't than do. It may come up during a telephone screening when the screener attempts to determine your salary expectations. The same could happen during the actual interview. You need to be prepared for the discussion, and possibly negotiation, whenever it arises.

If asked about salary or your earning history, have a sense of how much you should say and be willing to discuss. The employer often will ask for a salary history with your letter of interest or presenting resume and will use this information to screen away people they feel are expecting salaries higher than they are expecting or willing to pay.

Also have a sense of the salaries the occupation commands and if any differences exist because specific demands of the roles or where the position may be located. Computer programmers, for example, get paid more in New York City than they do in York, Pennsylvania.

The basic rule is to determine and set in advance of any negotiation the salary it will take for you to accept the job or change positions. The last thing you want to have happen is to accept a salary that you will regret afterward. Be aware that postings that suggest a salary range of $55,000 to $70,000 represent a range. Candidates with basic knowledge, skill, and competencies are unlikely to command a salary at the higher end.

You may or may not have to answer the salary question specifically before the interview ends, and it is far better to present your qualifications, experiences, and personal characteristics before any money issues are discussed. You may wish to address compensation by stating a specific number with the follow-up statement to the effect that you are open to discussion and negotiation.

Approach any salary discussions with a realistic sense of your worth and never apologize or become defensive in stating what you believe that worth to be. Most employers are positioned to pay you more than their first offer or the lowest figure in the range they present, and your failure to negotiate effectively could result in your not getting the best salary. Acknowledge the salary proposal (after all, they are telling you they want you to work for them), and then go on to indicate that your assessment of yourself and understanding of the pay for similar positions requires that they increase the offer.

This subject of compensation and salary will be examined in greater detail in the "accept or not accept" information presented in chapter 18.

Approach video interviews in an identical manner
Given the visual and audio capabilities in many employers' communications arsenal (i.e., Zoom, Skype, GoTo Meeting, etc.), you may be asked to participate in a long-distance interview. Telephonic interviews took on a whole new identity when the coronavirus pandemic generated protocols restricting people distancing, travel, and meeting management.

Long distance can mean across town or on the other side of the globe. You will be having a face-to-face experience, but you and your interviewer will be at different ends of a camera and a microphone. If your interview is to be conducted in this manner, all of the rules presented herein are still applicable, as well as a handful of others.

Individuals participating in video interviews should make certain they are familiar and comfortable with the technological equipment that is being used so the experience goes forward without any technical glitches. Care must also be taken to ensure that the surroundings, lighting, and general privacy is appropriate for the formal activity. For example, one should never attempt to participate in a video interview from an environment (i.e., current job location, Starbucks, etc.) where they cannot speak freely and be heard or a location where the interview might be disturbed by people, telephones, and other intrusions.

Close the interview and move forward

At the close of any interview, make your interest in the position known once again and possibly more firmly than previously. Your enthusiasm will be governed, in large measure, to how the interview proceeded. Interviews can affirm for candidates their interest in a particular job, and if that occurs, you may wish to exit the interview with a strong affirmation of your interest in the position. Remember, too, that some employers use a multiple interview format or require a "call back" for the candidate to be interviewed by another individual.

The interview ends, but does it? You have shaken hands again, offered your gratitude and commentary on the experience, and departed. Now, it's okay to turn your cell phone back on and unbutton the top of your shirt or blouse.

In the period immediately following the interview, you should take some time for personal reflection. What are the things that you did well and in what areas could you have responded differently or provided a better answer to a particular question? Critiquing your experience, if only a mental review, will prepare you to do a more effective job the next time. Each interview is a learning experience and can teach you some valuable dos and don'ts.

Take the time to prepare and send a written or email note to the interviewer, expressing once again your enthusiasm and interest in the position. Often, a handwritten message on a card can be very effective. If you don't have the best handwriting, a typed or emailed message will be fine.

Be certain to provide any follow-up information that may have come up during the interview, information such as a list of references that will complete your application and interview and allow the employer to move forward to the decision stage. Finally, if you have not heard from the employer within the time frame in which they indicated they would make a decision, it is appropriate to follow-up by either telephone or electronic mail.

One of the features found in the interview process is the "call back" or "pass along" tactic. Often, the second, third, or later interview is with another individual who is only talking with the candidates screened by the human resource officer or staff. This person may be the manager or supervisor who oversees the particular position. Other "call back" interviews focus on a different stage of the screening process with the interviewee being asked an entirely new and different set of questions, including hypothetical and situational questions where knowledge and understanding must be applied.

Note: In the preceding section the word "interviewer" was used, but job applicants are often interviewed by interview teams or by multiple individuals during the process.

THE ROLE OF BEHAVIORAL INTERVIEWING

Behavioral interviewing occurs when the employer poses hypothetical situations or questions to determine how the candidate responds to real circumstances in the workplace. This often occurs when you are engaged in a multiphase interview and the second or third phase calls upon you to demonstrate behaviors to respond to hypothetical cases or situations. The responses you offer are thought to be indicative of your general thought processing and problem-solving ability, processes the interviewer would like to observe and evaluate. Following are several behavioral interview questions:

- Describe a time in your work when you were faced with a particularly complex problem. What did you do?
- Identify an experience in your work where you were called upon to exert personal leadership in order to achieve your employer's goal or objective. How did you respond?
- Cite an example of how your personal creativity and ingenuity were called upon to address a work-related matter?

When faced with questions that require answers about behaviors you have either used or would use to address a work situation, you should use what human resource managers refer to as the STAR technique, a method of answering an interview question that addresses Situation, Task, Action, and Response.

First, think of a situation similar to one in any of the three questions above. In stating the situation, you might say, "I recall a situation when our work team was spinning our wheels and floundering, unable to address an important production matter." Next, offer the task or strategy that reflected your cognizance of the situation and what it required. Your response might be that you believed it necessary to go back to the beginning and review what outcomes were desired and what steps would likely result in their achievement.

This would be followed by the action you performed and requested of your coworkers in order to resolve the situation. Here, you might state that you took an active leadership role and organized team members in a way that required each to expend a certain level of energy in developing an effective plan. You might add how you oversaw this effort and the time requirements you set for its completion. Finally, inform the interviewer of the result that occurred from your attention and behavior.

Applying the STAR technique is not difficult but doesn't always play itself out positively in a spontaneous situation. You may have to think of behavior situations in advance, committing the application of the STAR technique in each instance to memory and then interjecting your prepared response into the interview when appropriate.

STRAIGHT TALK ABOUT JOB INTERVIEWS

Getting the interview means you are viewed positively in the eyes of the employer. Now, all that remains—and it's a major challenge—is to talk yourself into being hired by demonstrating that you're the right person for the job. Learn to control the controllable and minimize the impact of the things you can't. And most importantly, learn from each interview you have and factor that analysis into the next experience. Enjoy the experience and learn from it. Remember the Barbara Walters quote at the beginning of this chapter. Should something humorous occur or be said during the interview, don't be afraid to laugh.

Being intelligent, skilled, and capable will not be enough. Most of those being interviewed have these qualifications. Differentiate how you are different and show your agility, as well as your desire to learn and grow. Conduct yourself using an etiquette that leaves the impression or image that you would be a fantastic coworker or staff member.

Interviews result in one of three things. You are offered a position, your involvement in the search process continues with a prospective employer, or you are eliminated from future consideration. Here's hoping one of the first two is in your future.

CHAPTER 15

Challenge: Writing Proficiency as a Job Search Ally

I hate writing. I like having written.

—DOROTHY PARKER (1893–1967), AMERICAN POET, SHORT
STORY WRITER, CRITIC, AND SATIRIST, BEST KNOWN FOR HER
HUMOROUS PERSPECTIVE ON LIFE AND LIVING

IT WAS ONCE CALLED THE "POWER OF THE PEN." TODAY, IT'S MORE
appropriately the "power of the keyboard," and it certainly applies in
the world of job acquisition. Your ability to write and deliver a powerful
message in your cover letter or job application can be more influential
than you realize.

Cover letters, either in print or email form, serve as front pieces for
resumes, and you can never underestimate the influence this letter will
have on whether the reviewer is going to flip the letter over to examine
the resume. A strong letter is one that is well written and presents your
case for employment in a concise and effective statement. What good is
a great resume if a poor cover letter shields it from ever being seen?

Applications, for the employers that still use them, force you to present full and complete information in short, clear, and concise passages
that offer the application reviewer a lot of information in a relatively

short amount of space. There are examples of lengthy, detailed employment applications (i.e., federal government employment forms), but for the most part, employment applications are one- or two-page documents.

There may also be opportunities for you to exchange communications with a prospective employer who seeks additional information or clarification regarding something in your resume or growing out of an early interview. Some employers ask candidates to prepare written answers to a series of hypothetical questions or create written responses to case situations as a part of the screening process. Often, you will be asked to provide a writing sample, and it may be focused on an employer-driven topic or question. You need to be as sensitive about these types of communication as you would be to cover letters, emails, and resumes.

All of the above will require your personal attention, and your movement forward in the job acquisition process may depend totally on the quality, clarity, and style of these written communications.

PREPARATION OF COVER LETTERS AND EMAILS
The instrument used most often to present a candidate for employment is either a written or email letter, the latter of which has significantly grown in popularity over the past decade or two. It's important to know when to go with paper, or when to go paperless, or if there isn't a preference. Whether you send your letter via the U.S. Postal Service or communicate via an email transmission, a number of issues need to be addressed, and the implementation of a series of protocols and strategies will bring you the best results.

Make a great first impression
Consider the introductory letter or email as your first opportunity to grab the reader's attention, as well as the first time to "turn them off." Incorrect names or titles, confused job descriptions, and any number of other erroneous details tell the reader you didn't care enough to get things right. The same is true for the rest of the letter or email. Grammar errors, misspellings, and an unattractive presentation will also kill or diminish your chances of moving forward.

One of the dangers associated with using cover letters and emails is that you often create and file the letter as a template document in your word-processing system. Be careful when you go to that file and use it a second, third, or additional time. A letter containing references to or information about a position with the XYZ Information Technology, Inc., is not going to be favorably received by ABC Information Technology, Inc. Make certain all of your attachments are properly identified. Proofread, proofread, and proofread again.

Lead with your best

The first line in many popular novels is the one that readers remember the most. *A Tale of Two Cities* by Charles Dickens begins with "It was the best of times; it was the worst of times." Many who don't remember the story remember the opening sentence. Dickens enticed the reader to continue, and that is exactly what you want the opening of your cover letter or email to do.

An opening sentence like the following captures the attention of the reader and often produces the desired results. "Since graduating from college and entering the field of pharmaceutical sales, I have achieved $___ in annual sales and had oversight responsibility for the work of ten members of the northeast regional sales team. Now, I would like to bring that record of success to F. E. Brown Pharmaceuticals."

This opening sentence speaks to the writer's education background and sales experience. It presents evidence of sales success and mentions the supervisory role that the applicant has undertaken, including the number of people whose work is being managed. It also tells the reader about the sales geography with which the applicant is familiar. All of these points are made in a single sentence. The writer has led with a message of achievement, capability, and experience.

The second sentence opens the door to bringing that talent and experience to the employer posting the position and suggests both interest in the firm and a belief that such a transition would be a good one.

Revise until you get it right

Your first writing is not always your best writing. From your days as a student, you know that good results occur when you create, review, edit, and then submit a revision as your best work. Apply the same principle in any written documents that you prepare as a part of the job-seeking process.

Be clear about destination

Make certain your letter and resume make it to the proper destination. Email messages with documents attached to them have a propensity for becoming lost in cyberspace in what many refer to as the "deep black hole." If there is a specific contact that you are certain will give your letter and resume the appropriate attention, send or email it directly to that individual. General letters and emails to the chief executive officer, human resource officer, or another high-ranking official are likely to find their way to the delete button or the office shredder.

Create the right size message

Some cover letters and emails are too long. Others are too short. Tell the readers what they need to hear and let the resume do the rest. Letters and emails aren't dumping grounds for all the things you couldn't find a place for in your resume. Furthermore, don't repeat everything that you've already placed in your resume. Redundancy and repetition are taboo. Similarly, being overly chummy or gratuitous can also be taken the wrong way.

Many human resource officers and recruiters say that a cover letter or introductory email can do what it needs to do in 250 words or less. Shorter is better if shorter will do the job. This means you must be selective and focused, opting for the most salient information and descriptors. These are sometimes called "grabbers" and cause the reviewer to give your resume a good look.

Be positive, but cautious

Be wary of too much self-praise and too much criticism of previous work situations and relationships with managers and colleagues. Citing your strengths and any personal competencies that may be useful in the position is a good thing. Suggesting you are the "perfect" candidate for addressing the employer's concerns may be a little too strong. If you know about problems and issues the targeted employer is experiencing, use the interview to validate your beliefs, and then proceed to offer a solution or correction if warranted.

Finally, don't let your letter, email, or interview profile you as a "know-it-all," especially if you're applying for an entry-level job. There is often a thin line between the presentation of important self-information and being boastful. Emit a positive tone without being overly aggressive.

Avoid storytelling

If storytelling is appropriate and will help you in presenting yourself, save it for the interview, and don't clutter your letter or email with this kind of passage. It seldom adds substance to your letter or email.

Offer an original piece of work

In earlier chapters, you were cautioned against letting a coach "package" or "prep" you for the various phases of the job search process. The same is true with all written communications. Reviewers see so many letters and resumes that they begin to know the internet template or publication that offered the original message they are holding in their hand.

Personalize your letter or email, and stay away from statements like "To whom it may concern" and clichés like "I'm writing to express my interest in your posted position of _____" or "Enclosed please find my resume for the _____ position you have posted." Your understanding of the prospective employer and the position it is attempting to fill will help you personalize your message.

Include only the necessary and the relevant

Your successes as a marathon runner or service as a Big Brother/Big Sister volunteer may fit during the interview, but emphasis on extraneous achievements may have the opposite effect on your letter or email reader. In fact, if you say too much about preparing and running in marathons, you may create an impression that your away-from-work interests may be more important than your work interests and habits.

One additional point should be made about relevance given the major increases in the use of email to communicate with prospective employers. Make certain you know exactly what you are attaching to your emails. Stories can be found all over the internet about job applicants, often students, who attach a totally inappropriate photo, link, or document to a formal or professional communique they are exchanging with a prospective employer.

PREPARATION OF APPLICATIONS

There are still quite a few employers that use a standardized form or group of forms to gather information they wish to collect from job applicants. Many firms that employ a lot of people or have large numbers of facilities or stores—Walmart, Target, McDonald's—use a standardized application form. Many occupational specialties (i.e., automotive service technician, health care assistant, etc.) use a standard application development with questions that cut across settings and help standardize the application process.

Similarly, the internet is being used increasingly as a vehicle for you to complete an online application that is submitted directly to the employer and inserted into the screening process. Like with print applications, make a copy of any online applications for your job search portfolio. While the majority of these applications ask for the same basic information, each is just different enough to require that the applicant stop and complete it. In some instances, firms will ask applicants to complete an electronic application on the internet. Proofread everything you place on the form before you hit the submit button.

As one of the largest employers in the world, the U.S. federal government offers an incredible mix of occupational positions at every level of training and experience. Included are accountants, IT engineers, researchers, lawyers, inspectors, park rangers, doctors, mechanics, and any number of different professionals and service workers.

At www.USAJobs.gov, an applicant for federal employment can search a comprehensive list of vacancies and create an account that can then be used to process a formal application for federal employment. Many state and local governments have a similar system.

The task of completing a job application is sometimes as simple as transferring information the applicant has already collected for the resume and then addressing any questions or requests for information that are unique to the application. If you have created a resume, be certain to take a copy with you at the time of application, as it will allow for the smooth transference of data. If at all possible, make a copy of any completed applications for inclusion in your career portfolio. Expect more firms to use this type of electronic connection with prospective employees in the future.

STRAIGHT TALK ABOUT GOOD WRITING

Poor writing can take many forms. The same things that your English teacher in high school or college marked you down for in the past are the same things that will get your job-seeking communication strategies in trouble. Poor sentence structure, word choice, grammar, and spelling contained in cover letters and emails have stopped many resumes from ever being reviewed.

Good writing is just the opposite. Whether you are creating a cover letter or email to accompany your resume or inserting the information a prospective employer is calling for in a formal employment application, you must approach every written communication with determination and zeal. Take whatever time is required to craft sound documents, messages that if prepared properly, will open job, occupation, and career doors for you.

CHAPTER 16

Challenge: Managing Career and Education Transitions

When one door closes, another opens; but we often look so long and so regretfully upon the closed door that we do not see the one which has opened for us.

—ALEXANDER GRAHAM BELL (1847–1922), INVENTOR,
SCIENTIST, AND FOUNDING MEMBER OF THE NATIONAL
GEOGRAPHIC SOCIETY WHO IS CREDITED WITH THE
INVENTION OF THE TELEPHONE

IN HER BEST-SELLING BOOK, *PASSAGES: PREDICTABLE CRISES OF ADULT LIFE*, author Gail Sheehy discusses the transitions facing young adults and adults in a manner that had not been previously broached. Much had been published about child and adolescent transitions, but Sheehy brought the adult into full focus, and her journalistic and storytelling style had many readers thinking they were reading about themselves.

Although written in 1976, with some time and event modifications, this could be your story. Depending on your age, reading *Passages* and studying the vignettes of real people is like reviewing many of the life experiences you have already had. Just as importantly, Sheehy projects many of the career and life challenges you can expect to face in the future.

Passages examines in detail the twenties, thirties, and forties and the development tasks that you will confront during these years. If there is any comfort in having company, the book will tell you you're not the only one experiencing these challenges. They have an "evergreen" effect, reappearing in each new generation of adults.

TRANSITIONS HAVE A BEGINNING, A MIDDLE, AND AN END

The transitions that you will experience in your career development are natural. They appear often and stretch across a number of years, all the way to the slowing down, exiting, and retirement period. The missteps most common in both career and education development tend to relate to your failure to start soon enough to affect a positive transition and then allow time for evaluation once the passage has occurred. Imagine a sandwich without bread or a roll. Then imagine an employment search without adequate preparation and follow-up. They are incredibly similar.

Another frame used to look at transitions is through the eyes of the employer. A valued employee resigns to take another position. Too often businesses and firms think the transition ends the day the replacement employee reports to work. Nothing could be further from the truth. True normalcy doesn't occur until the replacement employee participates in a proper orientation to the job and the setting and rises to or surpasses the competency level of the person they replaced.

Career transitions overlap each other. Before you phase totally out of one transition, you often begin or ease into another. The three transitions faced by most adults are (1) school or college to employment, (2) employment to employment, and (3) employment to retirement. Each is a "passage." Before each passage, job seekers must determine the extent to which a position they are considering is one that will aid in the pursuit of their immediate and long-term goals. Being clear as to those goals will leave no doubt about what you want to accomplish and how the position before you represents a step in the right direction.

Each passage has a beginning, a middle, and an end, and many of them will be repeated multiple times as you progress in and move about the world of work. The worst that can happen, or the greatest challenge

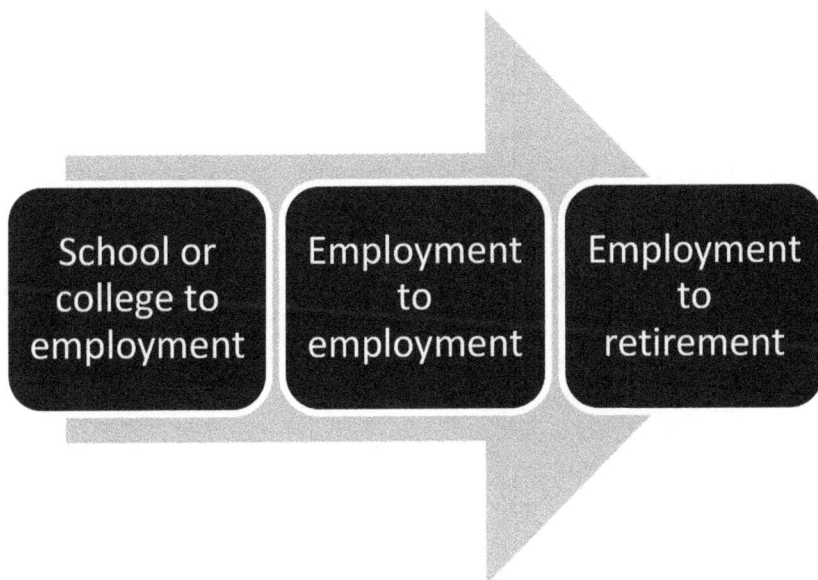

Figure 16.1 Career Transitions

you may have to confront, is that you reach a place in your life where you ask the question "Now . . . what am I supposed to do?" and not know the answer. If you have reached the end of an education experience, for example, it is a question you should have started asking long before you donned your cap and gown.

NAVIGATING THE NORMAL CAREER TRANSITIONS

At the risk of appearing to oversimplify what can be a complex issue, some are going to be challenged by the "you don't know what you don't know" condition. If you don't know what action or strategy will bring you the best results in effecting transitions, you will not make them or make them on the fly in order to make up for lost time. Let's look closely at three transitions.

School or college to employment

To avoid confusion and disarray as they relate to moving forward after schooling, you must begin the process of searching for a job before you complete your studies, long before. In addition to talking with educators, alumni, and all of the people in your various networks, use the counselors and resources of any career center you can access. Ideally, you want to graduate, possibly take a little break for rest and relaxation, and begin your employment shortly thereafter.

To do this, you have to begin the job search and acquisition process long before you graduate. The best transition is when you take off your graduation cap and put on your employment cap almost immediately. This will only happen if you begin your search, using the practices and tools outlined in previous chapters, at least a year ahead of completing your studies.

Employment to employment

Moving from one position to another can be either active or passive in nature. Search and staffing firms use these terms in describing how they work with individuals who are or may be candidates for employment or reemployment.

- Active—These candidates can be either employed or unemployed but actively searching for a full-time position. They are distinguished by their assertiveness in reviewing postings on electronic job boards and "help wanted" pages, sending out resumes, completing applications, and marketing themselves to prospective employers. They are likely to interview for any position that matches their qualifications and preferences (i.e., location, compensation, etc.).

- Selectively active—Individuals in this category are either working full-time now or considering a return to the workplace following a planned leave (i.e., maternity, medical, etc.) or a leave of absence for retraining purposes. They have circulated some feelers, contacted their networks, and are usually willing to interview when an excellent opportunity presents itself.

- Passive—These are employed individuals who are relatively satisfied with their current work situation and have not mounted a systematic search. They would consider employment elsewhere if the right opportunity were brought to their attention.

Surveys of employees regarding their looking outside the organization regularly for a new position vary dramatically, but it is not unusual for as many as a third of the workforce to state that they are actively pursuing other opportunities at any point in time. The number of passive job changers is more difficult to assess.

Numerous studies by HR professionals have identified the most frequent reasons individuals become active candidates for job relocation. They include:

- Uncomfortable business, corporate, organization, or firm culture or climate
- Poor relationships with managers, supervisors, and colleagues
- Absence of engagement and appreciation
- Lack of support and assistance
- Limited or no opportunity for growth, mobility, and advancement
- Competitive or fair compensation and benefits

It should be noted that compensation, while more relevant for some more than others, often gets a "bad rap" as to why employees are dissatisfied. Research conducted by the Society for Human Resource Management (SHRM) and others suggests the employment characteristics that lessen turnover and promote retention represent a mosaic of the above work and workplace qualities—not a single factor. It must also be recognized that some environments are simply restrictive (i.e., growth options), and relocation to achieve personal growth and development is inevitable.

The reasons why you might wish to change jobs might be any one or all six of the above. Career advancement and mobility, woven with the psychological factors of seeking new environments and loftier opportunities, can often turn normally satisfied individuals into job changers. People who see their current work as temporary or a bridge to their "career of choice" will certainly add to the number of job changers. And some employees simply want to move on to what they perceive to be "greener pastures."

Everyone in the workforce must be vigilant regarding the impact that change will have on a satisfying employment experience. Any change (i.e., workplace philosophy, setting, manager, etc.) can turn a good work experience into a bad one. When this occurs, many good jobs don't look so great any longer. If a situation like this is happening to you, it might be time to dust the cobwebs off of your resume.

Successful change for all of these candidates depends on distinct actions within the various passages of the career or job change process, but the one common denominator in each is the need to engage in some form of awareness and exploration experiences that will lead to good decision-making should the right opportunity emerge. This doesn't occur overnight.

The significant rise of employed individuals resigning or seeking job changes as the devastating effects of the coronavirus pandemic subsided in 2021 and 2022 could be testimony to the number of people who were uncomfortable in their current employment and sensing that the economic momentum that accompanied the "new normal" was a good time to switch. The Great Resignation, sometimes referred to as the Big Quit, helped these members of the workforce achieve career objectives that had been stymied or interrupted by COVID-19. Correspondingly, the unusually high turnover of the period resulted in confusion and disorder in hiring practices of many employers.

Employment to retirement

The trickiest, and most delicate transition for many, and the one that is often perplexing and generates a "now what" response is the one that comes late in the career. You may want to move into a different work pattern (i.e., reduced hours, telecommuting, job sharing, etc.). More dramatic would be your desire to try a totally different career. Or you may wish to simply exit the work world and enjoy the benefits of full retirement.

Whatever you aspire to do late in or after your employment, none of these passages will succeed if a proactive plan is not set in motion long before the actual transition is to occur. Sadly, too few prepare adequately for this passage, and many suffer the consequences for their lack of preparation. That lack of preparation for some is financial, and for others it may also be emotional and social. You can't just stop working one day without planning effectively for all of the changes that will be set into motion the next.

JOB CHANGE OR CAREER MAKEOVER

A time may occur in the career development process when circumstances call for a more intensive and complicated adjustment—the consideration of a total career makeover. Job change is usually the appropriate solution when the individual is in the right career but employed in the wrong setting or with an unsuitable employer. Makeover comes into play when the employed individuals determine they are in the wrong career altogether and are experiencing a measure of "career regret." However, makeover as a solution for getting one's career back on track is a circumstance that warrants careful examination and thoughtful action.

When comfort issues are so significant that they cannot be resolved by simply changing jobs, the solution—as difficult as it will be—is the abandonment of one's career and the move toward an entirely different career direction. In other words, it entails going back to square one. It is a circumstance that many cannot even consider because of the cost, age, and time requirements, as well as one's personal and family situation.

The ultimate challenge for any individual undergoing career change is returning or recycling through the self-awareness, exploration, decision-making, and goal-setting stages of the career development process (see chapter 1) and repeating these stages and behaviors. Career makeovers typically require a reinvestment of energy, time, and commitment in order to learn the knowledge and skill set that must be mastered to complete the makeover.

CHALLENGES THAT ACCOMPANY TRANSITIONS

Navigating transitions are fraught with challenges. An employer offers you an attractive first job, the solid opportunity to grow or move to a different one, or an appealing "early out" retirement package. Offers of this nature require a response for the new worker as do change opportunities for those already in the workforce.

Do you jump at the first opportunity in a tight job market or competitive field? Do you leave the familiar surroundings of something you know well to move to the unknown? How adequately have you prepared yourself for the transition that may suddenly appear in front of you? The unready often find themselves in the uncomfortable "put up or shut up" position. The elation of being offered employment or a different position is tempered by the challenge associated with whether you should accept it or not. While acceptance or rejection may be a nice problem to have, you will be a better decision-maker if you have identified in advance what it will take in order for you to make the next move.

STRAIGHT TALK ABOUT DEALING WITH TRANSITIONS

The Boy Scout motto, "Be prepared," can also be applied as you move into, through, and out of the life and career transitions you are going to face as a young adult and adult. Throughout the search and selection process, doors will open, and opportunities will present themselves. Never embark on a new career or life path without looking as far down that path as you can. Those who are prepared will enjoy options and be able to act proactively. Those who don't will face a certain amount of "risk" and often find themselves acting reactively.

Beginning early in each transition, you need to have contingencies in place that answer the "now what" question. If this issue is not systematically addressed, you are likely to find yourself at a dead-end point in your career development.

CHAPTER 17

Challenge: Dealing with Career Setbacks and Obstacles

"If at first you don't succeed, try, try again."

—A PROVERB THAT HAS BEEN TRACED TO AMERICAN
EDUCATOR THOMAS H. PALMER (1782–1861) AND HIS
"TEACHER'S MANUAL" PUBLICATION

YOU DIDN'T GET THE JOB AND YOU'RE NOT CERTAIN WHY? YOU DIDN'T recognize and deal with an obstacle that stood in your path? Why some people get hired and others do not remains a mystery for you? The expression, "when thrown from a horse, get right back on," may be applicable here. The answer is often as simple as not standing out or causing those doing the hiring to see you in the position you are seeking.

Sometimes, you find out quickly. Other times, the process drags on forever before you learn you've been unsuccessful. At the point of rejection, you have to engage in analysis of what happened to determine why a job offer wasn't extended to you. That analysis can only occur when you get the answers to as many of the following questions as possible:

1. At what point in the job search and acquisition process were you eliminated?

2. Did you do something wrong in the hiring process? Did you make the right moves at the required times?

3. Did you create the best job search tools and employ the best practices?

4. Did you apply for a job or jobs that you were qualified for? Were you right for the job? Was the job right for you?

5. Were you the kind of candidate they were looking for?

6. Did you devote the appropriate energy and time in your pursuit of this job?

7. Did you control the things you could control?

8. Did you solicit and use the right help and use the proper resources?

9. Were you proactive rather than reactive?

10. Are you disappointed? How are you handling the disappointment?

What you learn from the answers to these ten questions will help you in your next job-seeking venture. It's time to apply the wise admonition of Thomas H. Palmer at the opening of this chapter.

RISING ABOVE THE COMPETITION AND GETTING HIRED

The greatest truism of the job search and acquisition process is that all candidates are not created equal, nor are they seen equally by those assigned to screen and hire. Why do some people get hired while others are passed over? Surveys of human resource officers and recruiters consistently report that personality, demeanor, and presentation rank highest in reasons why people do not get hired.

Your experience and education, and to some extent your skills, are quantifiable by reviewing your resume, and the interview will dig deeper into these areas, especially if your resume was less than forthcoming or complete. But in reality, and stated earlier, the interview is your opportunity to put a face on you the candidate. Resumes cannot answer questions. People can! Resumes don't have personalities. People do!

If IQ stands for intelligence quotient, you need to display a "PQ" throughout the job-seeking process. PQ, in this case, stands for passion quotient. Your resume, interview, and every other interaction that you have with a prospective employer are being examined through a PQ lens as the employer seeks to determine if your interest is genuine and your motives are clear.

Whatever the reason, the candidate's ability to impress the interviewer(s) will govern the ability to compete for the position and eventually get the job. The impression the candidate needs to make is two pronged. First, the interviewer needs to be convinced that you are capable of doing the work. Of equal importance, however, is your ability to communicate how well you will fit into the culture of the organization and become a contributing member.

In this regard, the interviewer is assessing personality and other attributes in the hopes of determining "fit." You must stand out in the pack. There are many ordinary and acceptable candidates. The extraordinary and exemplary applicants are the ones that get hired.

A MATTER OF CONTROL

Earlier you were encouraged to reflect on the manner in which you went about the application process and more specifically, the things you may have done right and wrong. If you performed that assessment, you are certain to have observed any number of controllable factors, any of which may have affected the process and resulted in your being rejected.

Following is a discussion of the issues or problems in the job-seeking process that could have derailed your prospects of getting hired.

Poorly targeted applications

Targeting can be too broad, too narrow, or just right. You send your resume everywhere and hope that it lands favorably in a place that has an opening that you will like. Known in some circles as the "spray and pray" approach, it is often picked up by employers who will then question just how much research you actually did or whether you are simply throwing your resume into the wind and hoping for the best. Limiting your search can also work against you. If you make too few contacts and distribute too few resumes and applications, you're limiting the exposure that may bring positive results.

Insufficient evidence of fit

Interviewers want to know that you're the best person for the job and once hired you're going to be with the employer for a long, long time. Stated differently, the employer wants to be certain that the investment made in you is going to pay the highest dividends for both you and them. Applicants who lack knowledge, skill, and experience often overcome any fit questions by proving their willingness to learn and grow and fit into the culture of the employer. You may come across as a "Jack or Jill of all trades," but that won't work if that isn't what the employer is seeking.

So-so or weak interview

Any number or things can happen during the course of an interview for which you will be graded downward. You may have not done the right or enough research or preparation. Interviewers want to see an upbeat, pro-active you—not an applicant that is reactive and defensive. The passion and enthusiasm the interviewer was expecting may have been missing. You may have appeared indecisive, lacking confidence, or unfocused. Your handling of questions or hypothetical situations may have been inadequate.

The worst interviews can often be linked to specific behaviors—you displayed poor etiquette and manners, your body language was offensive, you dressed inappropriately, or you didn't cover your tattoos and body piercings. Any one or a combination of the above could have been your nemesis.

Emitting the desperation vibe

The worst signal you can send during the entire search and hiring process is one of desperation. It is one that recent grads give off when repeated job search efforts result in rejection. It is also seen in the unemployed individual attempting to get back among the ranks of the working. Regardless of the circumstances that surround your search, avoid appearing desperate and despondent about your situation. Positive, forward-thinking candidates give off the best vibe.

Overtalking and underlistening

In all interviews and interactions, there is a time to speak and a time to be quiet. By overtalking or rambling aimlessly, you may come across as trying to manage the interview by not giving up the microphone. In failing to listen, you will not be able to guide the interview toward your strengths and "push the right buttons." You may also miss cues that would have allowed you to take the interview in a positive direction. Interviewers seek a balance, and if you haven't offered the depth in your responses they were hoping for, they will present a follow-up question.

Poor social media presence

To complement what they derive from the interview and reference and background checks, a growing number of employers are turning to social media sites to learn more about their candidates. If you've posted anything that will work against you if seen by one browsing the internet, take steps to remove or block it from general examination.

Discovery of lies and exaggerations

Employers check references and conduct background searches, and if anything is incorrect or overblown in your resume, it's going to eventually be discovered. The same is true for your response to interview questions. Candidates, for example, often don't know how to respond to questions about time interruptions or voids on their resume. The remedy is to be honest, candid, and forthright in everything you present as a candidate. The worst thing would be for a lie or exaggeration to be learned after you are hired and result in the grounds for dismissal.

Faulty move from the resume to the interview

Many candidates or applicants look great on paper but don't look as appealing in person. If you look at the transition from the resume to the interview as a bridge, exactly what do you need to learn, do, and execute to make a successful crossing? You can expect that any red flags that may have been picked up in reviewing your resume will likely be raised in the interview process. Be sensitive to concerns about your candidacy that the employer may have and be prepared to respond.

Faulty or nonexistent postinterview follow-up

The thank-you note or email is a signal of your continued interest in the position. It allows you to expand on questions and drive home any final points you'd like to make. This brief note also calls the attention of the interviewer back to you; a factor may move your candidacy from a casual impression to a more indelible one.

Inadequate search plan

Many of the controllable factors mentioned to this point are ones that deal with a specific job. Your failure to get the job or jobs you want may be larger than that. Do you have a job search and acquisition plan? Are you following all the "dos" and avoiding all of the "don'ts"? How solid is your plan? If questionable, a visit to the career counselor or career services center may be in order.

Any one or more of the above factors could have led to your being dismissed as a candidate. If you can pinpoint those that may have been influential and either corrected or learned how to avoid them, you may be able to move on in the hiring process the next time.

SOME THINGS ARE SIMPLY UNCONTROLLABLE

There are going to be times when your job quest finds you banging your head against the proverbial brick wall. This usually occurs when, for no reasons that you understand, you are eliminated from consideration for a particular job. Any of the following could factor into your failure to get the job and most are absolutely uncontrollable:

- More impressive candidates caught the employer's attention.
- A poor economy resulted in a flood of competitive applicants.
- Someone didn't capture the real you from your resume.

- Candidate value and salary expectations exceeded what the employer was willing to pay.
- Generational gap between candidate and interviewers was too great to span.
- Personalities clashed.

While these six factors may not be controllable on your part, they may tell you something about you and the way you went about getting the job. If you wanted more money, additional research up front may have told you what comparable positions were paying and what you should expect. Falling victim to a bad economy usually passes with time, but recovery sometimes seems to take forever. It would be a mistake to become a whiner and play the "blame game." Persistent exploration of opportunities is the only path to overcoming the challenges of a national or global economy.

Competing with a surplus of equally knowledgeable, skilled, and competent candidates could also be altered if the demographics change in your favor or a more favorable economic climate were to reoccur. The demographics also show up in the supply and demand statistics. At any given time, there could be an increase in the number of degree, diploma, or certificate achievers, and that number may drop in a year or two.

Today, there may be a shortage of people to fill education, health care, and engineering jobs. A year from now those needs may be in sales and marketing, hospitality, and finance. You may be helpless in changing the numbers, but as a job seeker, you can constantly take the pulse of the specific occupational specialty and general work world.

The personality issue is totally outside of your control, but your future as an applicant and employee may be dependent on forming a positive bond or connection with the people you meet, especially those that interview you. Interviewers have preferences and base their decisions by viewing applicants through a lens through which you may never appear positive.

Equally challenging, but not always impossible to overcome, is the generational gap. Baby boomers (born between 1946 and 1964) are doing a lot of the hiring, and the candidates are likely to be Generation Xers (born between 1965 and 1979) and Generation Yers and millennials (born 1980 and later). The mix doesn't always work. However, you must recognize that human resource officers and recruiters have a simple goal—placing the right person in the right job—and if you are that person, your age and lifestyle preferences won't make a difference.

STRAIGHT TALK ABOUT ASSESSING FAILURE TO GET A JOB

Accept the challenges you must face in order to land the job you want. Work from a position of strength and display all of the reasons your candidacy stands above the competition. But recognize that while successful candidates stand out for their positive attributes, others stand out for all the wrong reasons. The latter will not get the job.

You are going to have a "bad day" on occasion. It happens to everyone. When you don't feel well or fail to be on "top of your game," it usually results in not getting the job. Don't take rejection personally. It is a fact of life, and the road to the work world is littered with knowledgeable and skilled people that didn't get the jobs they wanted.

Examine the experience that resulted in rejection. Learn from it. Challenge any obstacles, put any failures behind you, and vow to do a better job the next time. Make certain you are using the right tools and procedures and that they are current. The way your grandfather found employment is not going to cut it today, and you may have to seek professional assistance to become skilled in the behaviors that will lead to a paycheck.

Control the controllable and learn from each experience. Don't dwell on or cry about the things you can't control. Move on. Attempt to anticipate as much of the uncontrollable, and if possible, develop a scheme for countering it. You may win. You may lose. But keep trying.

CHAPTER 18

Challenge: Accepting the Right Job Offer

I'm gonna make him an offer he can't refuse.

—Don Vito Corleone (played by Academy Award–
winning actor Marlon Brando) in the film *The
Godfather* (1972)

You are offered a job. Better yet, you're offered multiple jobs. It may seem hard to believe, but many err in what others think is an easy decision to make. Just like any other aspect of the career development process that involves decision-making, choosing whether to accept or reject an offer of employment is a task that requires considerable attention and thought.

Your consideration of an offer of employment is one that you will have to examine through two lenses. What are the things about this position that you like and that you believe will have a positive impact on your career development? Second, what elements of this position are not to your liking? You must ask yourself if you can live with the things you don't like or if you can find ways to eliminate or reduce them upon accepting the position.

Decision-making takes time, but indecision takes more. When offered employment, you share control over that time with the firm, organization, agency, or institution offering you the job. At the risk of sounding overly repetitive, think about the process you followed to choose a career and then study and prepare for it. The same kind of exploration and analysis need to be done again before you are postured to accept or reject a job offer. This might be a good time to return to chapter 3 and read again what Benjamin Franklin had to say about how good decisions are made.

Accept your first or any other job for the right reasons, not because you're attracted to some false notion of what the position will be like or a salary you think is too good to refuse. Search and staffing firms see thousands of resumes from workers seeking to correct an earlier misstep in their decision-making. It may be difficult, but you must walk away from an offer that will only imprison you in a position that you will find unbearable.

POSITIVE VS. NEGATIVE ELEMENTS OF THE JOB OFFER

Studies conducted by human resource professionals have isolated the issues that will lead to employee engagement and retention, a goal that represents a win-win situation for both the employee and the employer. These are the same issues that you will factor into the decision to accept or reject an offer of employment. The basic difficulty in examining some work and workplace characteristics (i.e., job, fit, workplace culture,

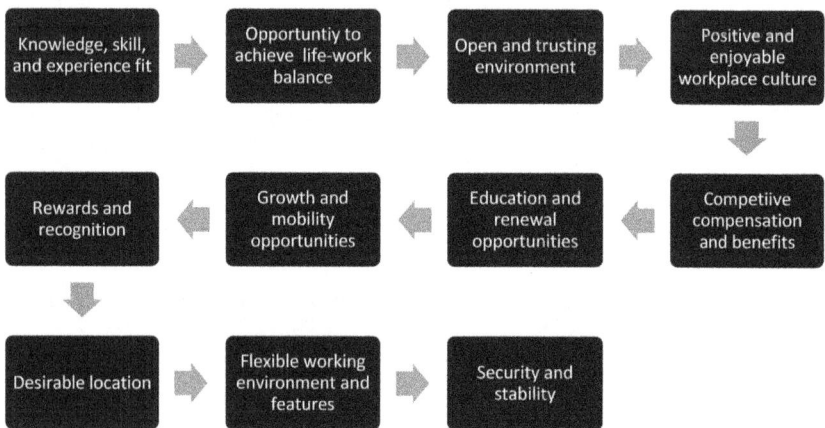

Figure 18.1 Factors Influencing Acceptance of Job Offer

collegial attitudes, etc.) is that they have to be experienced to some degree before they can be assessed.

To engage and retain desirable employees, firms, organizations, agencies, and institutions must create a position and a workplace culture that:

- Fits your knowledge, skill, and experience levels and appears to be something you're going to truly enjoy doing
- Satisfies life–work balance issues by addressing personal, cognitive, emotional, and social needs
- Offers an open and trusting work structure and culture, one where free and open communication and multidirectional interaction are encouraged
- Presents a positive workplace culture and enjoyable place to work
- Offers competitive compensation and benefits
- Provides opportunities for you to achieve full career potential, including education, training, and renewal options
- Recognizes and rewards the achievements of individual employees
- Is located in the community, region, state, or country where you want to work and in a setting (i.e., urban, suburban, rural, etc.) that appeals to you
- Presents a flexible working environment that is responsive to the varying needs of different employees, as well as workplace features that are compatible with your preferences and interests (i.e., tuition assistance, travel opportunities, remote work, etc.)
- Offers security and stability

How many of these elements are present in the offer before you? The vibes you got from your research, interviews, and networks are one way to find out. One thing is certain, if one or more of these elements is important to you, yet missing from the job offer in ways that you deem critical, you most likely have the negative elements that will lead you to rejecting it.

Most of the positive elements outlined above are typically offered by employers with a solid, established reputation, as well as a record of success in doing whatever it is that they do. To many, the credibility and reputation of their employer is as important as the actual work that they perform.

If you've been offered a job at one of the firms profiled in the annual *Forbes Magazine* 100 Best Firms to Work for in America listing, the life–work balance question may be a no-brainer. The *Forbes* list and others like it (often conducted in cities—Best Places to Work in Boston, for example) rate and include the firms and businesses that meet a significant number of workplace features. Most place a high premium on responding to the employee's life–work balance concerns, and each has to get high marks in order to make the list.

Throughout the job search process, you must use these issues, and any that you wish to add, as your personal yardstick for grading prospective employers. When they are present, they make the offer or offers more attractive. When they are not present, they make consideration of the job offer more challenging.

Before leaving the elements of a job offer, you need to consider the emotional reaction that may be associated with rejecting a position. Turning down a position can be a difficult thing to do and may leave you with a "did I do the right thing?" feeling. Fit is incredibly important for your immediate and long-term future, and you will likely get a sense of that fit as you move through the transition and information-gathering process. Don't accept just any job unless you are disparate. Accept the job that fits best.

The best part is you are now the evaluator. They, after all, got to grade you. Now, it's your turn.

OPERATE FROM A POSITION OF POWER AND UNDERSTANDING

Powerless and poorly informed people make bad decisions. You have a certain level of power to wield in the job selection and negotiating world, and all you have to do is use it. Take stock of where you are, where you want to go, and the best path to follow to get there. Will the job offer you received facilitate those concerns?

Part of your power base has to be your belief in your personal competence and ability to do the job. That belief will help guide you through the job consideration maze. Be prepared to communicate with mentors, colleagues, and others who can provide input to your decision. Don't ask or expect them to make the decision for you, but welcome their understanding as you gather the intelligence you require.

Resist pressure, both the internal and external variety. Self-inflicted pressure usually relates back to procrastination and indecisiveness, and you lose your power when you don't act in accordance with a reasonable timeline. External pressure usually takes the form of the employer telling you that it wants your answer yesterday. This demand may be a legitimate one, especially if the vacant position is creating havoc within the organization, but should be no reason for your giving up your consideration and negotiating power.

Active applicants are often unemployed or underemployed or dislike their present work so much that they want to change. Succumbing to pressure of this nature can lead to hasty and poor decisions. Passive applicants are better situated and under considerably less pressure. While working and not necessarily looking for a new job, they will need to be convinced that they are looking at a great opportunity, one that will take them to a new level in their personal career development.

In the final analysis, if you are considering a job offer, you need to sort through and evaluate all of the options—just like you did way back at the exploration stage of the career development process.

WORTH, EXPECTATIONS, AND SALARY

Trying to make sense of the U.S. and global salary structure may be more difficult than choosing the numbers that will win the state lottery. Often, you separate positions from the outset in either a real or imagined belief of what that job will pay. You may also have a magical number that you must attain in order to consider a new job or move from the one you currently hold. Knowing and understanding your worth is a critical element in the process.

The expression, "It shouldn't be about the money," is often a difficult factor to implement in the real world. When employers offer ridiculously weak salaries and poor benefits, it may be symptomatic of a larger issue. If they don't compensate their employees competitively, where else are they likely to cut corners? In these situations, the job offer may be symptomatic of a larger problem.

Salary concerns become bartering points at two places. First, the candidate must determine if the job, the employer, the environment, and the other life–work balance factors are strong enough to offset a salary offer that comes in below expectations. The second is the job that you really want to get but one where you are going to have to negotiate the salary you believe you should command or one that is competitive for the occupation.

In the first instance, you are bartering with yourself. In the latter, you are negotiating with the employer. In both instances, a certain amount of elasticity must be present. How much must you have or are you willing to give to get the job. Deciding exactly what that number should be may be difficult, but in the end, you should not have to compromise your sense of worth or accept a position for a salary significantly below the accepted norm.

There may be other trade-offs. Some positions offer an introductory salary until a probationary status has been completed and then raise that number to a more acceptable and competitive level. Others offer work characteristics and features that result in cost savings. For example, the job in the suburbs where parking is free is going to keep more money in your pocket than the downtown job where you have to pay for transportation and parking costs.

Often, the trade-off you make isn't about money. Using the location example from above, working in the suburbs or an outlying community may offer life–work balance benefits that neutralize a higher salary in the urban center. Shorter commutes and fewer traffic snarls may have a value that can't be calculated in dollars and cents. In conclusion, the employer that may not be able to offer you the salary that you want may be able to offer flexible working hours, tuition assistance, and other perks. In the final analysis, make certain you comprehend and factor in the value of all of the nonmonetary benefits.

EXAMINING THE SALARY WITHIN THE JOB OFFER

Let's examine a job offer you'd like to accept, one for which the salary offer is below your expectations. What salary figure will it take to move the offer into a more favorable position? What strategies can you employ to get the employer to sweeten the offer?

If you find yourself in a salary negotiation position, the following guidelines may apply:

1. Don't let it only be about money. People who only work for a paycheck often learn that money can't buy happiness or contentment. Working to meet your needs and address your responsibilities should be the strongest motivation and far more understandable.

2. Do your homework. Are there specific knowledge and skill set shortages in your community or the employment sector that have generated a greater demand? How long has the position been vacant? Long-running vacancies may indicate that the employer is having difficulty filling the position. Knowing these simple facts can work in your favor.

3. Go into any salary discussion or negotiation only after using one or more of the internet salary checkers, PayScale, CareerBuilder, or Monster. Each will tell you what comparable work in comparable situations is paying.

4. Select the right time to play the salary card. This may or not be controllable, but keep as much control over the timing of the salary discussion as you can. It is far better to remove yourself from consideration after being offered a job than to allow salary expectations to keep you from getting that offer.

5. Expect to play somewhat of a salary negotiation game. Most employers expect you to negotiate and have more experience than you in playing the game. Questions like "What are your salary

expectations?" or "What would it take in the way of salary to get you to come to work for us?" can sometimes be countered by your asking "What is the salary or salary range you are offering?"

6. Your success as a salary negotiator is dependent on your ability to push the employer's buttons. It begins with offering interview answers that fully highlight your achievements by way of performance and productivity standards. It follows by your showing how much you understand the workings of the employer and all of the places where you can contribute. It's no longer about the salary; it's about your worth.

7. Offers stating an exact salary are sometimes an introductory offer, and in other instances, a starting point for negotiations. If your research tells you that the employers have a history of higher salaries, let it be known that you are aware of that fact.

8. Be realistic in your expectations. If you respond to a job posting with an annual salary in the $60,000 to $75,000 range, don't expect to always walk away with the higher figure. Unless you're a candidate with impeccable credentials and a wealth of experience, you can expect to be offered something short of the top of the range. Determine where you believe your worth falls in that range and aim for that amount. You might aim a little higher and be prepared to accept a counter.

9. If the salary discussion is occurring in the latter stages of the interview process, recognize that you may be competing with others who look as good as you but are willing to accept less than you are asking.

10. The salary issue can be the most uncomfortable aspect of the interview or hiring process. However, you have to look out for number one, and that may mean rejecting a reasonable job offer that doesn't meet your occupational worth and salary expectations.

FUNDAMENTAL EMPLOYMENT ACCEPTANCE TEST (FEAT)

All jobs have their good qualities and hopefully, to a lesser extent, their deficiencies. Early in this book, there was a discussion about values and preferences as they relate to career choice. Now, you are going to use values and preferences to evaluate the job offer or offers you are considering.

The Fundamental Employment Acceptance Test (FEAT) that follows examines the appeal of six elements:

- The work
- Employment security

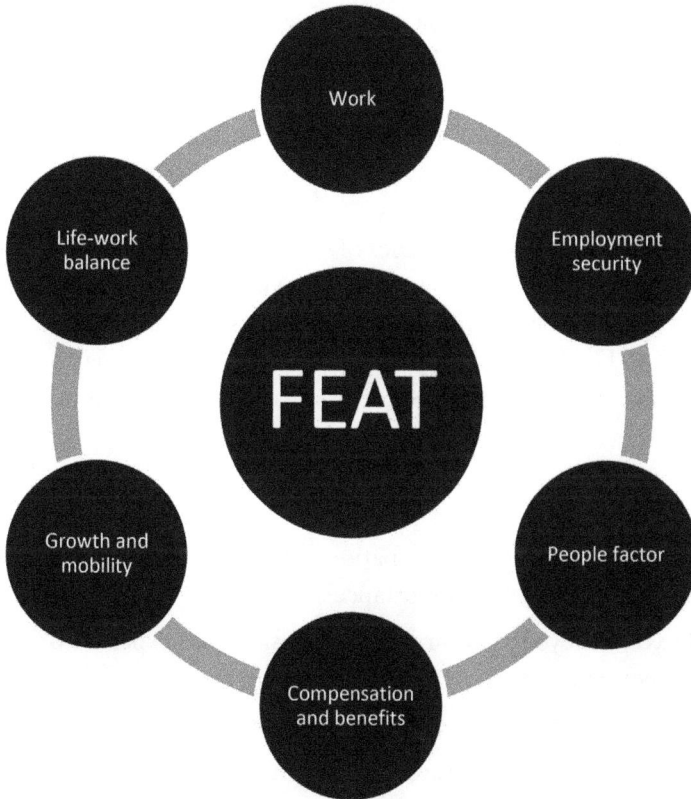

Figure 18.2 Factors in the Fundamental Employment Acceptance Test

- People factor
- Compensation and benefits
- Growth and mobility opportunities
- Life–work balance

Using FEAT, the decision-maker creates a "yardstick" for measuring the acceptability of the job offer. Active job seekers may find themselves willing to accept a position that has less than perfect scores. Passive job seekers, especially those that are working and reasonably comfortable in their present roles, will likely want a higher FEAT score in order to make a job change.

Apply all of the information you have gathered in your research, your interaction with family, friends, colleagues, and your networks. If necessary, extend the process by taking more time to get answers to questions that are critical to you. After you have gathered everything you can about the job, the employer, and all of the position attributes, this becomes a personal assessment. You have to answer the questions and rate the factors.

Following, you will find a series of questions that will help you determine how to rate each of the seven factors. When rating a factor, examine all of the questions and come up with a composite rating for each. Circle that number. Don't consider this list exhaustive, and you may have other concerns that can be tied to the factors that have particular significance for you.

Work test questions

- How important is the occupation that you perform, and does the position address that importance?
- Do you believe that your knowledge, skill, and experience fit the job requirements?
- Does the work culture and environment appeal to you?
- Does the employer reward and recognize those who are productive and successful in their work pursuits?

- Do you have a sense of how success will be measured?
- Does the position place you in a slot consistent with your career development plan?
- If currently working, does this job have desirable elements your present one doesn't?

Rating the work

Excellent		Adequate		Poor	Not applicable
5	4	3	2	1	NA

Employment security test questions

- Does the specific position appear to be a secure one within the employer's structure specifically and the sector or industry generally?
- Does the employer have a history of success and performance in the sector or industry?
- Are there any internal threats (i.e., emergence of robotics, offshoring of employment, etc.) that would impact that security?
- Are there any external threats (i.e., economic downturn) that would jeopardize that security?
- Does the position offer opportunities to enhance your personal security?

Rating employment security

Excellent		Adequate		Poor	Not applicable
5	4	3	2	1	NA

The people factor test questions

- Will the position present the comfort level you desire to have with peers and fellow workers?

- Does the workplace culture foster open and trusting communication?
- Does the position offer the type and level of people engagement that you wish to have with managers and supervisors?

Rating the people factor

Excellent		Adequate		Poor	Not applicable
5	4	3	2	1	NA

Compensation and benefits test questions

- Is the salary and benefits package being offered what you expected?
- Is the salary and benefits package competitive with comparable positions?
- Is the salary and benefits package competitive with similar positions in the area?
- Did the salary offered take your knowledge, skill, experience levels, and "market value" into account?
- Will the salary permit you to meet existing cost of living challenges?
- Does the position offer salary increases for merit and/or longevity?
- Do any nonmonetary rewards exist for productivity and successful performance?
- For job changers, is the salary and benefits package sufficient to get you to change jobs?

Rating compensation and benefits

Excellent		Adequate		Poor	Not applicable
5	4	3	2	1	NA

Growth and mobility opportunities test questions

- Does the position offer opportunities for growth and mobility?
- Can your short-term (five years) career goals be met in this position?
- Can your long-term career goals be met with this employer?
- Does the employer encourage and support education and training initiatives?
- Does the employer have a history of promoting within the organization?

Rating growth and mobility opportunities

Excellent		Adequate		Poor	Not applicable
5	4	3	2	1	NA

Life–work balance test questions

- Will the work permit you to fulfill nonwork interests and objectives?
- Does the work have time and calendar demands that are acceptable to you?
- Does the work satisfy social, cognitive, and emotional preferences that you deem important?

Rating life–work balance issues

Excellent		Adequate		Poor	Not applicable
5	4	3	2	1	NA

After you have applied the evaluation scale to each of the questions, total your score. If you're comparing job offers, the math will identify the offer that has earned the best mark. If you're looking at a single job, you have to determine if that score is sufficient for you to accept the position or if you should keep searching.

A LOOK AHEAD

Any new job is a beginning. As a part of looking ahead, make certain the magnetism of the offer is such that taking this important step is a positive one and you are drawn to all the right things. Far too many people accept less-than-good fits, with the belief that they can change things once they start working. This belief fails more often than it succeeds. The last thing you want to say six months into the future is "If I had only known _____."

STRAIGHT TALK ABOUT ACCEPTING OR REJECTING A JOB

The positive side of getting a job offer is that the employer wants you. The negative side may be a role that isn't exactly what you anticipated, or an employer who isn't willing to compensate you at your market value. As job-changers during the COVID-19 pandemic have learned and recurring economic downtrends have shown, the FEAT test will allow you to evaluate offers and opportunities more thoroughly and make better career adjustments.

All negotiation must be entered into with your knowing exactly how strong your hand is. Aim for fairness and an employment arrangement that satisfies your current wants and needs. Accept a job offer where you truly believe you can be successful and fight for everything you can get. If you present an effective negotiation, reasonable employers will at least listen to your case, but in the end, you may have to accept conditions that are not perfect or a salary that is lower than desired. Either can make an offer not attractive enough to accept.

Depending on your mindset, preferences, and circumstances, each job offer will present tempting elements. Make certain the positive aspects of the job offer outweigh any negative ones. When it's not a good fit, walk away.

CHAPTER 19

Challenge: Coping with the New Job Anxieties and Stresses

Your work is going to fill a large part of your life, and the only way to be truly satisfied is to do what you believe is great work. And the only way to do great work is to love what you do. If you haven't found it yet, keep looking. Don't settle. As with all matters of the heart, you'll know when you find it.

—STEVE JOBS (1955–2011), CHAIRMAN, CHIEF EXECUTIVE OFFICER, AND COFOUNDER OF APPLE, INC., A BUSINESS, COMMUNICATIONS, AND TECHNOLOGY PIONEER WHO WAS AT THE FOREFRONT OF THE GLOBAL MICROCOMPUTER REVOLUTION AT THE END OF THE LAST MILLENNIUM.

IN THE CAREER DEVELOPMENT STAGES OUTLINED IN CHAPTER 1, THERE is a description of a stage called Orientation/Entry/Adjustment. This is the period that you will experience each time you enter or change jobs. It focuses on all of the adjustments and changes you will need to make as you move into your new job.

Employers refer to this period as "onboarding," a systematic set of actions and experiences through which new employees move into and become effective contributors to the organization that has just hired them. As the first step in the engagement process, it is a time when you will learn all of the operational protocols and procedures that will be required in order for you to make a smooth transition. It is also a time when you may have your fingers crossed hoping that you made the right decision to accept the offer of employment.

Studies by a mix of employers have revealed that the adjustments made during onboarding have a link to later employee satisfaction, performance, productivity, and loyalty—all matters that lead to employee retention. These same studies have also shown that the return on investment (ROI) for your employer grows as the organization becomes more efficient at onboarding.

Onboarding can also be a period when anxiety or stress appears as you move into the ranks of the "newly employed" regardless of whether this is your first job or the fifth. You are the "new kid on the block" or the "fresh face" in the building. The first days on the job represent a time when you have to learn how things are done and become acquainted with the cast of workers who are now your colleagues.

The adjustments that occur in moving into any new job are social, emotional, and cognitive ones. The social experiences involve your meeting and developing a way of working with your colleagues and supervisors. The emotional experiences will require that you address the mental demands (i.e., meeting deadlines, managing time, etc.) of the workplace. And finally, all cognitive experiences relate to how successful you are at learning what is expected in your new role, acquiring any new knowledge or skills, and then displaying everything as a part of your performance and productivity.

ENGAGEMENT NEED NOT BE MYSTERIOUS

In various polls, the Gallup Organization has found as few as three in ten workers saying they are engaged in their work. If correct, the vast majority (70 percent) are not achieving their full potential. Engaged employees are effective at building relationships with customers, clients, and colleagues and are more likely to transmit a signal of confidence in the organization through their personal commitment and loyalty. An engaged relationship is one that you and your employer should seek from day one on the job.

Studies have shown that engaged employees accept, support, and are faithful to the organization they have joined. They see their contributions as both personal performance and as contributing to organizational performance. Engaged employees are "self-starters," respond to evaluation and feedback, and require a minimal amount of supervision. Through their personal growth and development, they become more productive and valuable. Finally, they take great pride in their work and have a positive influence on the entire organization.

Not engaged workers display a number of contradictory characteristics. They lack enthusiastic commitment, display limited loyalty, and are often indifferent as to how their contributions are considered as long as they do what is asked of them. Not engaged employees often require greater managerial and supervisory attention. They contribute at a satisfactory level but seldom exceed the basic expectations laid out in their job description. Finally, not engaged workers don't grasp the concept of career and its importance in their personal growth and development.

In reviewing these characteristics, you can see how engaged workers represent a win-win scenario. When you are engaged, you are more likely to enjoy your work and travel a progressive path to your personal career goals and objectives. At the same time, your employer is benefiting from your productivity, as well as the other benefits of having you and your colleagues fully engaged.

A NEW JOB, A NEW BEGINNING

Some have compared the beginning of a new job to an artist's placing a blank canvas on the easel for the first time. Everyone starting a new job wants to make a strong impression from the first day in their new job. From the moment you accept the job to the time you are fully functioning is a time period that will vary dramatically.

Each mark you place on the canvas is distinctively yours and a reflection of the identity you will bring to the workplace. That transition is often about you and how fast you learn and adjust. In other circumstances, full functioning is governed by how much freedom the employer will give you to enter, adjust, and become entrenched in the work.

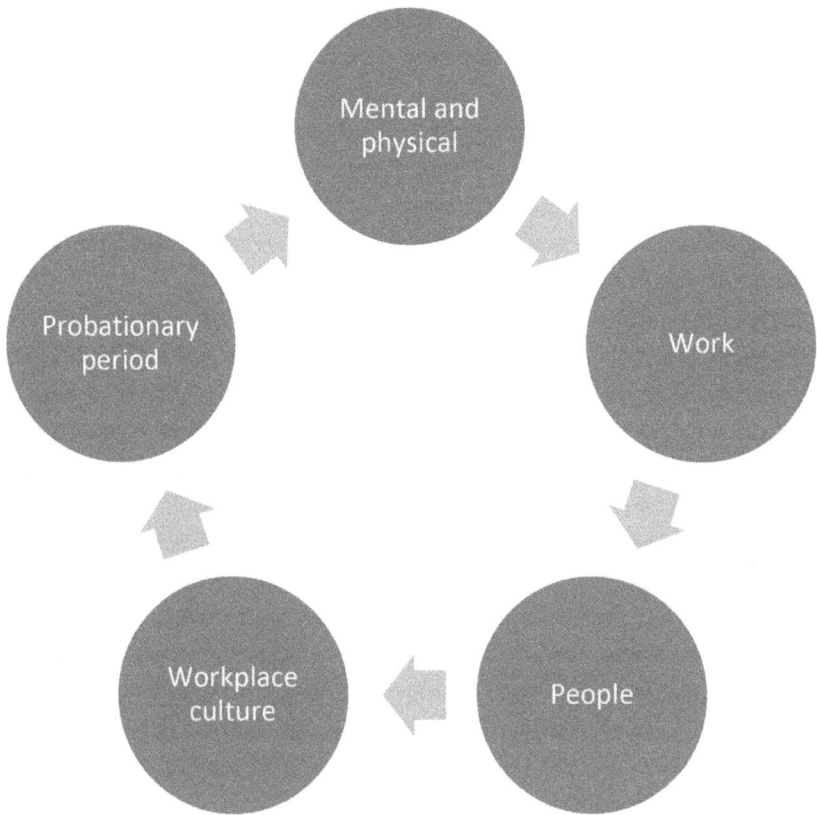

Figure 19.1 Onboarding Challenges

Following are a number of challenges facing you during the onboarding process:

Preparing mentally and physically
The first days on a new job can be both stimulating and exhausting at the same time. There is much about operations that needs to be learned. There are countless people to meet. You have to establish and organize your workspace. Each has to happen while you begin to play the occupational role the employer hired you to perform.

Whether this is your first real job or you are changing positions, it's important to look forward, not backward. Education and work may have resulted in a certain level of "burnout" for you, and you need to rid yourself of any anchors either school or work have created. Remember that all behavior is learned. Move into the new job intent on learning or applying the new behaviors it will take for you to be successful. Any poor habits that you learned or displayed in a previous job need to be left behind, and you must view your new position as a fresh start with new behaviors. If you changed positions because the old one was too stressful, don't carry the old stressors to the new workplace. Refresh!

Eating properly, exercising, and getting sufficient sleep will be critical to the demands of the new work you are performing. Healthy habits have a positive effect on performance, and there are challenges in any transition that will require the healthiest you. Often, it is advisable to take a brief "stop out" before starting or between jobs to clear out the cobwebs and reinvigorate yourself.

Confronting work challenges

New positions present challenges that you have never experienced before, including some that your former position didn't present. In moving about the career lattice, you will find that every change places different demands on you. While you may have been hired to interject new ideas and innovative ways of doing things, established protocols still rule the day and need to be learned. This is especially true when the new job is a growth position where you not only have to do good work but also manage others who now report to you. Different skills must be displayed and practiced and may require a heightened level of energy and attention from you.

Once you gain command of the protocols in place, employers are looking at two transitions and the speed with which each occurs. If you're replacing someone, how fast will it take you to reach or exceed the work quality and production level of the previous staff member? If in a new position, how long will it take you to reach the expected quality and production levels? You got the job because the employer thought you could do the work. Now you have to prove it.

Confronting people challenges
The people challenges of the new job will range from remembering names to acquiring a sense of what roles your colleagues or coworkers play within the organization. Work groups are often like community groups—with different individuals performing roles in making the community function. Once you have completed the onboarding process, it is likely that you will assume one of these positions and it will mark your status in the organization. There are also hierarchies (i.e., chain of command, organizational flow charts, etc.) that you will have to learn in the early stages of the new job and use throughout your employment.

You may need to grasp how people come together to form teams to take on work projects. The greatest "turnoff" in the established organization is the new employee who gives off the "know it all" vibe. Even if you know more than may be of expected of you in the early going, you may want to make it grow out of your performance and not your proclamations.

Every organization usually has one person who knows more of the history of the employer and can offer insights into operations and procedures more than anyone. Usually, this person has been around for some time or occupies a position from which astute observations can be made. This individual is a good one for you to get to know because they will help in your "learning the ropes."

The final people challenge, and possibly the most important one, is to learn the management style of the person to whom you will report. Understanding expectations early in the new job and discovering ways to build a good working relationship with your superiors will remove many of the anxieties associated with how your performance will be evaluated.

Learning the workplace culture
The quickest way to take the organizational and cultural pulse of the workplace is to use a derivative of "management by wandering around" (MBWA), an administrative style addressed by Tom Peters and Robert H. Waterman in their book *In Search of Excellence: Lessons from America's Best-Run Companies.*

Peters and Waterman suggest that managers use unstructured and impromptu movements around the workplace as a tool for understanding the effectiveness of the organization and spotting issues requiring attention before they become problems. Substitute "learning" for "management," and a "learning by wandering around" style on your part will help you acquire valuable orientation information. These exposures allow you to see, hear, and touch the workplace that you have entered.

Dealing with probationary status

The first part of every new job is a test or trial period during which you will be on probation while you learn what is expected of you and move forward to fulfill the work role you were hired to perform. Treat any probationary period as part of the onboarding process and learn everything you need to know. It is a good thing to watch, listen, and touch all of the things that are being done by your peers because they typically represent how the employer wants the work to be performed.

STRAIGHT TALK ABOUT ADJUSTING TO A NEW JOB

The early days in any new job represent a new adventure, one filled with excitement and anticipation. Although you possess the knowledge and skills to do what the job demands, you are now in a different venue, and you must prove yourself again. Make certain you make the social, emotional, and cognitive adjustments that are critical to a successful job launch. It is a time for you to be attentive and organized.

Organizational attention will be required to learn the protocols (i.e., how things are done) in your new environment and a number of "one and done" tasks (i.e., completing forms, acquiring ID badges and parking permits, etc.). Surviving the onboarding period requires forming and asking questions. You become a student of the new workplace.

As you become acclimated to your work role, seize every opportunity to become engaged. Engagement is a two-way street, and you must make every effort to capture any elements of the process that will allow you to enter, adjust, and contribute to a new work environment. Hopefully, your employer will facilitate this objective.

Enter your new work role in sound physical and mental health and pay attention to this aspect of your well-being all of the years you are employed. From an emotional experience, view it as a new beginning.

Dedicate yourself to achieving and enjoying the success that this new role will contribute to your long-term career goals. Confront all of the challenges presented by onboarding and do whatever it takes to make a seamless transition.

CHAPTER 20

Challenge: Holding Out for the "Dream" Job

Perfection is not attainable, but if we chase perfection, we can catch excellence.

—Vince Lombardi (1913–1970), National Football League Hall of Fame coach who led the Green Bay Packers to victories in Super Bowls I and II

When it comes to measuring success in the world of work, many set out to find their "dream" job. While perfection as an objective is something to be encouraged, it may be more elusive than it often appears. In the real world, each individual can identify the factors or elements that they would like to see present in their work and workplace and then embark on discovering the environment where a reasonable array of those conditions exists.

Following a meta-analysis of numerous studies and essays about why people love or hate their jobs, your author has concluded that an individual's definition of a "dream job" is mostly about expectations, preferences, and values, and an examination of what those studies and experts have put forth suggests that candidates for employment would do well to carefully scrutinize those characteristics under a special lens to determine the level to which these desired factors are present.

CPR AS A CAREER OR JOB SAVER

Acknowledging that the commonly known CPR (cardiopulmonary resuscitation) is a lifesaver, the CPR strategy advanced here may have relevance as a career or job saver. When the following culture (C), people (P), and reward (R) factors or conditions are present, the odds are favorable that individuals will like their job. When they are absent those same people are more likely to become active candidates for change and relocation.

THE MIXTURE THAT BREEDS SATISFACTION

Seldom does a single factor fully contribute to total job satisfaction. Rather, when individuals speak highly of their position or place in the work world, the superlatives of the most satisfied are often a combination of the CPR factors. Highly satisfied workforce members tend to rate the work and the environment in which it is expected to be performed as contributing to a desirable culture—the C factor.

Equally important to contented workers is a healthy dose of the interaction their work allows for interaction with people at every level and in various capacities—the P factor. Happy employees seek balance, fairness, and equity in peer work roles and consistent, respectful, and supportive guidance from their managers, supervisors, and leaders. Finally, following closely in the CPR equation, a reasonable measure of rewards—the R factor—will add icing to the work and workplace cake.

While it usually takes a combination of CPR factors to ensure satisfaction and pleasure, the presence of a solitary factor (i.e., conflict issues with a manager) can be powerful enough to result in an intolerable working situation. Such situations can be a driving motivation for the victim to seek a job change.

Figure 20.1 Dream Job CPR: Culture Factors / People Factors / Reward Factors

INDIVIDUAL DIFFERENCES YIELD INDIVIDUAL PRIORITIES

Prior to the consideration of any position, job seekers should engage in a "pulse taking" designed to assess and prioritize the factors that they are seeking to find as movement into and around the workplace proceeds. Playing on the old "different strokes for different folks" adage, it is likely that most of the factors are similar for many, but how they are prioritized will vary from person to person. Like a good pot of vegetable stew—the ingredients may be to an extent identical, but the amounts and preparation techniques may be what make one recipe different from another.

Similarly, different individuals will require the presence of different recipes to ensure career and job satisfaction.

The fifteen ingredients in the following recipe for career satisfaction and success are those most frequently cited by people claiming to love their careers and jobs. Concomitantly, one can assume that when these factors are missing, they will be contributing elements in why individuals seem to relocate.

FACTORS CONTRIBUTING TO EMPLOYEE SATISFACTION AND SUCCESS

Following are the work and workplace factors that are most likely to generate career and job satisfaction:

Culture factors

- Freedom, flexibility, and autonomy to contribute to the mission of the employer
- Practices, protocols, and policies that encourage "buy-in" by the employee
- Environment that invites participation and sharing
- Presence of the right tools, equipment, and information to perform work role
- Absence of interfering and nonproductive politics

People factors

- Respect for coworkers leading to a feeling of making contributions to a team effort and "all pulling together" spirit
- Respect for the direction offered by leadership and management and a confidence in the guidance of one's immediate supervisor(s)
- Sense of a collaborative spirit and energy
- Presence of overall honesty, fairness, impartiality, and evenhandedness
- Peer equality at every level on the chain of command

Reward factors

- Sense of worth, as well as recognition for achievements and accomplishments, recognized in both tangible (i.e., raise, bonus, promotion) and subtle (i.e., pat on the back) rewards
- Presence of personal career growth and development opportunities
- Work role that includes reasonable and achievable challenges
- Fair and competitive compensation and benefits
- Respect for the employee's life away from work

Any review of the fifteen CPR factors, will show that they represent a mix of the tangible and intangible, the visible and the less evident. Among the R factors, for example, tangible rewards are most likely to fall into the compensation and benefits arena. Intangible rewards, however, may be valued just as highly. These include subtle and difficult to define conditions like feeling recognized, taking pride in accomplishments, and the sense that one is contributing to an effort in an important way.

Some CPR factors emerge in the onboarding process and grow over time. Others, however, are associated with performance and productivity and will not be obvious until they are fully earned. Until their presence can be determined, individuals in transition must rely on their instincts and their study of the particular workplace to ascertain their level of existence.

STRAIGHT TALK ABOUT HOLDING OUT FOR THE "DREAM" JOB

The quote offered by Coach Lombardi at the beginning of this chapter should not be construed as a reason for not setting lofty goals with respect to career and job satisfaction. As long as those goals are realistic—meaning attainable—they will become the yardstick by which satisfaction can be measured. Each individual, however, must understand that perfection is surrounded by all sorts of excellence.

Initial job satisfaction is most likely to happen when the CPR method has been applied to the search process from beginning to end. This entails an assessment of individual needs, preferences, and values—a personal profile, if you will—that is then compared to what is known about the culture, people, and rewards that are present in positions under consideration. Continued career fulfillment will occur when the individual is able to grow and develop in that job.

CHAPTER 21

Challenge: Managing Positive Encounters with Career Helpers

If you don't have a competitive advantage, don't compete.

—JACK WELCH (1935–2020), PROMINENT BUSINESS EXECUTIVE
AND COAUTHOR OF THE BEST-SELLING BOOK, *WINNING*. FROM
1981 TO 2001, HE WAS THE CHAIRMAN AND CHIEF EXECUTIVE
OFFICER OF GENERAL ELECTRIC, A PERIOD IN WHICH THE
COMPANY STOCK EXPERIENCED PHENOMENAL GROWTH AND
GREW TO BECOME A GLOBAL FORCE.

INDIVIDUALS IN TRANSITION OFTEN FAIL TO USE THE AVAILABLE
resources that can give them the competitive advantage in their quest
for career satisfaction and success. This was addressed in chapter 10 as
the failure to use counseling and support services in moving about the
early stages of the career development process and making education and
training decisions. It must, however, be examined again because you need
to consider utilizing career counseling and other services in the times
following school and college.

If your first and only experiences with counselors to this point
took place in schools or colleges, you have now progressed to a point
where another set of counselors working in a variety of venues may be

positioned to help you find a job and progress through your early career development.

In addition to the counselors in institutions, organizations, agencies, and private practice, you will need to consider how focused services offered by employee assistance programs (EAPs) and search and staffing firms may be useful in supporting your various job, occupational, and career transitions. The problem is that too few recognize their value or know how to use these counselors and services effectively.

INTERVENTIONS WITH PROFESSIONAL COUNSELORS

Tied to this failure to utilize the helpers and helping services is a belief that seems to emanate from an "island" mentality. Outside of your family, close friends, and trusted mentors, you may be reluctant to reach out beyond your personal comfort zone to acquire the assistance in helping you identify potential jobs and then move assertively through the systematic steps to acquire your first or next job. Similarly, when you experience personal issues or problems across the career span, you are reluctant to seek assistance.

In far too many instances, the "I can do it on my own" attitude results in inefficient and ineffective transitions—or no transitions at all. When these transitions fail, your life–work balance will be threatened, and your career goals will not be realized. Learn about the resources and services available to you and reach out to utilize them.

Following is a listing of personal and career interventions where professional counselors are likely to be of assistance to you:

- Job identification and acquisition
- Workplace adjustment and orientation
- General career growth, mobility, and maintenance
- Specific career change
- Continuing education and training
- Workplace stress and anxiety

Figure 21.1 Career Helpers

- Personal, emotional, and social issues that have workplace implications
- Interest and personality assessment and evaluation
- Life–work balance issues
- Late-career adjustment and exit

The counseling professionals who can help you tackle the issues above are found in institutions, agencies, organizations, and private practice environments. Employment counselors, for example, can be found in numerous state and local government agencies (i.e., Virginia Employment Commission, Colorado Department of Labor and Employment, etc.) whose primary role is to work with clients in addressing employment issues. Make certain you are dealing with properly prepared and credentialed professionals, ones certified by a national body (e.g., National Board of Certified Counselors) or licensed or certified by the state. Further, be wary of untrained and noncredentialed individuals calling themselves "coaches" and "consultants" and claiming expertise in helping people with their career development transitions.

Many confront their career challenges effectively all by themselves. A significant number do not. Why struggle with one or more of these issues when there are professional counselors who can help you deal with each? The challenge becomes more formidable when you are working and want to change positions, escape a bad situation, or deal with life–work stresses. In some instances that assistance should come from professionals with career and education counseling backgrounds. In others, you will want the counselor that possesses mental health skills and experience in addressing personal, emotional, and social concerns.

Different counselors address different needs and play a variety of roles. Counselors can help you appraise a career situation, aid in the identification and consideration of options, and provide guidance as you chart a future course of action. They can help you learn more about yourself through the use and interpretation of interest and personality inventories. At other times, counselors will serve as a "sounding board" where you lay out a personal strategy and obtain assistance in its analysis. But there will also be times when counselors play a rescuer role, people you turn to to deal with a problem or crisis.

INTERVENTIONS WITH SUPPORTING INDIVIDUALS AND SERVICES

Throughout the early-, mid-, and late-career development stages, any number of individuals and services can come to the aid of those pursuing or changing jobs. The people and programs include:

- Colleagues and networks
- Mentors (early and contemporary)

- College and school career services offices
- State and local government agencies
- Professional and trade associations
- Community organizations
- Employee assistance programs

The contributions of any or all of the above may be useful as you consider each and every career transition.

INTERVENTIONS WITH SEARCH AND STAFFING FIRMS

When you are able to find and successfully use recruiters and direct-hire consultants within the search and staff industry, you are likely to form connections that will have a positive influence on your career development. In every community in the land, job seekers and changers will find experienced search and staffing firms that are in the business of linking the "right people to the right job."

While it may sound like a fairly simplistic objective, linking talent to opportunity is a challenging proposition, and reputable, experienced search and staffing firms do it very well. From placing recent graduates to helping mid- or late-career changers, capable recruiters can be invaluable at the job search points in your career development.

All search and staffing industry professionals are not equal and should be chosen for their performance record in helping active and passive applicants find employment and move into employment settings where they are most effective. Some are generalists, and others specialize in career cluster placement (i.e., information technology and engineering, health care, hospitality, etc.).

Staffing industry professionals also have their own credentials and work in accordance with professional and ethical standards. The Certified Personnel Consultant (CPC) and Certified Employee Retention Specialist (CERS) credentials of the National Association of Personnel Services (NAPS), for example, are industry-developed and -administered certifications. The CPC certification examination focuses on all of the laws governing the hiring and employment transition process. In addition, NAPS requires certificate holders to adhere to industry-developed professional and ethical standards and engage in continuing education experiences.

BUYER BEWARE

As previously stated, avoid the shyster who wants to "package" you for your career success. Many adhere to few or no professional or ethical standards, and a significant number have not been trained to perform the services they purport to deliver. The questionable, and sometimes unethical, practices of these coaches and consultants range from exaggerating their placement success to the writing, not assisting in the creation, of client resumes and cover letters. And most significantly, their fees for doing these things are likely to be outrageous.

STRAIGHT TALK ABOUT THE CAREER HELPERS

Too often, job seekers and changers fail to utilize the talented people and competent services that will take them from one end of an employment transition to the next. Professional counselors, offering individual and group services to clients in institution, organization, agency, employment, and private practice, possess the talent and experience to aid in any of these transitions. Select those who are properly credentialed and adhere to the professional and ethical standards advanced by the American Counseling Association, National Board for Certified Counselors, and other reputable organizations.

Search and staffing firms can serve as connectors between those with vacant positions and those seeking to find or change jobs. Again, every effort should be made to deal only with reputable individuals and firms, those who have a history of service to candidates for employment and taken steps to display their professionalism via their credentials and adherence to peer established ethical standards.

Each of the helpers identified here should be considered a "path lighter," one who will help you identify any challenges that might appear before you, as well as outline the varied options and directions you may wish to consider in moving forward.

PART 3

ACHIEVING CAREER SATISFACTION AND DEALING WITH THE OCCASIONAL CRISIS

CHAPTER 22

Challenge: Maximizing Career Growth, Mobility, and Maintenance Opportunities

Yesterday I was a dog. Today, I'm a dog. Tomorrow I'll probably still be a dog. Sigh! There's so little hope for advancement.

—SNOOPY, POPULAR *PEANUTS* CARTOON CHARACTER CREATED BY CHARLES M. SCHULTZ

DURING THIS STAGE OF THE CAREER DEVELOPMENT PROCESS, MANY engaged and satisfied individuals reach a competency level that calls for new or expanded responsibilities. It could mean taking on a new role with your current employer or exiting and moving to an identical or expanded role with another employer. It represents a period of career maturity in which positive change will call upon your self-assessment, exploration, and decision-making skills once again.

Every American worker, with reasonable foresight, should be able to assess their occupational and career progress. Once understood, the next step is to take both developmental and corrective measures needed to grow, become more mobile, and deal with the occasional career crisis. This analysis should be conducted in a manner that also deals with the personal and social adjustments you are making away from the work-place. At the same time, every employer would like to keep its strongest workers engaged, producing, growing, and satisfied, all factors that will lead to their retention. Individual success is an essential ingredient within organizational success.

ENTER CAREER GROWTH, MOBILITY, AND MAINTENANCE

Growth and mobility and your achieving your full career potential are forever linked. When you slow down or stop, you move from a passive applicant to external employment to a very active one. Full realization of that potential is dependent on your ability to consider opportunities and seize the ones that fit. Think back to the way in which you chose your first real job. Now fast forward and update all of the information that you used to make that decision and apply it in dealing with the new options that are appearing on your career radar.

To maximize your growth and mobility, you must visit and answer the following two questions throughout the career development process: Are you in the place that will allow you to fulfill your career mission or objective? Is your current job or occupation a viable "stepping-stone"? Earlier you were challenged to invest in or "own" your decisions—to play an active role in making each decision that will take you to the place in your larger career schema. The degree to which you are engaged in your employment will play a huge role in determining the extent to which each decision is fully realized.

Except for the most monotonous of occupations, you are likely to be in a job or workplace environment that is constantly changing and presenting new challenges. Growth and mobility are tied to those changes and are also related to the challenges that you are experiencing personally, socially, and emotionally. You are not the same person you were in high school or college. You have learned more, acquired greater skills, and become more competent than the day you walked into your place of employment for the first time.

Any growth that you experience will have an impact on mobility options as they occur internally (within your current employment situation) or externally (other employers who would benefit from your knowledge and skills) and lead to the competence level that brings security and satisfaction with it.

Maintenance is more fundamental. This a point in the career development process when you must examine the "big picture" when determining if you achieved the milestones that you set or are in a place to do so. Much of it has to do with effective performance on the job, but it doesn't end there. Maintenance also means the acquisition of any new knowledge or skills that will be required to keep you current in your work role. When the American workplace concentrated on industrial and manufacturing jobs, all that many had to do was appear there each day and perform the same tasks as the previous day. Change was more minimal then than it is today.

Working to ensure personal career growth, mobility, and maintenance is made more challenging by the adjustments that are occurring all around us. In part 5, Challenges to Career Development in the Future, the reader will be exposed to how American work, workers, and the workplace today are incredibly different from yesterday.

ENGAGEMENT RESULTS IN RETENTION

Studies conducted by human resource officers and staffing firms are clear about the importance of employee engagement as a factor in employers being able to retain their best workers. A number of these workplace studies have sought to identify the elements that are most influential in the engagement and retention of employees. Consistently, these studies have found that satisfied employees:

- Like their job
- Like the environment in which they work, including colleagues and setting
- Feel a connection to the mission of the organization
- Sense they are surrounded by competent colleagues and are having their work managed by capable supervisors
- Believe their compensation, benefits, and related rewards are competitive

- Recognize opportunities for growth, mobility, and advancement
- Feel treated as valued contributors

RETENTION RESULTS IN GROWTH AND DEVELOPMENT

If there are secrets to getting promoted in the workplace and developing within your career, you don't have to dig too deeply to unearth the magical formula. Growth and development emanate from engaged employees being retained in work they find satisfying. Satisfied employees exude a certain manner that is likely to result in their being targeted for promotion and advancement. That manner includes:

- Visibility—Be an active player in the workplace and a positive contributor to the culture. You will never get promoted if no one knows you're there and you don't express your desire to grow, develop, and take on new challenges. Volunteer for assignments that will increase your exposures.
- Performance—Do your job and display the skills (i.e., organization, evaluation, leadership) of the position you aspire to acquire. Accept and respond to feedback. Exhibit the mix of roles you are capable of performing in order to showcase your flexibility and versatility.
- Work ethic and demeanor—Carry yourself in a professional manner. Put in the hours needed to get the work done and be prepared to go above and beyond when conditions demand or even when they don't demand. Zealous behavior is often rewarded. Meet deadlines and use time effectively. Display a desire to learn more and jump on every chance to participate in education and training experiences.
- Communication and interpersonal relationships—Ask relevant questions and answer the questions of others when the opportunity presents itself. Find a mentor in the workplace environment, that individual with whom you can talk and discussion work matters. Be a mentor when the opportunity arises.

When these elements are present, they will be noticed. When they become a pattern, they represent the traits that employers use to make promotion decisions. Those promotions lead to rewards (i.e., compensation, office location, amenities, etc.) and recognition (i.e., position, authority, etc.) within the firm, organization, agency, or institution.

THE ABSENCE OF GROWTH AND MOBILITY

When employees doesn't merit growth and promotion attention or when such opportunities don't exist in a particular workplace, there is a strong chance they will become disenchanted, even to the point of feeling mired or stuck in their job. Often, it goes beyond being unhappy to a level of dissatisfaction, even dislike, for their job and the place where they work.

Information about dissatisfaction, gathered via exit interviews, suggest it manifests itself in a variety of ways, most of which run counter to the satisfaction engagement "magnets" identified early in this chapter. Dissatisfaction is typically based on one or more of the following:

- Loss of passion and the onset of boredom and discontent with both the work and the workplace
- Absence of meaningfulness in the work and corresponding challenges
- Values and philosophical conflict
- Sense of job insecurity
- Limited or nonexistent growth opportunities
- Limited or nonexistent continuing education and training opportunities
- Poor relationships with employer, managers, and coworkers
- Belief that better opportunities exist elsewhere
- Failure of the work to contribute to your overall career development

When one or more of the above is present, many employees have one foot already out the door. This is especially hard on the employer who has failed to create a culture of acceptance, opportunity, and reward. These characteristics form the basis for why you will seek other employment.

ABSENCE OF AN EFFECTIVE CAREER PLAN CAN BE THE DEATH KNELL TO MOBILITY

The establishment of career goals and a corresponding career plan, introduced in chapter 3, are factors that arise again during the growth, mobility, and maintenance phase of adult and senior life. When an individual considers any occupational and job changes, they must be viewed within the context of one's overall career development.

An effective career plan will aid in the achievement of a set of objectives that will keep candidates from the perils suggested in the words of Yogi earlier. Minimally, the plan will:

- Identify long- and short-term goals (ends)
- Offer an operational apparatus to achieve those goals (means to the end)
- Pinpoint the decisions that must be made to facilitate the plan (choice points on plan path)
- Define the indicators or outcomes signaling when goals have been achieved (benchmarks indicating progress)
- Establish a timetable for when those decisions must be made and indicators and outcomes will be realized (calendar)
- Include monitoring mechanisms that will allow for the evaluation of the plan and making adjustments or updates as deemed necessary (progress assessment)

BENEFITS DERIVED FROM A CAREER PLAN

The development and maintenance of a career plan is likely to produce multiple benefits to the individual, including these:

- Ongoing personal assessment—Career plans afford the makers the opportunity to examine their aptitudes, achievements, interests, traits, values, and lifestyle preferences over time and plot a course that meets their unique characteristics, needs, and ambitions.

• Empowerment and control—Each plan empowers the makers to control the career development process over the long term, as well as the various experiences and events at every step along the way. Further, the plan developers are fully at the controls of the career development process and can guide all activity in whatever direction they choose.

• Investment opportunity—A quality plan affords individuals the unique opportunity to "buy-in" to both the process and the selected target. Buy-in leads to ownership, a sense of commitment to doing whatever it takes to bring the plan to fruition.

• Aura of confidence—A well-thought-out and meticulously executed career plan sends a signal to prospective employers that they are dealing with poised and confident individuals who have a sense of career direction and their own GPS system or map for getting there. Whether the first job, third job, or umpteenth job, such confidence can be the asset that leads to a desirable job offer.

Career plans can range in formality from written plans to informal schemes that add adventuresome thought to those "in a perfect world" moments of imagination that often pop up in the young and mid-adult years. Irrespective of the formality of the plan, it can be a very germane conversation topic between the candidate and recruiter.

Achieving career satisfaction and success doesn't just happen. It requires work—hard work. Each step along the way, whether, choice, preparation, entry or movement, can be piloted more effectively and efficiently if a well-thought-out plan is in place. From a recruiting and placement perspective, it diminishes the prospects that one's candidacy won't be "dead on arrival."

THE NEXT JOB: WHERE IS IT?

Candidates for growth and promotion will find their next job in a variety of different locations, including:

- Doing the same thing for another employer
- Engaging in an enhanced version of what you are doing now for your current employer or another one
- Doing what you do independently as a contractor or a consultant
- Doing something completely new and different
- Venturing out into the entrepreneurial world and starting a business or service

A century ago, it was common to start a job and work in that role, often for the same employer, for one's entire career. Today, you will likely experience multiple growth and promotion transitions over the course of your career.

NO MAGICAL FORMUAL FOR MOBILITY

Throughout this book, it has been repeatedly stated that there are no one-size-fits-all solutions to the achievement of career satisfaction and success. There may be a common objective—life–work balance—but there is no superhighway to getting there. You will create your own plan and then proceed to implement it. Anytime you make a significant change, be certain to have a Plan B in case Plan A doesn't turn out to be what you expected. Counselors and others can assist you, but the degree to which you achieve your goals is mostly up to you.

Opportunities for career mobility are typically tied to readiness, a metric that is measured in different ways, including:

- Knowledge—Do you know what you need to know in order to move vertically, horizontally, or to a new place in the work world? Are you willing to learn more?
- Skill set—Have you converted that knowledge into skills that your current employer or prospective employers find desirable?
- Experience—Have you been engaged in employment tasks long enough for them to become ingrained?
- Competence—Are you good at what you do?

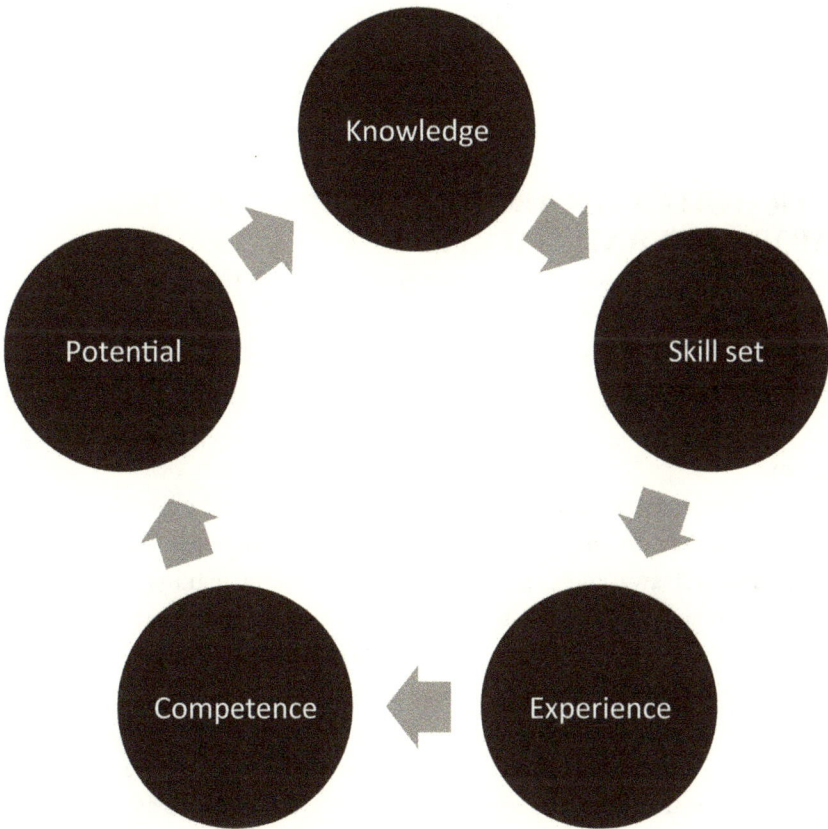

Figure 22.1 Measures Affecting Career Growth and Mobility

- Potential—Do you have the capacity for growing even more?

REASONS EMPLOYERS WANT TO RETAIN GOOD EMPLOYEES

When you abandon your current position and move to a similar or different position with another employer, any investment made in you walks out the door with you. Any return on investment (ROI) the employer was expecting to gain from your presence just dropped to zero. The metrics are clear. When you depart, a new person can be put in your place fairly quickly. Getting your replacement up to the performance level you achieved is a whole different matter.

For this reason and many others, there is a new emphasis in the human resource community on engaging employees and helping them grow and develop—factors that weigh heavily on employee retention. Expect even greater attention of engagement and retention in the future.

STRAIGHT TALK ABOUT CAREER GROWTH, MOBILITY, AND MAINTENANCE

Career growth, mobility, and maintenance have a lot to do with opening doors. When open, you must determine if you are prepared for what is on the other side and then act accordingly. Often, these doors remain open, and you can pass through whenever you wish. Sometimes, they open just a crack and close again quickly if you're not ready to slip quickly through them.

As you consider and implement change, you must exercise many of the same behaviors that you've applied earlier in your career development, including self-awareness, exploration, and decision-making. A personal assessment will validate the things you discovered earlier that sent you in this career direction. That may reopen the door to additional exploration and present new decisions for consideration.

Seizing opportunity is tied directly to awareness and readiness. When you possess both, you will be prepared for a host of new and different options. Unlike Snoopy, you will have great hope for advancement.

CHAPTER 23

Challenge: Attaining Career Success, Satisfaction, and Life–Work Balance

You should not confuse your career with your life.

—DAVE BARRY, PULITZER PRIZE–WINNING COLUMNIST AND
AUTHOR WHOSE SYNDICATED HUMOR COLUMN FOR THE *MIAMI
HERALD* RAN FOR MORE THAN TWENTY YEARS

WORK IS NOT THE ONLY IMPORTANT THING THAT YOU WILL DO IN YOUR life. It is one of the important things, but it must be balanced in a way in which you achieve life–work balance. A Society of Human Resource Development study earlier this millennium found that six in ten (58 percent) workers stated they wanted their work to provide the flexibility that allowed them to balance their life and work. It was the most sought-after workplace trait, one that many believe will keep their career from running or ruining their life.

The print and electronic media are prone to use the term "work–life" balance. This book reverses the terms and in doing so, places greater emphasis on the larger picture. After all, your workday is not a 24/7 arrangement, and what you do at work should be balanced with what you do the rest of your life. They are indelibly connected but need to be considered separately.

Life–work balance and career satisfaction are difficult to define, and no attempt will be made to define them here. That definition is an individual one and can only be created by the reader. It should be noted, however, that life and work are inexplicably tied to each other.

As you grow and develop, you become comfortable with a certain set of lifestyle preferences and interests. These, as stated in chapter 1, are the things you favor and like doing. They are your life lens. It stands to reason that you will seek a career that is consistent with these preferences and interests or one that allows you to achieve them away from the workplace.

A second lens is your job, your occupation, and eventually your career. Achieving career satisfaction is also a matter of paramount importance for you, one that exists throughout life. You want to prepare for, enter, and progress through a series of occupational experiences that you will one day look back on as a successful and rewarding career.

CAREER SATISFACTION AS A STEPPING-STONE TO LIFE–WORK BALANCE

Everyone would like to find their dream career. Many, however, find it an elusive challenge and certainly not something that happens quickly. A more realistic objective may be attaining a level of career satisfaction in which you enjoy the work, the people, and the place where you do it. Career satisfaction, for most, can be measured by both tangible (i.e., compensation, benefits, etc.) and intangible (i.e., life–work balance, recognition for good work performed, positive engagement with managers and peers, etc.) attributes. That satisfaction then becomes the stepping-stone to life–work balance.

THE REALITIES OF FAILED LIFE–WORK BALANCE

A number of realities come into perspective when you find your life–work balance is not what you had hoped it would be. Because these represent a mixture of both personal and work circumstances, you may find the need to separate them for the purposes of resolving. You may have:

- Set personal and career goals that are not achievable
- Failed to master the art of decision-making

- Prepared academically and vocationally for a career that is not a good fit
- Studied something different from what you really want to pursue
- Accepted a job with an employer that is not a good fit
- Started an occupation or career that isn't the right one
- Failed to take advantage of growth and mobility opportunities
- Failed to address personal, social, and emotional issues that require counseling attention

If any one or more of these factors fits your developmental scheme, you may have to revisit the career development process and examine possible corrective actions. Recognize fully that any personal, social, and emotional issues that impinge on your life–work balance may have to be dealt with through appropriate counseling.

Another reality in the contemporary workplace is that trade-offs may be expected in return for the benefits derived. Most welcome the new flexibility (i.e., casual dress, telecommuting, etc.) that exists in many places of employment today, but does some of the flexibility come with a price? Is flexible scheduling interpreted by the employer as you are "on call" 24/7? Are you presented a business cell phone and then expected to answer it anytime and anywhere? Is your life being regulated or monetized by your employer in return for the freedoms and flexibilities being afforded you? Life–work balance requires a level of separation, and you should never abandon your personal life when you accept a work role.

The Gallup Organization regularly conducts opinion polls of how the U.S. workforce feels about their work and workplace. The findings of a number of their *State of the American Workplace* studies can be found at Gallup.com.

CHANGE REQUIRES BALANCE ADJUSTMENT

Recognize that throughout the growth, mobility, and maintenance period of your career development, considerable change is occurring. You are changing. Your personal needs and responsibilities (i.e., spouse, partner, children, etc.) are likely to have changed, as well as many of your personal, emotional, and social needs.

Add to the above all of the changes that are taking place in your work and the workplace, and you have a formula for upsetting any life–work balance you have been able to achieve. The result is what has been popularly referred to as "midlife crisis" or "burnout."

SIGNS LIFE–WORK BALANCE IS IN JEOPARDY

There are a number of signals to watch for in achieving and sustaining life–work balance. When one or more of these characteristics emerge, what was once a desirable work situation may move in the totally opposite direction. They include:

- The work becomes boring and mundane.
- The passion for performing the work diminishes or disappears.
- Relationships with colleagues sour.
- Relationships with managers and supervisors become contentious.
- Salary adjustments are not forthcoming, or job security is lacking.
- Politics become unbearable.
- Rules, hours, and other working conditions affect freedom and flexibility.
- Growth opportunities fail to emerge.
- Factors (i.e., family matters, unexpected debt, etc.) away from work begin to impact employment.
- Work has a negative effect on life (i.e., missing family obligations, relationship suffering, loss of sleep due to stress and anxiety).
- Recognition that previous career decisions were faulty and need to be corrected.

Often, challenges of this nature are correctable. You address them and move forward. Other times, they are the "wakeup call" that your employment is not what it once was and it is time for a new setting or a total career makeover.

STRATEGIES FOR IMPROVING AND ENSURING LIFE–WORK BALANCE

Achieving life–work balance is a two-way street. Behaviors will be required both at work and away from work in order for you to achieve it. Different workplace environments offer an atmosphere and culture that will influence how you feel about your work, but one thing is certain— the engaged employee is most likely to be more satisfied. The following six strategies represent behaviors you can exhibit that will contribute to that satisfaction.

Do your job consistently

Apply the knowledge and skills you possess consistently and thoroughly each workday or to each work assignment. Expect more of yourself than your employer expects of you. Practice good time management principles and develop regimens that promote performance and productivity.

Draw a distinct line between life and work

Separate your personal life from your work life. This may involve turning off your cell phone and refusing to carry your work back and forth between home and work. Setting these boundaries will ensure that your "downtime" is yours to enjoy your family and friends and participate in leisurely pursuits. Take care of personal, family, and nonwork issues before or after work or on weekends. Try not to allow personal and family matters to form a cloud over the time you are working.

Create and sustain relationships

Perform your role in a manner that contributes to and feeds off of the work of your coworkers. Create and sustain relationships with all of the people with whom you interact in your work roles. Determine the expectations of your manager or supervisor and seek evaluative feedback regarding your performance and productivity. Most importantly, cultivate the communication that is needed in all of your interpersonal relationships.

Strive for good physical and mental health

Eat the right things. Get the appropriate amount of exercise and sleep. All will aid in your enjoyment of life–work balance when it is achieved. Avoid stressful and anxiety-producing situations when possible. Determine the tasks that are most stressful and determine ways to address these challenges by learning and practicing appropriate coping skills. When possible, resolve conflict as an "issue" and keep it from becoming a "problem." Avoid being defensive and look to collaborative avenues for problem solving.

Blend life and work when the situation calls for it

Without appearing to contradict number 2 above, there may be instances when life away from and at work can be merged. Transfer behaviors learned and practiced in one setting to the other.

If you can multitask at home, you can do the same in the workplace and vice versa. Look for additional ways to exchange positive and productive behaviors. Create one calendar that has both personal and work information on it. This blend will allow you to better understand the mix of events and ensure that everything that needs attention gets attention.

Enjoy life and career simultaneously

Don't allow your life or career to become your personal prison or quicksand. If you have prepared properly and chosen wisely, you can have both. The younger members of the U.S. workforce are the ones who have championed life–work balance. They were the ones who brought telecommuting, casual Friday, flextime, and other features to the U.S. workplace. The entire workforce has reaped the rewards.

STRAIGHT TALK ABOUT CAREER SUCCESS, SATISFACTION, AND LIFE–WORK BALANCE

There is nothing wrong with dreaming and hoping that you will find the perfect job, in the perfect place, and paying you a great salary. It gets even better if that position allows you to do all the things that you want to do in your personal life and career. Aim high but not beyond a set of reasonable targets.

Success and satisfaction grow with time and experience and often don't show up until you've been doing something for a while. How are you measuring satisfaction and success? Life–work balance, ability to get along with managers and colleagues, growth potential, compensation, security, and any number of other factors are likely to be ingredients in your personal recipe for career contentment.

Life–work balance need not be elusive. It may not exist at the beginning of a job or career, but it is likely to begin and grow with time and experience. When poor life–work balance takes a significant foothold, it can result in a number of things, the impact of which can range from running your life to ruining your life. Many end up hating their jobs, the people they work with, and for the lousy decisions they have made over time. The passion and excitement that accompanied the onset of employment is blemished by a sense of frustration and defeat.

A growing body of evidence is telling employers that performance and productivity are enhanced when workers achieve their desirable life–work balance, and fewer are reporting "burnout" and discontent. Clearly, a workplace that offers opportunities for full engagement of its employees will meet you halfway, but how you define life–work balance and what you will contribute to achieve it are totally up to you. Possibly, there will come a time in the future when all employers recognize that performance, productivity, and sustainability are inexplicably tied to the retention of a happy, satisfied workforce.

Life–work balance requires putting yourself and the things that you want higher on your goal list than they may be presently. If you are realistic in your expectations and reasonable in your behaviors, you should be able to achieve the flexibility and balance you desire. Avoid allowing your career to run or ruin your life.

CHAPTER 24

Challenge: Dealing with Termination, Job Loss, and Other Dilemmas

It's a recession when your neighbor loses his job; it's a depression when you lose yours.

—HARRY S. TRUMAN (1884–1972), THIRTY-THIRD PRESIDENT OF THE UNITED STATES. HE WAS A FARMER, ADMINISTRATIVE JUDGE, U.S. SENATOR, AND VICE PRESIDENT, AND WAS UNSUCCESSFUL IN SEVERAL VENTURES INTO THE BUSINESS WORLD.

DURING THE GROWTH/MOBILITY/MAINTENANCE STAGE OF YOUR CAREER development is when you will face the difficult situations like termination and job loss or you must confront any number of difficult situations in the workplace. The onset and continuance of these situations can result in personal chaos for you and play havoc with the career development plan you have created. Each requires your immediate attention and full energy.

Work termination can take a number of forms. In many instances, job loss is your fault as seen when you underperform or fail to meet the expectations of your employer. There can also be circumstances beyond your control that lead to termination. Too often people lose their employment because of downsizing and economic conditions that have a negative impact on the industry in which they work. Others are hurt when businesses merge and need fewer people or when "offshoring" sends U.S. jobs to other places on the globe. Still others become the victims of job obsolescence.

Work dilemmas are different and will vary in severity from those that are correctible to those that will force you to want to look for a new job or a different employer. The worst dilemma may be you're finding yourself in the wrong career with the only salutation being that you must start the entire process all over again.

FIFTEEN REASONS PEOPLE GET FIRED

Consider the following list of notable, and by all accounts, successful women and men: Michael Bloomberg (former New York City mayor), Walt Disney (cartoonist and entrepreneur), Steve Jobs (Apple founder), J. K. Rowling (author), Howard Stern (radio personality), and Oprah Winfrey (television host and entrepreneur). What is the one thing they all have in common?

All of them were fired at some time in their career. Imagine the manager of the Grand Ole Opry in Nashville telling Elvis Presley to keep his job as a truck driver because he had no future as a singer. They all took their dismissal in stride and used the experience to move on to future challenges or to career changes where they eventually found success.

Workers can run afoul of their employer for many reasons. One or more of the following concerns are likely to result in termination:

1. Poor performance—The most common reason people are likely to be fired is poor or substandard performance. Inferior work is not acceptable from either the new or seasoned employee. It can be detected as early as during the probationary period or come up as a part of a performance evaluation. For some, this is simply a matter of being in "over their heads," while for others, it is represented in a display of unsatisfactory work habits. In either case, productivity and performance are affected negatively.

2. Attitude—Commitment to your work and workplace are measured in how effectively you engage yourself in the role you have accepted with your employer and how hard you work. All employees are expected to contribute to the level of their capability and competence, and those who slack off are likely to be identified instantly.

3. Attendance—Absenteeism, tardiness, and poor time management speak to dependability. When you miss work, arrive late, and fail to manage your time appropriately when you are there, your commitment to your job and your employer comes into question. An unusually large volume of personal phone calls and other nonwork activities are also frowned upon.

4. Lying and misrepresentation—Anytime you falsify or exaggerate anything on your resume or job application, there is a great likelihood that these inaccurate claims will be discovered. If these inaccuracies are found after you have been hired, they will likely result in termination. Similarly, dishonesty about any aspect of your work (i.e., falsifying reports, etc.) of any sort is going to be dealt with in the most severe of ways. Little lies can have huge consequences.

5. Personality issues—Confrontational or arrogant employees who fail to function effectively as individuals or team members are putting their employment in jeopardy. Any number of unacceptable personality traits can endanger your employment. It's basically a "fit" issue and often emerges when a personality trait produces a behavior that runs counter to the workplace culture and affects overall performance and productivity.

6. Distractions—When you cannot separate your work from all that is going on in the rest of your life, these distractions are likely to impact negatively on your work. While many personal, family, and other external issues may be unavoidable, every effort should be directed to not allowing them to become workplace distractions.

7. Behavioral issues—Employees who have too much to drink at the holiday party or staff golf outing and exhibit behaviors that

are totally in contrast with their work persona are going to set off alarm bells. Further, team members who constantly undermine the contributions of fellow team members are going to be seen as malcontents. These and many other behavioral issues can eventually flag these individuals for possible termination.

8. Unlawful conduct—Behavior away from the workplace that is unlawful and results in your arrest can be considered a character flaw, one that your employer may use to affect your future relationship with the firm, organization, institution, or agency.

9. Violation of protocols—When your employer prescribes a manner in which things are to be done and you step outside or beyond these protocols, the consequences can often result in your termination. If you don't like the way an employer does things, don't go or continue to work there.

10. Insubordination—The fastest way to get fired is to refuse to accept or adhere to a directive from a supervisor or manager. While many employers will encourage innovation and experimentation, your refusal to follow orders will likely produce the wrong results.

11. Social media behavior—When your Facebook, Twitter, or other social media profile shows you acting in an unprofessional manner, it may be viewed by your employer as unsuitable. When those social media images are derogatory with respect to the employer and workplace colleagues, they are almost certain to result in firing.

12. Sexual harassment—Sexual harassment can be defined in two ways. Quid pro quo harassment occurs when you make sexual overtures or demands of a fellow worker. Hostile environment harassment is best described as any behavior (i.e., using profanity, accessing inappropriate websites, etc.) that makes coworkers uncomfortable. Either can be the grounds for dismissal.

13. Unauthorized use of the internet—Many employers have specific rules on the use of the internet in the workplace. These rules range from using business email for personal purposes to spending time

visiting non-work-related websites. Violations can result in the loss of employment.

14. Working under the influence of alcohol or drugs—Almost every employer has rules about the use of alcohol and drugs in the workplace, and they are usually extended to addressing the employee who comes to work under the influence of these substances.

15. Work politics, gossiping, and other human interaction issues—While less job threatening than many of the behaviors presented above, your participation in workplace politics, gossiping, and other interpersonal issues may be viewed negatively and seen as a lack of concentration on work tasks and responsibilities. When the politics run counter to the views of your employer, you are taking a risk that could impact your employment status.

REASONS PEOPLE LOSE THEIR JOBS

Losing your job may also have nothing to do with you. Various circumstances may arise in your industry or field that result in positions being reduced or lost. In cases like this, the consequences can range from your being laid off temporarily to the more permanent condition of job abolition. Included among these conditions are the following:

- Economics—Any time the economic conditions of the nation and the world go into a downward spiral, many places of employment will be affected. The influence of Wall Street on Main Street is one that can result in termination and layoff notices being delivered. History has shown that every economics "boon" is followed by a downward adjustment of some kind. The trick is to learn from history and find ways to avoid or minimize the next downturn.

- Downsizing—There are situations when companies and organizations go through a mission review that results in a downsizing of the workforce. This also happens when two or more firms merge, resulting in duplicative staff members doing the same thing. Surplus workers in these types of situations lose or are required to change their positions.

- Offshoring—Downsizing of a different nature, offshoring occurs when a firm or business elects to move its operations to another global location. It can be caused by either a merger or the simple desire to place the work in an environment where it is less expensive to operate and products can be produced for less.

- Job obsolescence—Technology and the discovery of new ways to do things have dramatically altered the workplace and resulted in the downsizing and abolition of many jobs. The U.S. Department of Labor projects that total employment in the United States will grow from 153.5 million to 165.4 million during the 2020–2030 decade, an increase of 11.9 million jobs. At the same time, a significant number of others will become totally obsolete, meaning they are no longer needed or require far fewer people.

ADDRESSING THE REALITIES OF JOB LOSS

Unlike the early days when you were moving forward from school and college and without work, true job loss takes on some dimensions you may have not had to deal with before. First, you must deal with the reality that you're unemployed. After your final severance check, your normal compensation will cease.

Forced job change has been known to be a blessing in disguise. Many of the notable personalities cited earlier look back at getting fired and say it was the best thing that ever happened to them. It is certainly a time for self-reflection and if handled properly, need not be as negative as it may appear.

When you were at the front end of your career, circumstances gave you a little more freedom and flexibility to consider options. Those who lose their jobs often have spouses, partners, and families that depend on them and bills (i.e., mortgage, car, credit card debt, student loans, etc.) that limit their independence and structure exactly the course of action you follow to become reemployed.

Following any form of job loss, you have to put into motion a plan that gets you to a work situation that minimizes the impact of the transition but, hopefully, will allow you to extend the career development journey that has been interrupted. That plan should include the following:

- Be positive and do everything from a position of strength. Mount an aggressive job-seeking campaign, one with you squarely in control.

- Give your resume a complete scrubbing. Don't just "dust it off." Review every word and make it reflect you today, not the person who created it originally.

- Avoid being angry and defensive. Both behaviors reek of negativism, something that will likely be noted by prospective employers. Take the high road and refrain from "bad-mouthing" your previous employer.

- Tell the world you're unemployed, including all of your personal, social, and professional/trade networks. Avoiding any of the gory details, seek their assistance in learning of work opportunities for which you might apply.

- Join LinkedIn, Facebook, Twitter, and any other social media community to increase the exposures that may result in new employment. If already active in these networks, make certain your profile is current and accurate.

- Register immediately for any compensation and benefits (i.e., COBRA health insurance extension) to which you're entitled. Know the laws that affect the unemployed, especially if you believe you were the victim of discrimination or your termination may have violated a contract or a union protection.

- Examine your budget and make any necessary spending adjustments.

- Pursue temporary or part-time work if needed to get you through the economic challenges not having a paycheck will create.

- Learn from the last time you looked for employment. Repeat the things you did right and steer clear of the mistakes you made.

- Get the sleep, diet, and exercise that will sustain you through this challenging period.

- Examine and reflect on the larger career picture. Are you in the right place? Is this a time to move in a new direction? Should you stop working for others and form a business of your own? Are you positioned to make such a bold move?

Job loss has personal, social, emotional, and economic ramifications. Once again, finding full-time employment must be your full-time job in order to rectify or minimize those ramifications.

THE CHALLENGES OF A CAREER MAKEOVER

If you believe that you've made poor decisions over time that led to your termination or job loss, the decision to "make over" your career is one that has to be entered into with great care. When the career hole you have fallen into is too deep to crawl out of, you must get answers to a series of questions and concerns, or you may repeat an earlier misstep. There is also the question of degree: Do you need to restart your career or simply jump-start the existing one?

The most important question is a very basic one. Is your career situation irreparable or can you rework your work in some manner that allows you to salvage the time and energy you have invested to date? When the answer is yes, you need to recycle yourself through the awareness, exploration, and decision-making stages of the career development process in a manner that yields more positive results.

Anytime one engages in a career makeover, whether early or later along in adulthood, they usually do not have either the personal freedom or the economic security to do it the way they originally transitioned from school or college to work. Preparation for the new career is going to require all of the things your original career did, but this time you may have to approach it according to an entirely different set of learning strategies and employing a greatly modified clock and calendar. Part-time and online education, as well as volunteer experiences, may become the only mechanism that will allow you to learn what you need to learn in order to change course.

When the education and training part of the makeover is completed, the job search and selection process has to be tackled once again. This is followed by an orientation and adjustment period where you will be viewed as a "rookie" once again.

Those moving from working for an employer to becoming self-employed face a significant number of organizational challenges. Workspace may need to be rented, equipment and furnishings may need to be purchased, and all of the protocols (i.e., licenses, insurance, marketing, etc.) associated with moving into the entrepreneurial world need to be addressed.

The challenges of the career makeover are formidable and need to be approached with forethought, planning, and thoroughness. Starting over is never easy. You will likely take steps backward before you move forward again.

A HOST OF OTHER WORK DILEMMAS

Termination and job loss aren't the only issues that bring havoc to your personal career development. Not getting the promotion you sought or the raise you expected is often difficult to swallow. A workplace culture that fails to recognize your contributions or an employer that is stingy with compensation will leave you feeling unappreciated. Your inability to gain acceptance as a contributing team member can leave a bad taste in your mouth. When any of these situations occur, the best tactic is to voice them with those who are in a position to do something about them or guide you in what you need to do to see them resolved. One final thought: you may be in the right occupation or career—you may just be in the wrong place of employment.

There is one other two-part dilemma that merits consideration. You may have exhausted all of the career growth and development options afforded to you in your current work situation. You will know it when you feel mired or stuck in your current work. Even a job you are in and enjoy may offer nothing in support of your career development. You may also feel "in over your head" and faced with challenges beyond your knowledge, skill, and competence levels. Often, these situations are self-correcting, but they can still generate anxiety and stress. When either situation occurs, passive job candidates may need to become active candidates. It may be time to move on.

Avoiding the blame game and depending on defense mechanisms
Career and workplace crises, while they appear to place you in a victim role, seldom are totally your fault or totally the fault of others. Unfortunately, in assuming the role of victim, you may want to play the "blame game." Job loss can be a fact of life. Whether you are fired or lose your employment to conditions you cannot control, blaming others will only serve as an impediment to moving forward.

If you were the reason you were fired, accept responsibility, consider what corrective action you need to take, and proceed onward. Behavior is controllable; you simply have to grasp what you are doing wrong and take measures to remedy it. In other words, you must learn new behaviors.

Those who believe people issues are the reason they were fired (i.e., boss, manager, supervisor, or colleagues) have a different type of assessment to conduct. In most interpersonal conflicts, both or all parties may need to give a little in order for a positive resolution to be achieved. It begins by sitting down, placing the issue on the table, and talking about it.

By the same token, when you believe you are the victim of substandard compensation and benefits or you don't receive the recognition you feel you deserve for the work that you perform, it is a matter that should be raised in a nonthreatening manner with the person or persons who can do something about it.

Turning to defense mechanisms
Termination, job loss, and the inability to resolve workplace problems finds many turning to defense mechanisms to escape taking responsibility. Defense mechanisms are psychological strategies, often acted out unconsciously, that help you cope with the situation and sustain your self-image. You will go to great lengths to disguise your disappointment or hide your anxiety and inner pain from others. The science of psychology has identified an array of defense mechanisms. Following are some of the common ones that you may use to confront dilemmas in your personal career development:

- Compartmentalization—A form of disassociation in which you explain away the negative by referencing another value.
"I was destined to fail. My employer never discovered my true talents."

- Displacement—Redirecting of behavior or thoughts from one situation to another.
"I apologize for my behavior in the team meeting today. I'm having some problems at home that are distracting me."

- Conversion—Using an escape device rather than face the challenges of life and work.
"I'm stressed to the limit, and my physical health is at risk. It's time for a vacation."

- Denial—Failing to accept fact or reality.
"I did everything they asked me to do, but nothing seemed to satisfy them."

- Rationalization—Offering an explanation of a situation that is beyond reality.
"I didn't discuss the problem with my supervisor because I'm certain she wouldn't have done anything to help me resolve it."

- Sublimation—Channeling anxiety in an alternate direction through the use of fantasy, imagination, or humor (i.e., laughing it off).
"Sure, I've been fired from my last three jobs, but that won't stop me from achieving my ultimate career objective."

- Anticipation—Dealing with the trials of the present by facing future life events with optimism.
"Just five more years and I'll be retired and playing golf three times a week."

Often, people use defense mechanisms as a means of explaining to themselves why a challenging situation got the best of them. Mature defenses can, in fact, help to ease the anxiety and stress you're currently experiencing. Healthy people use them as an emotional bridge.

Not-so-healthy people use them as a permanent crutch. When the defense mechanisms become too intense and frequent, it may be time to seek counseling or therapeutic assistance.

You may also use defense mechanisms to explain away negative things that happen to you in your work, including your failure to do a good job or be as productive as your employer would like you to be. They also appear when your quest to fit in and be liked or accepted by your colleagues is unsuccessful. Finally, they often allow you to deal with the stress and anxiety, even "burnout," that is self-inflicted or brought on by relationships with your colleagues or managers.

Mental health professionals today label "burnout" at the job one loves and enjoys as "compassion fatigue," a condition that arises, which among other circumstances, results in a draining of emotional energy by simply carrying out your day-to-day responsibilities.

STRAIGHT TALK ABOUT DEALING WITH TERMINATION, JOB LOSS, AND OTHER DILEMMAS

People lose their jobs or have difficulty in the workplace for many reasons; some they can control and others they cannot. Each, however, is likely to interrupt or derail your career development plan. Dealing with termination or job loss is likely to be difficult. Dealing with workplace issues, setbacks, and stumbles are less threatening but need to be addressed appropriately before they reach the problem stage.

The task before you is to steer your career back in the direction you want it to go and keep it there. It begins with a thorough assessment of why you were fired, lost your job, or are experiencing difficulties in the workplace. This assessment is necessary if you are to right your career ship. It will require both proactive (i.e., reexamining the future) and reactive (i.e., repairing mistakes you are currently making) attention.

If any of this self-analysis and assessment finds that it is your behavior and personality that are the heart of your work problems or the source of job loss, you need to seek out the assistance of a professional counselor or therapist. If not addressed now, they can be a lingering or repeated concern.

In some instances, you will need to recycle aspects of the career development process and engage in self-awareness, exploration, and decision-making tasks that you've performed earlier. Career development is cyclical, not linear, and there are multiple entry and reentry points. Consider all of them.

Job loss or termination have personal, social, emotional, and economic ramifications that often shape both the outlook and demeanor of workers at a time when they need to display a sense of strength and stability. When individuals have made poor choices leading to their job loss, the solution may be as simple as engaging in the behavioral modification strategies that will rectify the situation. More serious deficiencies and problem behaviors may require more thoughtful solutions and interventions with the appropriate helping professionals.

CHAPTER 25

Challenge: Benefiting from the Knowledge Explosion

If we don't change, we don't grow. If we don't grow, we aren't really living.

—GAIL SHEEHY (1936–2020), AMERICAN AUTHOR,
JOURNALIST, AND LECTURER. SHE WROTE *PASSAGES, PATHFINDER:
OVERCOMING THE CRISES OF ADULT LIFE*, AND *CHARACTER:
AMERICA'S SEARCH FOR LEADERSHIP*.

READINESS FROM THE POINT OF JOB ENTRY TO EVERY STEP ALONG YOUR personal career development is dependent on lifelong learning. A century ago, you would have prepared yourself for occupational entry, found a job, and then learned new and different things "on the job." While that way of learning is still present in the American workforce, formal education and training have become a force in career growth, mobility, and maintenance.

Continuing education can be voluntary or required. You may be motivated to study and learn new things by your personal desire to succeed in your occupation and grow into a new and varied role. The committed, motivated worker lays out a continuing education or renewal plan and then sets out to fulfill it. The term *renewal* here is focused on the things (i.e., reading, networking, study, etc.) you will do to extend your experiences and lead to greater competence.

At other times, you won't have a choice. Many careers, including those in medicine, education, business, and law, require continuing education. The renewal of many licenses and certifications in these and other occupations occurs only after you show evidence of ongoing study. You could even run into a situation where to sustain the accreditation of an organization or agency where you work that body will have to meet continuing education requirements for professional and technical staff. Situations might also exist where work performance (i.e., automotive technician, medical technician, etc.) is required by your employer in order to ensure competence.

In many work settings, continuing education is expected of any employee who seeks to advance to higher levels within the organization. In order to move up the career ladder and about the career lattice, additional study is usually required. Lifelong learning has become a fixture in the contemporary work world, one that will only grow in the years to come.

THE INFLUENCE OF THE KNOWLEDGE EXPLOSION

You work or will work in a dynamic, volatile workplace that has over the last half century experienced an incredible knowledge explosion. Experts in the field of health and medicine, for example, have estimated that more knowledge has been generated in the past century than in the previous five thousand years. This explosion of knowledge is not restricted to health and medicine. Any career environment (i.e., communications, industry, engineering, etc.) that fails to keep abreast of new knowledge and invest in research is flirting with obsolescence.

There is no end in sight to the knowledge explosion. If anything, the explosion is going to grow in magnitude and affect more workers and work settings than it currently touches. Because of the knowledge explosion, those twenty-five and younger are going to enter and proceed through a work world that is dramatically different from that experienced by their parents and grandparents.

TRADITIONAL AND NONTRADITIONAL LEARNING OPPORTUNITIES

In order to remain current with the emerging knowledge and skills in any career field and the impact that innovative practices and new technologies are having on your work, you must utilize both traditional and nontraditional learning vehicles, including the schools, colleges, and training centers where you had your original education experiences. Those education venues are profiled in chapter 5. These institutions that prepared you for entry into the world of work will now contribute to your continuing education and development.

The emerging continuing education formats possess characteristics that enhance their accessibility and accommodate the personal and work lives of their participants. Even traditional institutions are becoming more flexible, as they offer focused career training and targeted certification programs along with degree completion opportunities. They are also making the return to study for graduates and "stop-outs" (i.e., former students who haven't met degree requirements) more accessible.

While many will return to traditional venues, others are likely to become engaged in the new and innovative learning formats that are being created. An ever-growing number of education opportunities, many leading to certification and endorsement, are being offered in the work or industry environment. The extensive and ongoing training offered by major employers like Microsoft, General Motors, McDonald's, and others ensures that their professionals, managers, and technicians are keeping abreast of the newest information and trends. Many go so far as to offer credentials for the attainment of this expertise.

Professional and trade associations have also become havens of continuing education. Annual conferences of these organizations, which in the past were the prominent knowledge exchange offered, are now complemented by an ongoing series of webinars, podcasts, seminars, workshops, and other learning formats designed to educate their members. Industry-and association-driven continuing education programs focus on the teaching of knowledge and skills that are relevant, applicable, and competitive. This type of learning activity ensures that industry standards are set and achieved.

A PERSONAL LEARNING PLAN

A personal learning plan will help you achieve both your short- and long-term career objectives. Assess what you need to learn, where you will be able to study, and how to weave it into your personal and work schedule. You will likely be working as you seek to fulfill this plan, and you need to make certain your situation allows you to fulfill the education objective that you have embarked upon. The last thing you want to have happen is to have education interfere with either the quality or quantity of your work.

You may have to depend on a flexible work schedule, evening and weekend study, or a leave of absence in order to concentrate on the learning that will facilitate your personal development. Learning can become more accessible if you learn about and evaluate how to use the various distance learning tools or systems that are now available and will continue to emerge in the immediate future.

Employers are finding that support (i.e., financial, schedules that permit study, etc.) pay dividends in multiple ways. In another of those win-win situations, you strengthen your knowledge and skills, and your employer benefits from what you have learned. It is little wonder then that many are creating tuition assistance and cost reimbursement programs, along with working with you, to weave learning and study into your work calendar.

LEARNING IN THE FUTURE

Certainly, schools and colleges will change, and new venues, like the workplace itself, will extend learning opportunities to its employees. As stated above, education and training will not be restricted to traditional institutions and organizations.

How will education and training be delivered in both traditional and nontraditional learning environments? While the changes of the recent past have been somewhat subtle, those in the future are destined to be more dramatic. Consider the following projections:

- Learning will be adapted to the individual and available on demand or through assignment. Learners will have to change in order to facilitate how they will learn.

- Immersion or concentrated study within a body of knowledge, skill, or area of focus will become common. Shorter, focused learning experiences will replace the longer curricula and programs of studies of today.

- Accountability and effectiveness will be driven by the application of learning in real work situations and relevant environments. Personalized proficiency will become an even stronger element in worker evaluation.

- Learners will be able to access learning from anywhere in the world. E-learning (i.e., Blackboard, WebEx, Massive Open Online Courses [MOOCs], etc.) are becoming more widespread, along with other technology-based, interactive instruction and electronic conferencing. These tools connect the learner with experts and mentors anywhere in the global community.

- Upskilling and renewal will be constant and built into the routine work experience. A formal portion of the work experience will be devoted specifically to continuing education.

- Teachers will be replaced by learning coordinators who will organize the resources and tools from which students will learn and monitor their achievement during and following study. The teacher-focused classroom box of today will give way to virtual classrooms that will turn the content, style, design, and delivery of learning upside down.

- Textbooks and learning tools will give way to contemporary contrivances.

- The workplace of today will add a new dimension in the future; it will become a virtual classroom where learning will be as important as the work that is performed there.

- Employee assistance programs (EAPs) will expand to include a greater emphasis on career and education counseling, as well as accessibility flexibility and financial support to offset education costs.

As early as the next decade, you may no longer be able to predict what you will learn, how you will learn, or where you will learn.

LEARNING INFLUENCES EARNING

Studies conducted by the U.S. Department of Labor's Bureau of Labor Statistics and the U.S. Census Bureau give meaning to the theory that "the more you learn—the more you earn." Following are the findings of a recent Bureau of Labor Statistics study of median annual income by the educational attainment level of the worker:

- Less than high school—$30,784
- High school diploma—$38,792
- Some college, no degree—$43,316
- Associate degree—$46,124
- Bachelor's degree—$64,896
- Master's degree—$77,844
- Advanced graduate professional (medicine, law, etc.)—$96,772
- Doctorate—$97,916

Another important thing to note—unemployment rates go down for persons as their education attainment rates go up.

CHANGE, TECHNOLOGY, AND THE CONTEMPORARY WORKPLACE

As work changes, so must the education of the workforce. For example, the investigatory work once performed by law enforcement officers is now being done by crime scene investigators and laboratory technicians. Another example of a recent change has been with the counselors, psychologists, and other caregivers who have had to learn new things in order to assist the veterans of recent wars and victims of violence and natural disasters who suffer from posttraumatic stress disorder. In every career field, something is occurring that demands a change in learning.

These examples of change point to the need to conduct research, develop curricula, and design education and training experiences that bring this new knowledge to the worker in the workplace. Specialists in many career settings are assuming portions of roles once fulfilled by generalists. Consequently, the education and training of these individuals also become specialized.

The tools of the workplace have also improved significantly. The modern office, farm, factory, and related sites are using equipment today that has been influenced by the spread of technological advances. Things learned by the National Aeronautics and Space Administration (NASA) in the space program over the last half century, for example, are now being applied routinely by workers in countless settings.

In every career or occupational area, there are "hot button" issues where new theories are being discovered and new methods are being developed. In some instances, it means learning a new process. In others, it's mastering a new piece of equipment.

CAREER EDUCATION AND BEYOND

Learning today and into the future will not be restricted to the knowledge and skills that you will employ in your occupational roles. Every worker is going to be required to possess an improved understanding of the larger culture and environment and how your work influences and is influenced by the larger community and the world. One such issue will be to understand and address the role of diversity and inclusion in our personal and work lives and how you are and will be affected by multiculturalism.

Finally, education will play an important role in your personal life. Adult and continuing education programs include a recreational and leisure-time focus. Should you want to learn how to paint, take photographs, or learn a new language opportunities now exist in most communities to engage in such study. Recreational and leisure learning can have an extremely positive impact on your life–work balance.

STRAIGHT TALK ABOUT CONTINUED LEARNING AND EDUCATION

Lifelong learning is a fact of life in the United States and around the globe. Career maintenance will be dependent on how effectively the employee adapts to and learns how to perform the job in a contemporary workplace. It will also be tied to continuous education and training that results in the sustaining of the knowledge and skills needed in the workplace, while offering the employees to renew as a part of their career growth.

Career growth and mobility are similarly influenced by education, as advancement and promotion are generally dependent on your learning and practicing new things. Should that person wish to be considered for growth and promotion, ongoing study will not be a luxury; it will be a requirement. One trend readers should note about the future is that more education and training programs are going to be "competency based."

A volatile economy and difficult job market, like some in the United States have experienced sporadically over the course of history, will reward the workers who have committed themselves to continuing education and engaged in experiences to advance their knowledge and skills. When the nation experiences any economic recession, the more educated among the workforce are the most likely to keep their jobs.

The continuing technology revolution will demand new study for workers seeking to sustain their status in the workforce. The same technological advances that have changed the workplace have also changed the way you will learn and made it more accessible. Technology has been and will continue to be the greatest influence on the American workplace.

PART 4

WINDING DOWN AND EXITING YOUR CAREER

CHAPTER 26

Challenge: Posturing for Late Career and Retirement

There must be a goal at every stage of life! There must be a goal!

—Maggie Kuhn (1905–1995), American activist who
founded the Gray Panthers, an advocate group for
seniors

A TIME WILL COME IN YOUR LIFE WHEN CIRCUMSTANCES WILL CAUSE you to want to change course, wind down, and possibly exit your chosen career. It can be a time of positive reflection on a life and career that allowed you to achieve the goals you set for yourself, one that allowed you to utilize your full human potential to a level of personal satisfaction. The only certainty is that some kind of transition is going to occur. If conducted properly, it can be seamless and uneventful.

At other times, the prospects of these changes will be a time of hesitation and questioning. What does the future hold? How do you plan for it? How will the future separated from career be different? These and any number of other questions need to be addressed over time if you are to effect a reasonable plan to take you through the latter stages of your career and on to whatever you want your future to be. Like the creation of a career plan earlier in life, you now should have a corresponding plan that allows the adjustment of your work experience and movement on to retirement.

Studies conducted by the U.S. Census Bureau, the Department of Health and Human Services, and the Associated Press-NORC Center for Public Affairs Research all show that the population over age sixty-five is growing and seniors comprised 13 percent of the U.S. population in 2010. Projections for 2030 show that number growing to a point where older adults will comprise 19 percent of the population, which represents an estimated 72 million older adults. These demographic facts can be attributed to advances in medicine and adjustments in personal behavior (i.e., exercise, diet, ceasing or reduction in tobacco use, etc.).

Advances in health and medicine have had a profound effect on life expectancy. Healthier, active people who want to sustain their lifestyle and remain working are rejecting the rocking chair and staying longer among the ranks of the employed. Another reason why many are lingering in the workforce is both real and perceived fear that financial difficulty may lie ahead.

This book is about career development and because of that focus, will not attempt to address the financial and economic contingencies that are certain to influence you in the latter stages of life. Countless media sources, using both print and electronic venues, along with numerous government entities, offer an array of information and guidance as to how money can facilitate or hinder the way you will live and work in your senior years. You should, however, act cautiously when using this information and following these tips. There are multiple philosophies and opinions about the economic aspects of life, and like medical advice, you may wish to get a "second" opinion.

Before leaving the subject of finances, all indicators suggest that too few Americans have prepared adequately for retirement. As one example, a study of college professors, completed by Fidelity Investments in 2013, reported three-quarters of those age fifty-five and older recognized the need for financial guidance, but only 17 percent had a formal retirement strategy. Similar failings can be found in many occupations and careers.

It is important for you to recognize that any decisions you make or actions you take about adjusting or leaving your work role are yours and yours alone. Maggie Kuhn, whose quote introduces this chapter, founded the Grey Panthers, an advocacy group for the rights of seniors. She formed the organization after she was forced to retire at age sixty-five from her position with the Episcopal Church. The Age Discrimination in Employment Act of 1967 prohibits an employer from discriminating on the basis of age against any employee and candidate for employment who is forty years or older. You need to fully understand your rights as an employee and candidate for employment.

ATTITUDES OF OLDER AMERICAN WORKERS

A study conducted by the Associated Press NORC Center for Public Affairs following the Great Recession (2007–2009) revealed some interesting findings for those fifty and older, including:

- Before the Great Recession affected retirement planning, those reporting they retired before the recession averaged fifty-seven years of age. Following the recession, the age was sixty-two.
- Nearly half (47 percent) indicated that they are planning to retire later than they expected at age forty. Finances, benefits, and health were cited as the reasons.
- Eight in ten (82 percent) who are working expect to do some form of work for compensation during retirement.
- Two in ten report they have experienced age discrimination in the job market since turning fifty.
- Approximately half are working for someone younger than them.

While that recession has long since been replaced with better economic times, its historical impact remains. Experiences and events can make an indelible impression on the psyche of the individual, a mark that shapes attitudes and values for time to come.

CHANGE BROUGHT ON BY LATE CAREER AND RETIREMENT

Unfortunately, the miscalculations one makes in preparing for later career and retirement are too often restricted to the economic and financial situations that tend to dominate such situations. Too few prepare for the social, cultural, and emotional challenges that occur during this life stage. If you've followed a career development plan similar to that outlined in this book, the same aspects (i.e., self-awareness, exploration, decision-making, etc.) of that process will now apply to any adjustments to your career and the departure from it.

POSTURING TO WIND DOWN A CAREER AND RETIREMENT

Winding down and retirement planning needs to happen while you're still working. If that time has passed, you need to do a great deal in a hurry. Having such a guidance system in place is critical to moving forward.

Often, it is difficult to project yourself into the future—to engage in activities that are distant from the present—but force yourself to do it. The things that you should address at the beginning and throughout these transitions are presented below in random order, but they are all important:

- Create a portrait of you five, ten, etc., years from now—A number of options may appeal to you; remain working, modify your work, begin something new, or retire. What one or mix of these directions appears best for you?

- Don't wing it—Build everything into a formal or informal plan— the former is on paper; the latter is in your head. Don't overestimate what you have. Don't underestimate what you need. Engage those close to you (e.g., spouse, partner, family, friends, etc.) and impacted by your plan in its development.

- Talk to those who have preceded you down these paths—If not talk, observe the right and wrong things that other people do and incorporate them into your plan. Learn from their accomplishments and most importantly, their struggles and mistakes.

- Create a new calendar and routine(s)—Structure your world the way you want to live it. Include time for leisure, play, and occasional periods of rest. Stay active and limit the time you sit around idly and watch television.

- Prepare to live differently—Very noticeable will be the disappearance of things like alarm clocks, commuting snarls, deadlines, and meetings. Appearing in their place will be senior discounts, medical checkups, and life in a slower lane.

- Learn how to budget to fit your emerging lifestyle—Don't think of the reduction in costs associated with not working as savings. Any savings will likely be offset by a corresponding reduction in income.

- Address relationship transitions—Prepare for the absence of coworkers and managers and the possible emergence of new characters and old characters in new roles. Determine how family and friends will fit into your new life. Develop new friendships and make them age diverse. Being around older people exclusively can be hazardous to your social and emotional development.

- Put your life in order—Prepare a will if you haven't. Update it if you have. Make certain your wishes are clearly spelled out for those who may need to perform them.

- Prepare for the social changes that are certain to occur—Sustain relationships with colleagues, coworkers, and the networks you have established. The professional and skill networks that you constructed will now take on more of a social dimension. Become a mentor or a consultant.

- Prepare for the emotional changes that may occur—If you experienced stressors in your work, don't let them follow you into your later life. Wind down and retire unencumbered by the things that made you anxious all those years.

- Do the things (i.e., volunteer, home renovation, travel, etc.) you could never do or didn't do in sufficient quantity—Try to accomplish one specific task every day, but also take on projects that require additional time (i.e., closet and garage cleaning, planting a garden, etc.). Sell or give the things to charity that you no longer need.

- Engage helpers who can guide you through the transitions you're about to face—Determine who can help you—counselor, financial advisor, accountant, lawyer, spiritual adviser, etc.—find a good one, and get them involved in your guidance.

- Acquire a command of the internet and the new technologies—Even a limited understanding and skill set using cyberspace will open information (i.e., medical, education, etc.) and service (i.e., online shopping, etc.) doors. The Gallup Organization revealed that while nearly nine in ten (89 percent) of Americans used the internet in 2014, a third of seniors did not. This will likely change as younger internet users age.

- Confront your doubts and unknowns—Try to minimize the unexpected and don't be caught in a situation that embarrasses you.

- Concentrate on remaining healthy (physically and mentally)—Healthier living can be expected in later life if you participate in regular assessments and follow the advice of the caregivers.

- Learn new things—Return to education and learn the things that have interested you across the life span. Many schools and college have created noncredit learning opportunities (i.e., Senior College) to respond to the recreational and leisure education interests of seniors. Read for personal renewal and enjoyment.

- Practice entirely new things—Venture off into new areas of living. Try growing tomatoes and flowers, painting, writing, and learning a new language.

- Pace yourself—Create a "bucket list" and a schedule for accomplishing it. You've been dying (forgive the pun) to do these things, but you can't do them all in the first six months of your new life.

- First experiment, then lock in—Try everything to see how it "fits." Then insert the best into the new you.

- Prepare for loss of people close to you and the grieving it will create—Funerals will replace weddings on your calendar, and they will often have an impact far greater than you realize as you consider the loss and your personal mortality.

- Embrace retirement—It is not a dirty ten-letter word. Don't be afraid to tell people you are retired. Don't be embarrassed when offered a senior discount.

You had to make adjustments at the time you married, became a parent, and changed jobs. Similar adaptations will now be required as you adjust or exit your work. The final stages of your career and retirement don't have to be the end of anything. View it as a time for an adventurous new beginning.

Individuals not wanting to formally end their employment may elect to negotiate a new definition of their work (i.e., alternative schedule, task reassignment, telecommuting arrangement, job sharing, etc.) with their employer. Others may opt to work full-time for as long as their energy and interest permits.

STRAIGHT TALK ABOUT AGING AND CAREER DEVELOPMENT

Take a moment and reflect on all of the transitions you have made over time. You left the comfort and security of home and went to daycare and school. Education held numerous transitions as you moved from childhood to adolescence and then adulthood. The next transition was from education to work. Most recently, the transitions have helped facilitate your career growth and mobility. Winding down and exiting the world of work are likely to be your final transitions. Do them as well as all of the earlier transitions.

If full retirement looms in your future, enjoy the congratulatory party and parting and prepare for a "honeymoon" of sorts as you venture off into a lifestyle without work, or at least work as you've always known it.

Few cease working fully, choosing rather to direct their energies and talents in different directions. You will have to posture yourself in a way to enjoy your newfound flexibility, but don't fall into the "leave of absence" from life trap. Retirement is a transition, not an ending. You will establish a new identity and move forward to new challenges in different settings.

Should you decide to keep working for or change the work arrangement you have with your existing employer, look for new and innovative ways to perform the work role that you've been doing. If nothing else, doing things differently allows you to "refresh" as you continue to engage in your occupation or career. If you decide to move into a new career (i.e., consulting, creating a business, etc.) altogether, make certain you're fully prepared physically and mentally to accept such a daunting challenge.

Whatever you decide to do in your senior years, approach it with the same zeal that you have displayed all of your working life. The final stages of your career and retirement don't have to be the end of anything—view them as new beginnings.

CHAPTER 27

Challenge: Ensuring Positive Late-Career Adjustments

The shortest period of time lies between the minute you put some money away for a rainy day and the unexpected arrival of rain.

—JANE BRYANT QUINN, FINANCIAL WRITER AND JOURNALIST. BEFORE RETIRING, HER *STAYING AHEAD* COLUMN WAS PUBLISHED IN MORE THAN 250 NEWSPAPERS OVER A TWENTY-SEVEN-YEAR SPAN. SHE IS ONE OF THE LEADING COMMENTATORS ON MATTERS OF PERSONAL FINANCE, RETIREMENT, AND SOCIAL SECURITY.

MORE THAN POSSIBLY ANY OTHER STAGE OF THE CAREER DEVELOPMENT process, the winding down and exit phases abound with change. There are the adjustments required to redefine your work role while still employed, as well as the changes you will face when you exit your career for good. Additional changes will occur in your lifestyle, health and wellness, social networks, and many other aspects of your senior living.

Except when given the opportunity to open a holiday or birthday gift, people are generally ambivalent and sometimes even fearful of surprises. Surprises, however, do occur throughout the entire career development process but can be of greatest concern in the latter stages when there is limited time to deal with them if they present a problem. The unexpected can come in both positive and negative forms. A positive surprise would be when your assets of financial condition for retirement turn out to be more than you expected.

The opposite or negative form occurs when the unexpected stops, delays, or otherwise upsets the flow you were expecting to witness at this transitional stage of your career development. All negative surprises, however, do not deal with money. You may encounter an unexpected health or medical issue that prohibits you from moving into and through retirement according to the plan you had created. You may also find that your employer can no long accommodate the reduced or more flexible work plan you'd created for your senior years.

There can also be an array of matters outside your control. The death of a spouse, partner, or family member can often alter a plan and send you into a reconstruction period. A major recession, one that impacts the growth of stocks and retirement holdings or influences either the selling and/or purchasing of real estate can affect relocation objectives and force you to map out an alternative strategy.

Any abrupt or unplanned change can play havoc with the end of your career development and retirement. How well you make these late career and retirement adjustments will have a definite impact on the future, one that may present a limited time frame for the decisions you need to make and the actions you must perform. When you're younger, you have more time to resolve or detour your way around difficulty. Seniors don't always have the same luxury. This is definitely a place in life where it may be wise to have an emergency strategy or Plan B.

BABY BOOMER IMPACT ON THE WORKFORCE

What do we know about seniors in the United States? As the older population grows and becomes the focus of greater demographic attention, all sorts of facts are emerging. Information generated by a variety of agencies, organizations, and institutions contribute to the following profile of the U.S. baby boomer:

- U.S. Census Bureau data indicate that 78 million boomers were born during the 1946–1964 period with the first boomers turning age sixty-five in 2011. Of the people in the workforce in 2011, 16 percent were over the age of sixty-five.

- According to the Pew Research Center, approximately 10,000 boomers turn sixty-five every day, a pace that will continue until the year 2030. At that point, boomers will represent 18 percent of all Americans.

- Various authorities project the life expectancy for boomers to be age eighty-three.

As recently as the last half of the last century, the accepted retirement date was age sixty-five. No law dictated it, but many employers adopted sixty-five as their standard for directing people into retirement. Any firm time for retirement appears to have disappeared, and workforce members now have a voice in how long they would like to work. Those currently sixty-five and older exhibit behaviors and health conditions of the fifty-five-year-old's a decade or two ago, and they are adjusting and delaying many life and career actions. In fact, many think that eighty is the new sixty.

Boomers wanting or needing to remain employed are finding they are not as welcomed as they would like to be in the current U.S. work-force. This hostile trend runs counter to the federal Age Discrimination Act, which made it unlawful to discriminate against qualified and competent older workers over the age of forty, but nevertheless, many older workers are making claims of workplace bias based on age.

BOOMERS MAKE WAY FOR GEN X AND MILLENNIALS

In 2015, the boomers were replaced by the millennials or Gen Yers (born 1980–2000) as the largest population segment in the U.S. workforce. In between are the Gen Xers (born 1965–1979) who also comprise a sizable portion of the current working community. These generational groups are mentioned here because each has a distinguishable group identity (personal, lifestyle, social, and cultural characteristics) that differentiates them from the others. Seniors, working and retired, must interact with all of the generations, and the more we know about them, the more effective and positive those relations will be.

CHANGES AND CHALLENGES

Those winding down their careers and retiring can expect to experience a number of changes as those transitions progress. They will include physical, emotional, social, and financial changes and will need attention or resolution in order for you to manage both the expected and the unexpected. Following are a number of those changes, each accompanied with some explanatory words and the challenges the change may cause.

Change 1—Formal work, as presently constituted, will play a smaller role in your life and then may disappear altogether.
Challenges: Losing a job at any time can be difficult; losing it forever can be worse. Dealing with job change or retirement will call upon you to develop a new lifestyle, one in which career and work achievements are defined in different terms and replaced by new and different objectives for the future. Quite possibly, consulting, volunteering, or assuming an advisory role will allow you to sustain career interests and attachments under your terms.

Change 2—Routines and schedules will disappear as you have known them in your working life.
Challenges: The schedules, calendars, and clocks that you have gone by throughout your career will be discontinued and replaced. Establishing routines for your new lifestyle will require experimentation, and new calendars will need to be created. Emerging routines will be demanding initially, but once mastered, they will become the apparatus that supports your new lifestyle. You may also have to find ways to occupy the "spare time" you now possess. Most importantly, you need to be able to look back at each day and see something constructive, regardless of how big or small, that you accomplished.

Change 3—People will appear, exit, and change right before your eyes.
Challenges: Your retired world will be populated by familiar people in new roles and different people. The casual interaction you have had with family and friends will grow in intensity and time spent together. You will become more cognizant of changes in growth and maturity of the young around you and take special pride in family moments and the new role that an extended family plays in your life.

Change 4—People will see you differently.
Challenges: The work you is now the retired you. Fully retired individuals must first accept how they are perceived by family, friends, and former colleagues. The next step will be to determine what expectations these individuals have of the new you and how and if you are going to meet them. Simultaneously, you will need to make known how you wish to be perceived during and after this transition in order avoid intrusions and conflicts.

Change 5—Interactions with colleagues and coworkers will disappear and possibly reappear in a social context.
Challenges: Different types of friendships, to the extent desired, with colleagues and coworkers will have to be formed. Your active role in the workplace may now change to a mentoring, advising role—one in which others can learn from your achievements and successes over time. Don't be surprised if you're called upon occasionally by former colleagues to help with an issue or crisis. Your experience may be just what the doctor ordered.

Change 6—Retirement will place you in different social environments.
Challenges: Totally new friendships, to the extent desired, may fill your social needs, and they will be found in multiple places. Traveling new paths will acquaint you with a fresh set of faces and personalities, but you will need to determine the role expectations (i.e., coffee klatch partici-pation, traveling companions, tennis partners, etc.) you have for future members of your social network. Volunteerism will serve two purposes— as you will contribute something to the public good and be introduced to

a set of new social contacts. Social media that you may have used to this point in your life in a career or work context can now be expanded as a tool for connecting with people.

Change 7—*Wellness and health issues will arise.*
Challenges: Although baby boomers, as a rule, are healthier and enjoying a greater life expectancy, they are not immune to wellness and health issues. The senior years are fraught with the emergence of any number of new conditions (i.e., hearing loss, diminishing strength and mobility, beginning stages of Alzheimer's and other diseases, etc.). Alcohol, tobacco use, and addiction to prescribed medicines, while abated in recent times, remain a significant source of physical concern for seniors. Fortunately, there is a growing national trend focusing on responsible eating and exercising and the practicing of wellness behaviors. Checkups and examinations will be required more frequently, and health issues must be addressed before they become problems.

Change 8—*Everything about your financial and economic condition may be vulnerable.*
Challenge: Retirement requires a redefinition of the expression, "living according to your means." This is when you find out if your retirement and wealth management plan is working. Savings will slow down or cease and be replaced by a drawing down on pensions, retirement programs, and savings. New budgets will need to be created. You must also deal with the reality of inflation or another recession on your retirement plan and future spending. While Social Security will increase with inflation, the same is not true for many retirement and pension plans. Proceed cautiously with all major financial matters, selling the house, buying a vacation condo, etc., and don't forget to consider the possibility of older, unemployed children coming home to live or the care you might have to provide for your aging parents or grandchildren.

Change 9—*New learning opportunities appear.*
Challenges: Lifelong learning opportunities and enhanced education venues made possible by the new technologies are going to offer

innumerable education options. A growing number of seniors have found their way to the internet where the doors to learning are escalating with each passing day. If, as many education and medical professionals believe, you reach your cognitive peak between ages forty and sixty-five, extended learning can be both achievable and enjoyable. Learning computers and computer technology will tap that cognition and open many doors. Many traditional institutions offer special programs such as "Senior College," where topic-targeted courses for and by seniors are offered on a noncredit basis.

Change 10—Retirement may place you in a new living context or location.
Challenges: Determining any winding down or exit strategies must be created in concert with those (i.e., spouse, partner, family) who are affected by any decisions. The considerations will range from living styles (i.e., smaller residences, senior communities, and assisted living) all the way to geographic location. Geographic change can be a move to another location in the county, a different state, or an entirely new country.

Change 11—Mental and emotional issues will arise.
Challenge: For every "I can't wait until retirement day" believer, there are others who will struggle with the absence of work and the psychological challenges that detachment from it will bring. Engagement in new activities, calling for responsible contributions by you (i.e., not just busy work) can result in the establishment of goals and objectives similar to those you set during your working years. Accomplishing the tasks associated with the fulfillment of these goals will result in the achievements and successes you want to experience. Recognize first that mental and emotional challenges are occurring or about to occur and work on ways to address them.

Change 12—Loss will be experienced.
Challenge: This is a period when you can expect to attend more funerals than christenings and weddings. All loss is felt in some manner, but the closer the death is to you personally, the greater the impact on your

psyche. There is also an emotional loss brought on when health issues change relationships dramatically. Living with and caring for a loved one with severe Alzheimer's disease may present a feeling of loss that is the equivalent of death. You must address, not avoid, loss and do all that you can to move positively through the grieving process that accompanies it. While less likely at this stage of life, don't exclude the possibility that loss from divorce or separation may also be felt.

Change 13—Different interests, values, and personalities emerge.
Challenges: You will take your personality and most of your values with you into your senior years. The only thing different is you are now seventy, not thirty. Age doesn't make you happy or irritable. You've been who you will be later in life—content or cantankerous—all of your life. Age doesn't change Republicans into Democrats. Your faith and spiritual beliefs will likely be sustained. As your retirement freedom permits you to experiment new and different activities, your interests will expand, and you are likely to witness adjustments in priorities.

It's important to state that the above changes and challenges are not the only ones that you may experience in the latter stages of your career development. Entire books have been written about late adult development and aging. This book has attempted to identify a representative number of changes you may experience as a senior and the challenges associated with each.

Every change is an area where the senior can expect the unexpected. Some will resemble earlier changes in your life and career. If you call upon your life and career experiences to this point, you will be pleasantly surprised how capable you are of meeting these new challenges. The past few pages have dealt less with career and more about life challenges. Once work is removed fully from the life–work balance, all of your attention must be devoted to a life balance that is satisfactory to you and those close to you.

A professional counselor may help you manage the personal, social, and emotional challenges just like an investment counselor or wealth manager can be your best ally in dealing with all of the financial and economic concerns. Both can contribute valuable guidance at this place in your personal career development.

STRAIGHT TALK ABOUT HANDLING THE CHANGES OF LATER LIFE

Standing before a mirror is the surest way you can associate change with senior living. Look beyond the gray hair and growing number of wrinkles and find the new you that is emerging. Change is inevitable and fortunately, even though you are slowly joining them, you can learn from your elders. Their successes and missteps can be life lessons for you.

Take some time to experiment with all the things you didn't have time to do throughout life to this point. Discovering anything you like or enjoy should be followed with inserting it into your new life. Never allow yourself to get too old to do the things on your "bucket list." Accept and prepare for the time when you will not be able to do all the things you did throughout life and become accustomed to in your senior years.

No matter how much you considered and prepared for life's changes, you must have contingencies in place to deal with the unexpected and the uncontrollable. Lacking such contingencies, you're abdicating the power that you possess to exercise control and set direction during your senior years. You have a new voice—use it for your personal benefit and allow others to hear it.

Part 5

Challenges to Career Development in the Future

CHAPTER 28

The Work and Worker of the Future

You have to value skills and not just degrees.

—VIRGINIA "GINNI" ROMETTY, RETIRED AMERICAN BUSINESS
EXECUTIVE WHO SERVED AS CHAIRWOMAN, PRESIDENT, AND
CEO OF IBM, BECOMING THE FIRST WOMAN TO HEAD THE
COMPANY

THROUGHOUT THE PAGES OF *CAREER CHALLENGES*, THE READER HAS been exposed to numerous examples of how change has brought about the creation of new occupations and careers and influenced how long-standing occupations and careers would be performed in the modern world. New learning and operational techniques, coupled with technological advances, have led to occupations and careers that don't resemble the ones that dotted the American workplace a quarter or half century ago. As new and emerging careers and occupations are surfacing almost daily, one must work hard to keep up with the changes.

This chapter will analyze in a general fashion how occupations and careers are currently performed across America and around the globe and then explain how workers of tomorrow are going to have to make adjustments to achieve success and satisfaction in their work and career.

We will zero in on the current and emerging workplace and how accommodations are and will continue to be required in order for employers to ensure maximum employee performance and productivity. Noteworthy among these will be the coronavirus pandemic adjustments to workplace protocols and procedures that are likely to become fixed in the "new normal." Add in the usual and expected occupational alterations to the equation, and future workers will have to keep one eye on their work and another on the workplace where they will perform it.

CAREERS AND OCCUPATIONS ARE EVOLVING

The look of work and the individuals who perform it are remarkably different from yesteryear. The early twentieth-century emphasis of manufacturing and industry has given way to a new world emphasizing technology, service, and information exchange as witnessed by the ever-increasing number of jobs in areas such as health and personal care and the STEM (science, technology, engineering, and mathematics) fields.

New careers are being created as old ones are the subject of "makeovers." A good example is the teachers of an earlier time who complemented their lessons using chalk and a chalkboard. Today, those teachers are loading those same messages into a computer-based instructional system to be accessed digitally at specific times or at the leisure of the student. Another technological enhancement occurs when the class can take a "virtual field trip" to a historic site, museum, or even outer space without leaving their learning place.

Virtually every career and occupation have been touched in some fashion by the technological assault that has given us robots and mechanical tools capable of consuming a part or all of some of the most populated occupations of just a short time ago. Another very visible occupational role change is the bank teller or cashier whose functions have been taken over by automated teller machines (ATMs) and the deposit making, bill paying, and electronic management of other financial procedures via smartphones. One can only be left to wonder what careers and occupations are going to be affected by the technological discoveries of the future.

Not only is the work changing—so are the knowledge, skill sets, and personal characteristics that employers want to find in candidates for those careers and occupations. Thus, the worlds of education and work have had to discover and implement new ways of preparing a competent workforce.

Current and future members of the workforce must accept the fact that technology is going to be the constant that impacts efficiency, productivity, and many of the other protocols and procedures that guide the manner in which work is performed. Since that technology will come from many different directions and at varying speeds, career growth, mobility, and maintenance will demand acquiescence and eventual adoption. Resistance will most assuredly produce negative results.

CHALLENGES AND CHANGES NEEDING ATTENTION

The challenges and changes of careers and occupations that must be addressed from employees' perspective are both varied and of an evolving nature. Following are a number of conditions that have appeared on the radar of those exploring, preparing for, and already moving through their personal career situations. Keeping in mind that no list of this nature should ever be considered complete or exhaustive, the following work components need to be recognized and addressed.

Soft skills will join hard skills as prominent worker characteristics

Employers who have always emphasized hard skills (i.e., accounting, computer programming, editing, etc.) are now adding soft skills to their list of desirable worker characteristics. Soft skills include everything from competence in verbal and written communications and personality traits that allow the employee to fit more compatibly into the workplace culture to personal characteristics themselves, such as confidence, resourcefulness, and creativity. Varying soft skills can be associated with different workplace cultures.

Knowledge acquisition and skill set mastery will be continuous

Lifelong learning has been a common element in the contemporary workplace for more than a generation, but one of the most significant lessons learned from the COVID-19 experience was how much and how fast workers have had to learn and become competent at new workplace behaviors. Schools, colleges, and training programs will place greater emphasis on competency-based experiences that emphasize the hard and soft skill blends mentioned earlier.

Worker performance, productivity, and in the end, accountability, today and tomorrow, will be more tightly linked to one's keeping on top of the emerging knowledge and mastering the skill sets needed for maximum functioning. Competence is no longer defined just as "what you know and can do" but also by your capacity to learn, practice, and master new things.

Ability to work independently will be an essential worker asset

To the extent that remote working will represent a larger segment of the American occupational models, workers are going to have to be capable of contributing independently and discovering means of being heard during collaborative initiatives. If not currently present, it is an essential skill that will have to be mastered.

Virtual teams of workers will call for a different mindset

The good team member, for example, who relied previously on the verbal exchanges with colleagues in the office break room or around the water cooler must now be able to maximize what now must be generated by virtual teams and the different form of human interface they present. Similarly, relationships between managers and their subordinates may need to be reconstructed. Skills learned in social media interfaces may also be applicable here.

Time management and task adjustments will be inevitable

The "when" of the employees' world is likely to have been altered during recent times, especially for those engaged largely in remote working demanded during the coronavirus pandemic. As one example, many parents of school-age children who welcomed the remote work option found their work and parenting roles could not always be played harmoniously. Returning to in-person work and other unforeseen work and workplace adjustments may generate similar demands.

Where roles and responsibilities have changed, a new "modus operandi" may need to be established once final workplace protocols and procedures are put in place. The one certainty—employers will continue to make production and performance a priority.

Life and work balance may require a fresh examination

The life–work balance seekers that are so prevalent in the younger generation of workers may need to be reconsidered in light of the changes that have occurred to American workers and workplaces. The results of this assessment may vary from minor occupational adjustments to entire career makeovers.

The reader should note that the challenges identified above are more universal than specific from a career perspective. Individual occupations have changed exponentially, and one thing is certain—none of today's occupations are performed exactly the way they were a quarter century ago.

CHALLENGES FACING JOB SEEKERS AND CHANGERS

It has always been true that candidates for job change face different challenges during the relocation and transition process. That "truism" still applies, but the challenges may require reordering because of the unique circumstances. The successful rise out of unemployment for some may simply be the "reopening" of the America shutdown by the pandemic. Furloughed and terminated workers will simply return to the jobs they left, and life will hopefully return to some form of "normal."

Regardless of the circumstances, individuals engaged in any employment transition are required today to address a number of challenges as they seek employment or change. Those challenges are discussed below.

Personal challenges

Identifying opportunities, applying for employment, and engaging fully in job acquisition or relocation is work—hard, intensive, time-consuming work. Success in any career or job transition will require a personal commitment of energy and time to the process, followed by the creation of a

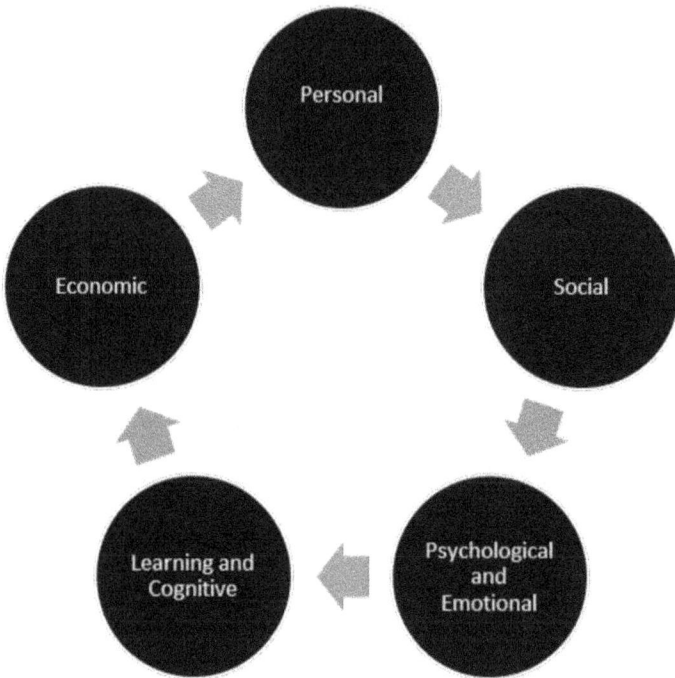

Figure 28.1 Career Challenges and Changes

search and transition plan that is appropriate and achievable. Failure will result in stagnation and eventually failure.

Social challenges

Family, friends, and work colleagues should be viewed as allies in the job change process, and their support and assistance should be sought during this time. Job seekers who withdraw socially from these support systems and networks are rejecting a valuable source of encouragement and validation.

Psychological or emotional challenges

Job loss or interruption or the threat of either can produce a distinct level of stress and anxiety. The same can be said for any failure to achieve career goals or aspirations.

The acts of registration for and acceptance of unemployment compensation and other forms of assistance can produce a negative blow to one's self-esteem, and care should be taken to ensure that mental health is given as much attention as physical health during these times of challenge and change.

Learning and cognitive challenges

Candidates seeking career growth, mobility, and maintenance often face the reality that additional education or training stands between them and where they would like to be in the world of work. In this fast-paced, changing world in which we live and work, yesterday's job skills are often obsolete today. Current and future American workers must invest in the concept of lifelong learning as a challenge that is here to stay.

Economic challenges

The loss of a paycheck, insurance, and other employment benefits almost always require lifestyle adjustments. Similar challenges exist for working individuals who feel that they are not being compensated at a competitive level for the work they perform. Bottom line: Any employee "belt tightening" that was necessitated during the pandemic may need to be retained until reemployment and job security are once again achieved.

This is by no means an exhaustive list of challenges that face the job seeker or changer of the future. It does, however, represent the types of challenges that need attention during the transition process. Challenges impact people in different ways—from being almost nonexistent to presenting major impediments to the overall career development process. A plan for addressing them must first include a means of identifying their presence and then designing coping or confronting strategies for minimizing or eliminating their impact. Success and satisfaction will stand a better chance when this happens.

STRAIGHT TALK ABOUT FUTURE WORK AND WORKERS

Individual differences and the extent to which employees are entrenched in a particular workstyle or manner are going to almost certainly play a role in how the American workers adjust to any "new normal" demands that appear in their particular work setting. When one discovers that these issues are not resolvable, relocation or even career change may enter the picture. But that's the way the world is today.

Few would have imagined at the beginning of the current millennium that electric cars, let alone electric, driverless cars, would occupy our highways as soon as they have. Even fewer would have predicted that drones and robots would be delivering packages and meals to your front door. Developments like these suggest that careers and occupations are going to be dramatically different in the future.

Coupled with the changes in the work of the future will be dramatic adjustments in career and occupational preparation. Expect tomorrow's employers to place a greater premium on competency (i.e., what you can do), rather than what diplomas, degrees, and certificates you possess. Depending on a careful analysis, anything from an updating of one's skill set to a major career makeover may be in order to ensure continuous career growth, mobility, and maintenance. Chapter 29 will now examine how the workplace of tomorrow will look.

CHAPTER 29

The Workplace of the Future

Don't be afraid of new arenas.

—ELON MUSK, COFOUNDER AND LEADER OF TESLA, SPACE X,
NEURALINK, AND THE BOEING COMPANY AND CONSIDERED A
PIONEER IN THE DESIGN, ENGINEERING, AND MANUFACTURING
OF ELECTRIC VEHICLES, BATTERY PRODUCTS, AND SOLAR
ENERGY SOLUTIONS

AS THE WORLD MOVES BEYOND THE EFFECTS OF THE ONGOING TECHNO-
logical changes and adjusts to the manner in which the coronavirus
pandemic may have altered work and workers, a similar analysis must
be made of how the workplace itself has been transformed and what
future workforce members will likely find when they enter their careers
or return to their places of employment.

Some of the adjustments required to sustain operations during these
extraordinary times, including those that were required to maximize
worker performance and productivity, are expected to remain. They will
be joined by the natural, evolutionary adjustments that every workplace
has become accustomed to throughout the twentieth century and on into
the current millennium.

Don't be surprised by the extent to which employers will continue
to polish and update the time-tested ways they have used to manage

their workplaces over time. The crème de la crème of existing operational practices and procedures will be blended with pandemic-driven ones to determine which are worthy of becoming a part of the "new normal."

The employer's goal is twofold. One is to successfully infuse any emerging technological advances that will enhance employee performance and increase overall productivity. At the same time a second and new goal has emerged. Employers are also seeking to determine if a "silver lining" can be found in any of the workplace adjustments that were made to survive the coronavirus pandemic. Most notable for continuation are the practices of remote work and flexible scheduling that were viable solutions to the social distancing and group concerns stirred up during the pandemic.

At the height of the coronavirus pandemic, the Pew Research Center reported that the percentage of the workforce working remotely had peaked at 71 percent. Following a leveling-off period, evidence lingers that suggests many employers are still considering the viability of making remote work a permanent component of how they define their workplace. Everything from full remote to a remote/in-person option to a full return to in-person work appears to be up for consideration.

As the pandemic interruptions eventually draw to a close, businesses, firms, organizations, institutions, and other employers are going to have to determine what lessons were learned during that time and which of those work protocols and practices merit being made permanent. Employees will then be required to make any adjustments required by these modifications in order to have normalcy, albeit a "new normal," once again.

WORKFORCE WELLNESS WILL GET UNPRECEDENTED ATTENTION

A recent study released by Leadership IQ, a leadership training and employee engagement survey firm, found that only a quarter of business leaders feel their workforce is currently thriving emotionally and mentally. Further examination of that report cited in a follow-up article in *Forbes* suggests that the layoffs, furloughs, and dismissals caused by the pandemic have been stress- and anxiety-producing for both the unemployed victims and the workers fearful for their career status and security.

Working from home or any other remote location, wearing masks, practicing social distancing, isolating from superiors and colleagues, and adjusting to new protocols for communication are just a few of the circumstances that have heightened "burnout" among the total workforce but most notably among high performers.

Emotional and mental challenges of this nature and magnitude demand continued employee assessment and engagement studies as the pandemic subsides and any changes become permanent. Since subsequent COVID-19 variants have interrupted plans for the return of employees to their pre–COVID-19 workplaces, new opportunities have been made available for employers to engage in employee pulse taking and employees to assess where they are in respect to their individual career plan. This assessment will aid in determining the levels of worker burnout and pandemic fatigue.

A *Washington Post* article in the second year of the COVID-19 pandemic reported that a number of major national companies and businesses were delaying the return of employees to their workplaces, some for a second, third, and even longer time. Employers of varying structures and sizes, facing adjustments in their return-to-work plans, are using this extended opportunity to engage the workforce and allow them to help shape how their workplace is going to look tomorrow.

Before leaving the impact of the coronavirus on the future, it is worth noting that employers and human resource professionals are placing a new premium on the impressions, attitudes, and feelings of their workers by asking them the four Ws—what is working, what is not, what can be fixed, and what should be made permanent in the post–COVID-19 workplace. Such engagement is recognized as a key contributor to employee retention.

QUESTIONS REQUIRING ANSWERS

As the American workplace consciously took on the COVID-19 challenges, employers and employees have been observed asking questions and seeking to determine how their answers would change the way work is to be conducted in the future. The following groupings, not exhaustive by any sense of the word, are representative of the questions requiring answers.

Is the prepandemic work model salvageable as it existed before or with modification?

If yes, those adjustments should be considered, finalized, and up and running when the doors swing open again. What factors must be present to return to full on-site work (or some variation) again? What factors must be present for a full return to occur?

When the COVID-19 crisis is in our rearview mirror, what protocols and practices that were used over the pandemic are worthy of permanent adoption?

Remote work, whether full or hybrid (partially in formal work settings and partially remote) or in some other form, is here to stay, and both employees and employers must recognize, prepare for, and accept it. Most affected, and likely the most resistant to change, will be experienced and senior workers who see little reward for the adjustments they will need to make this late in their career.

As an example, many employers, managers, and supervisors found that the fewer meetings and streamlined agendas that they used during the remote workdays of the coronavirus pandemic led to greater efficiency and a need for fewer meetings. Thus was born a practice that they and their subordinates didn't mind continuing.

If a mix of remote and hybrid work, flexible scheduling, and other practices is determined to be the best future course of action, what issues will need to be monitored during the "new normal" period?

To the degree that any of the new protocols and procedures require new knowledge or skills for implementation, employers are going to have to provide appropriate staff development and in-service training experiences to ensure that everyone on the team rises to the same level of understanding and confidence.

On a couple of other fronts, many employers feel that remote work has raised concerns about how to measure performance and production, how to ensure equitable work experiences in a mixed or hybrid workplace structure, and the best methods for connecting and communicating with dispersed staff members. These and others will need to be addressed as the "new normal" sets in.

Have the workers in any particular occupational grouping been influenced disproportionally by the coronavirus pandemic and required special attention?
When the coronavirus pandemic subsides, a number of occupations and occupational groupings will require explicit examination to determine if there is any evidence that the challenges and stresses of those particular positions resulted in a greater prevalence of burnout or any semblance of posttraumatic stress disorder. Such circumstances, most often identified with the added work and burdens assigned to health and medical personnel and other "essential personnel," have resulted in countless workers' decisions to modify their work roles, change careers, or exit the workforce completely. Where needed, continued care and attention must be directed toward these individuals.

STRAIGHT TALK ABOUT THE WORKPLACE OF THE FUTURE
America has survived a number of massive changes in the kinds of work that drove the nation, the people who performed those work tasks, and the environments where the work was done, a trend that continues today and can be expected to continue tomorrow. Few, if any, careers or occupations will be untouched.

The findings of a 2021 Gallup Organization study found that the workforce today, and most likely the future, is placing a higher premium on well-being and workforce members were prepared to leave their current position in order to find it. How did those survey respondents define well-being? Basically, it was comprised of the following five components: career (you like what you do), social (you desire meaningful people relationships in your life), financial (your money and finances are managed well), physical (you possess the energy and vitality to succeed), and community (you relish the environments in which you live). Additional information on the Gallup study can be found at https://www.gallup.com/workplace/352952/employees-wellbeing-job-leave-find.aspx.

These last two chapters have touched on some of the work, worker, and workplace issues that must be attended to, matters that have the potential to become problems if they are not addressed in an orderly, structured, and effective way.

CHAPTER 30

Experts Weigh In on Career Success and Satisfaction

Listening is being able to be changed by the other person.

—ALAN ALDA, EMMY- AND GOLDEN GLOBE AWARD–
WINNING ACTOR, AUTHOR, AND DIRECTOR MOST FREQUENTLY
IDENTIFIED WITH HIS PORTRAYAL OF DR. HAWKEYE PIERCE IN
THE TELEVISION SERIES *M*A*S*H*

UP UNTIL THIS POINT, THE READER HAS BEEN EXPOSED TO A COMPILA-
tion of strategies, recommendations, and opinions that the author has
formulated based on his personal career as a professional counselor,
counselor educator, consultant, and employer, as well as his observations
of thousands of individuals moving through the career development process. Further, my own career experiences have allowed me to observe the
contributions that multiple experts and authorities make to maximizing
career satisfaction and success.

Along my personal career journey, I've had the good fortune to
observe, listen, and learn from a number of women and men that I consider to be skilled experts in the process of helping people choose their
life's work and enter and progress in their careers in a manner that brings
maximum satisfaction and success.

Writing in the *Career Development Quarterly* at the beginning of the current millennium, counseling leader Edwin L. Herr of the Pennsylvania State University wrote that the twenty-first century would see career counselors and other specialists "increasingly expected to assist persons to identify and learn the skills by which they can be more effective in planning for and choosing careers, in making effective transitions and adjustments to work, in working cross-culturally and cross nationally and in managing their own careers and career transitions effectively."

The experts whose messages appear in this chapter correspond to the versatile career helper definition advanced by Dr. Herr. Individually and collectively, their words and ideas speak to the host of developmental issues raised in *Career Challenges*. Their expertise ranges from hands-on experiences as practicing counselors and counselor educators to search and recruiting professionals responsible for helping people identify and move into and about the workforce.

ESTABLISH A HEROIC MINDSET

Dr. Rich Feller is a retired professor of counseling and career development and University Distinguished Teaching Scholar at Colorado State University in Ft. Collins, Colorado, and a former president of the National Career Development Association. Rich believes that he and others "should retire into something, not from something." And that's what he has done.

In the following passage, Rich offers readers a provocative overview of how people seeking to achieve career satisfaction and success must create a "bouncing back" mindset from not getting what they want as they navigate a lifetime of transitions. The HEROIC mindset, as advanced in the following six-element paradigm, lays out how career satisfaction and success might be achieved:

- Hope (H) is a thinking process to actively pursue goals. It brings together "will" (a sense of investment and energy) and "way" (the resources used to generate options or pathways to finding purpose in learning).

- Self-efficacy (E) is the sense of "I can," where people trust their own ability to organize and execute a course of action to manage a loss, disappointment, or setback.

- Resilience (R) is crucial to moving beyond the stress and sense of failure brought about by change or unmet expectations. It results from defining, reframing, and constructing meaning of events that discourage people. Rigid or self-defeating thinking limits one's ability to bounce back and move ahead. Flexibility, objective thinking, and rational explanation of setbacks increase resiliency and acceptance of the unexpected.

- Optimism (O) is the ability to seek solutions, see the upside of things gone wrong, and reduce the gap between now and tomorrow's desires. Not personalizing or succumbing to failure, the mind stays open (rather than adopting helplessness) when performance or relationships set people back. Believing that (1) good events have a permanent cause, (2) causes of bad events are temporary, and (3) denying universal explanations for failure expands a student's perspective and opportunities.

- Intentional exploration (I) is looking for positive clues, welcoming planned (and unplanned) opportunities, and taking inspired action as a way to grow. These activities engage people to help them broaden, build, and test possibilities.

- Clarity and Curiosity (C) are clear intentions and acting on purposeful commitments to create focus, reduce distractions, and maximize energy. Being clear about internal motivation makes it easier to act intentionally, with integrity and curiosity. Curiosity is a readiness and openness to sparks of imagination.

Regardless of how one defines career success, the ability to adopt HEROIC mindsets offers support navigating a lifetime of transitions.

ENGAGE IN PERSONAL REFLECTION
Barbara J. Bruno, president of Good as Gold Training and HR Search, Inc., of Crown Point, Indiana, and past chair of the National Association

of Personnel Services (NAPS), believes that individuals can perform proactive behaviors that place positive momentum front and center into their job search, a trait consistently advanced in her personal and business philosophy. As a result, she represents that exceptional blend of entrepreneur, leader, mentor, and teacher and is widely respected for the unselfish manner in which she shares her personal career experiences with the larger search and staffing community.

When imparting "words of wisdom" to job seekers and changers, Barbara suggests beginning the journey by identifying "what they liked most and least about the jobs they've held—followed by the five things they would change to make their work more enjoyable." She contends that the "answer will provide the real reason one is contemplating a job or career change."

With that information in hand, she offers: "the individual is better equipped to embark on their search and prepared to isolate the factors that must be present in order for them to scrutinize options and accept a position if offered." In other words, "one needs to know why they want to work for that employer."

BECOME AN EFFECTIVE AND EFFICIENT INFORMATION AGENT

Job seekers and changers, according to Joe Madden, principal at Harbor Legal Search in Boston, Massachusetts, and past chairman of the board of the National Association of Personnel Services (NAPS), need to become effective and efficient information agents. He stands out in his work as an effective communicator—one who sends and receives—and will not rest until all points of view have been placed on the table. In addition, Joe is an advocate of the "leave no stone unturned" idiom by using every available resource in the completion of a task.

In advancing his belief regarding the importance of the information search and transition process, Joe stresses: "today's job seekers need to corral as much information on a particular position, company, and company leadership as possible prior to engagement. The more you know about what lies before you, the better you will be at understanding a prospective new opportunity or employer."

Joe adds that "being informed sends the message to a prospective employer that the job seeker is interested, has done their homework, and is well prepared for the next stage of the transition process. It will also cut down on a lot of time wasted by seekers exploring situations that possibly aren't right for either party." He concludes with the admonition: "The information is out there—job seekers need to go get it and use it."

ADVANCE A POSITIVE ATTITUDE
WITH QUALITY NETWORKS

According to Diane Post, president and founder of Pathfinders, Inc., in Atlanta, Georgia, and National Association of Personnel Services (NAPS) Hall of Fame honoree for her leadership, expertise, and innovation in the recruiting profession, "career-oriented people must—without exception—do their very best to establish and sustain a positive attitude throughout every phase of the career development process. It is this quality that causes others to notice their work and think of them in terms of advancement. It becomes a hallmark of their career reputation."

Diane adds that "the best opportunities for personal growth and advancement often grow out of a blend of people to people experiences during which the individual uses valuable interactive experiences to grow and nurture relationships that eventually impact their work." She amplifies that thought by suggesting: "A positive, cooperative approach to one's work that is focused on excellence will generate connections for a lifetime and lead to a reputation that will turn connections into opportunities."

MANAGE EXPECTATIONS AND MEET CHALLENGES

As people pursue their career dreams and aspirations, Danielle Irving-Johnson, career services specialist with the American Counseling Association (ACA) in Alexandria, Virginia, believes they must concentrate on "managing their expectations and even the expectations that others have of them." She bases that conviction on her experiences in facilitating the career transitions of a significant segment within the 55,000 ACA membership.

She adds: "Expectation management is a very important concept in life, but essential when it comes to career exploration, development, and management. Oftentimes, what we envisioned for our careers may not come to fruition as quickly as we planned. It is also possible that you may encounter some unanticipated challenges and obstacles throughout the career journey." That is why Danielle stresses that "it is imperative that individuals be in control at all times." In conclusion, she submits that "management will aid in the anticipation of problems, obstacles, and difficulties as perfection is unrealistic in the grand scheme of life. It is inevitable that you will in fact encounter some bumps in the road, and experience some uncertainties. Manage your expectations, expect the unexpected. As long as you prepare, plan/organize, and communicate effectively you will always succeed."

PLAN FOR SATISFACTION AND SUCCESS

Your author will wrap up these "words of wisdom" with a couple of thoughts of my own. In doing so, I will return to the quote by baseball great Yogi Berra that introduced chapter 3. Yogi once said: "If you don't know where you are going, you might wind up someplace else." The same can be said for one's personal career development.

Career satisfaction and success will stand a great chance of occurring if individuals have a good sense of the career development process and where they are at in that continuum. Knowing where you have been and where you are now are vital prerequisites to fully understanding the viability of the various options that may be ahead for you.

Finally, once new or revised career goals are formulated, it will take a well-constructed, reasonably paced, and doable plan of action to get individuals from where they are presently to where they want to be. That plan should consider the full ranges of options and choices.

Regardless of the past, any career or job change that you want to be successful should be put forth in the form of a "doable" plan. Just like the GPS system or map, there may be alternative routes to get you where you want to go, but your steady hand on the wheel or controls is essential to ensure you end up at the place you want to be.

STRAIGHT TALK FROM A GROUP
OF CAREER EXPERTS

There you have it—a network of veterans from different disciplines whose life work has been devoted to helping people achieve maximum career satisfaction and success. Each offers a personal take on various strategies for navigating the career development process. Uniformly, each offers valuable insights into the strategies you must initiate in order to light your personal career path into the future.

CONCLUSION

No one gets an iron-clad guarantee of success. Certainly, factors like opportunity, luck, and timing are important. But the backbone of success is usually found in old-fashioned, basic concepts like hard work, determination, good planning, and perseverance.

—MIA HAMM, FORMER UNIVERSITY OF NORTH CAROLINA AT CHAPEL HILL ALL-AMERICAN SOCCER PLAYER WHO EARNED TWO OLYMPIC GOLD MEDALS, AS WELL AS NATIONAL AND INTERNATIONAL HONORS

If you have read this book from the beginning, you have been exposed to thirty chapters that talked about a process that emphasized self-awareness, exploration, and decision-making as fundamental elements in career development. There have been list after list of "dos and don'ts" for you to consider at various life stages. You have been exposed to multiple strategies about how to achieve career satisfaction and success.

Hopefully, you haven't reached a "sky is falling" perspective on your personal career or education situation. Your career development will not be without its challenges, but the more you know about the options you have, the more likely you will achieve career success and satisfaction. For certain, missteps, mistakes, and even failures will occur. They are merely challenges that need to be addressed and put in your past. When you fall—get up, dust yourself off, determine what you need to do (or do differently), and move forward.

Consider a signature or defining moment in your career or education. Hopefully, it is a moment that required you to take action in some form. The moment doesn't have to be dramatic, simply an experience that has had a meaningful impact on you. What did you do that led you up to and through that moment? What was right about the actions you took? Signature moments will occur dozens, maybe hundreds, of times over the course of your career development. Allow every job, event, and decision to be a teacher. Identify, learn from, and build upon these successful moments.

No one knows you better than you. Your aptitudes, achievements, interests, traits, values, and lifestyle preferences have made you unique. That uniqueness must be considered at every life stage. There is nothing magical or mysterious about career development. It is you taking realistic, controlled, and careful steps.

Career satisfaction means different things to different people. If you haven't found your version, continue your quest and don't stop until you're there. Quite possibly, it is defined in how many "yeses" you can answer to the following list of statements:

- My career provides opportunities for me to achieve my full potential.
- My workplace offers a flexible yet stable working environment responsive to my needs and those of my colleagues.
- My career and workplace satisfy my life–work balance issues by addressing my personal, learning, emotional, and social needs.
- My workplace represents an environment where free and open communication and multidirectional interaction are encouraged.
- My compensation and benefits are competitive.
- My workplace celebrates diversity and does not tolerate discrimination of any form.

- My employer maintains working conditions that my fellow employees and I like and don't want to give up.

Hard work, determination, planning, and perseverance, as stated so succinctly by Mia Hamm, will place you in the best position to enter and progress through the series of life and career stages that lie before you. Be proactive and in control but reactive when the situation demands.

Challenges to career success and satisfaction are inescapable. Those that address those challenges properly and completely will create opportunities and options that lead to positive career outcomes.

Appendix

Careers and Occupations: Demographic Information
Careers/Occupations with Largest Employment
Value of Information: These occupations employ the greatest number of people in the United States and offer the largest number of growth and replacement opportunities.

Retail salesperson

Cashier

Food preparation and serving worker

Office clerk

Registered nurse

Customer service representative

Laborers and freight, stock and material mover

Waiter and waitress

Secretary and administrative assistant

Janitor and cleaner, except maid and housekeeping cleaner

General and operations manager

Personal care aide

Stock clerk and order filler

Heavy and tractor-trailer driver

Bookkeeper, accountant, and auditing clerk

First-line supervisor/manager of retail workers

Nursing assistant

First-line supervisor of office and administrative support workers

Sales representative

Main and housekeeping cleaner

Maintenance and repair worker

Elementary school teachers

Accountant and auditor

Teacher assistant

Cook

Construction laborer

Childcare worker

Landscaping worker

Team assembler

Security guard

Receptionist and information clerk

Farmer, rancher, and other agricultural manager

Carpenter

Business operations specialist

Secondary school teacher

Manager

Sales representative, all other

Light truck and delivery driver

First-line supervisor of food service and preparation workers

Home health aide

Food preparation worker

Software developer

Management analyst

Lawyer

Automotive service technician

Licensed practical nurse and vocational nurse

Packer and packager

Executive secretary and executive administrative assistant

Police and sheriff's patrol officer

Shipping, receiving, and traffic clerk

Careers/Occupations with Largest Employment Requiring a College Degree

Value of Information: For individuals aspiring to earn a college degree, these occupations employ the largest number of growth and replacement opportunities for occupations with this level of educational attainment.

Elementary school teacher, except special education

Accountant and auditor

Secondary school teachers, except special and career education

Management analyst

Middle school teacher, except special and career education

Computer systems analyst

Financial manager

Software developer—applications

Sales representative—wholesale manufacturing technical and scientific products

Software developer—systems software

Chief executive officer

Computer programmer

Network and computer systems administrator

Sales manager

Recreation worker

Securities, commodities, and financial services sales agent

Computer and information systems manager

Medical and health services manager

Information security analyst, web developer, and computer network architect

Child, family, and school social worker

Market research analysis and marketing specialist

Graphic designer

Civil engineer

Public relations specialist

Mechanical engineer

Industries or Settings with the Largest Employment (2010)

Value of Information: These industries and settings employ the largest number of people and offer growth and replacement opportunities. If the industry or setting is of interest to the career explorer or job changer, additional research regarding specific occupations will be required.

Elementary and secondary schools—local

Full-service restaurants

General medical and surgical hospitals—private

Grocery stores

Offices of physicians

Management of companies and enterprises

Colleges, universities, and professional schools—state

Computer systems and design and related services

Other general merchandise stores

Colleges, universities, and professional schools—private

Depository credit intermediation

Nursing care facilities

Services for the elderly and persons with disabilities

Management, scientific, and technical consulting services

Home health care services

Department stores

Automobile dealers

Legal services

Building materials and supplies dealers

Plumbing, heating, and air-conditioning contractors

Elementary and secondary schools—private

General freight/trucking

Clothing stores

Accounting, tax preparation, bookkeeping, and payroll services

Engineering services

Occupational Groups Projected for the Greatest Growth (Present—2022)
Value of Information: As groupings of occupations, these popular fields
are expected to grow at a pace that exceeds others.

Health care support occupations

Health care practitioners and technical occupations

Construction and extraction occupations

Personal care and service occupations

Computer and mathematical occupations

Community and social service occupations

Business and financial operations occupations

Building and grounds, cleaning, and maintenance occupations

Education, training, and library occupations

Legal occupations

Fastest Growing Occupations—Percentage (2021–2022)
Value of Information: Each reflects areas of percentage growth and
need as dictated greatly by the issues of technology development and
service providing (personal/health/social). Many represent emerging
occupations.

Industrial–organizational psychologist

Personal care aide

Home health aide

Insulation worker, mechanical

Interpreter and translator

Diagnostic medical sonographer

Helper—brick mason, block mason, stonemason, and tile worker

Occupational therapy assistant

Genetic counselor

Physical therapist assistant

Physical therapist aide

Skincare specialist

Physician assistant

Segmental paver

Helper—electrician

Information security analyst

Occupational therapy aide

Health specialties teacher, postsecondary

Medical secretary

Physical therapist

Orthotist and prosthetist

Brick mason and block mason

Nursing instructor and teacher, postsecondary

Nurse practitioner

Audiologist

Dental hygienist

Meeting, convention and event planner

Therapist, all other

Market research analyst and marketing specialist

Substance abuse and behavioral disorder counselor

Fastest Growing Occupations—Number (2021–2022)

Value of Information: These occupations will experience rapid growth. The number of new and replacement positions will be greater than other occupations.

Personal care aide

Registered nurse

Retail salesperson

Home health aide

Combined food preparation and serving worker, including fast food

Nursing assistant

Secretaries and administrative assistant, except legal, medical, and executive

Customer service representative

Janitor and cleaner, except maid and housekeeping cleaner

Construction laborer

General and operations manager

Laborer and freight, stock, and material mover

Carpenter

Bookkeeping, accounting, and auditing clerk

Heavy and tractor-trailer truck driver

Medical secretary

Childcare worker

Office clerk, general

Maid and housekeeping cleaner

Licensed practical and licensed vocational nurse

First-line supervisor of office and administrative support personnel

Elementary school teacher, except special education

Accountant and auditor

Medical assistant

Cook, restaurant

Software developer, applications

Landscaping and grounds keeping worker

Receptionist and information clerk

Management analyst

Sales representative, wholesale and manufacturing, except technical and scientific products

Note: The information presented above comes from a variety of occupational reports generated by the Bureau of Labor Statistics, U.S. Department of Labor; the U.S. Census Bureau; and CareerOneStop, Employment and Training Administration, U.S. Department of Labor.

CAREER AND COLLEGE WEBSITES
The internet can provide valuable information and assistance to students engaged in career and education transitions.

Note: Unfortunately, web addresses are constantly evolving, and some on this list may have become inactive or adopted a different web address. Every effort has been made to create a list of accurate and active URLs at the time of publication. Also, note that many websites require users to register before using services or accessing information. For privacy reasons, readers may elect not to visit these sites.

Career
Career exploration, www.careeronestop.org

Job boards/job search

www.careerbuilder.com

www.greenjobengine.com

www.helpwanted.com

www.indeed.com

www.justjobs.com

www.linkup.com

www.monster.com

www.mosthired.com

www.rileyguide.com

www.simplyhired.com

www.usajobs.gov

Military careers, www.todaysmilitary.com

Occupational Outlook Handbook, www.bls.gov/ooh

Women's career issues, www.dol.gov/wb/

College
Common Application, www.commonapplication.org

Admission testing and testing alternatives

ACT, www.act.org

College Board, www.collegeboard.com

FairTest (list of test-optional institutions), www.fairtest.org/optinit
.htm

GED Testing Service, www.acenet.edu/AM/Template.cfn?Section
=GED_TS

College exploration/search

www.asa.org.plan

www.collegeview.com

www.college-scholarships.com

www.howtogetin.com

www.nces.ed.gov/collegenavigator/

Higher education lists

www.schoolsintheusa.com

Catholic colleges, www.catholiccollegesonline.org

Historically Black colleges and universities,

www.wikipedia.org/wiki/List_of_historically_black_colleges_and
_universities

Hispanic serving institutions,

www.hacu.net/assnfe/CompanyDirectory.asp?STYLE=2&COM-
PANY_TYPE=1,5

Christian colleges, www.collegestats.org/colleges/christian

Women's colleges, en.wikipedia.org/wiki/
Women%27s_colleges_in_the_United_States

National Association for College Admission Counseling, www.
nacacnet.org

Financial Aid
General scholarship and financial aid

  www.finaid.org

  www.fastweb.com

  www.college-scholarships.com

  www.studentaid.gov

  www.wiredscholar.com

International scholarships
  www.InternationalScholarships.com

Scholarship Scams
  www.ftc.gov/scholarshipscams

Targeted Students
Minority students

  African American students, www.uncf.org, www.tmcf.org

  Latino, Hispanic students, www.lulac.org and www.hacu.org

  Native American students, www.engage.collegefund.org

General

Census Bureau, www.census.gov

U.S. Department of Education, www.ed.gov

U.S. Department of Labor, www.dol.gov

Study skills, www.how-to-study.com/

JOB BOARDS

The following job boards, culled from articles and stories that attest to their utility, are among the internet vehicles that help individuals explore job vacancies and apply for employment. Readers should be on the lookout for new job boards, as they are being created regularly, especially for niche occupations and careers. Job boards also have different access and registration procedures, including some that are fee charging. Where applicable, the occupational or user focus of the site is included in parentheses.

CareerBuilder.com

CareerJet.com

CollegeRecruiter.com (current college students and recent graduates)

CoolWorks.com (environmental jobs)

Craigslist.com

Dice.com (technology jobs)

Diversejobs.net (higher education positions)

energyjobline.com (energy jobs)

Everyjobforme.com

ihireEngineering.com (engineering jobs)

www.flexjobs.com (freelance and special arrangements, including seniors)

www.goodfoodjobs.com (hospitality and food service)

www.idealist.org/en/ (internships and volunteer positions)

www.indeed.com

www.internships.com (internships)

https://jobs.aarp.org and www.aarp.org/work/ (seniors)

https://jobs.google.com/about/

jobs.prsa.org (communication, media, and public relations)

www.linkedin.com

https://linkup.com

www.mediabistro.com (communications and media)

www.monster.com

https://newsolutions.org (older and experienced workers)

www.onewire.com (finance, accounting, and technology careers)

www.resume-library.com

www.retiredbrains.com/index.html (seniors)

www.seniors4hire.org (seniors)

www.simplyhired.com

www.snagajob.com (hourly wage earners)

www.upwork.com (independent contractors)

www.usajobs.gov (federal government jobs)

www.ziprecruiter.com

Note: Readers should be aware the many major city newspapers, once the larger purveyors of job information of the printed format, have established both paid and free job board sites that can be found at the internet site of the newspaper.

CAREER ABILITY, INTEREST, AND PERSONALITY INVENTORIES

Any number of career assessment tools may be used by professional counselors helping clients to explore career and education opportunities. The following list is not representative of the breadth of those instruments but does identify a number of free assessments that can be self-administered.

Career Maturity Inventory, www.vocopher.com

O*NET Ability Profiler, www.onetcenter.org/AP.html

CareerOneStop Skills Matcher, www.careeronestop.org/Toolkit/Skills/skills-matcher.aspx

O*NET Interest Profiler, www.onetcenter.org/IP.html

O*NET Work Importance Locator, www.onetcenter.org/WIL.html

Keirsey Temperament Sorter, www.keirsey.com

CAREER AND COLLEGE GUIDES AND DIRECTORIES

Following is a list of popular career and college publications with the names of the publisher in parentheses following each title. One or more of these titles will likely be found in public and school libraries. The guides and directories on the list are updated and published periodically and care should be taken to access the most recent edition available.

Career

Encyclopedia of Careers and Vocational Guidance (Ferguson/Facts on File)

Occupational Outlook Handbook (U.S. Department of Labor, Bureau of Labor Statistics)

What Color Is Your Parachute (Ten Speed Press)

College

College Admissions Data Sourcebook Hyper-Handbook (Wintergreen/ Orchard House)

Bound-for-College Guidebook (Rowman & Littlefield Education)

Bound-for-Career Guidebook (Rowman & Littlefield Education)

College Board Handbook (College Board)

Complete Book of Colleges (Princeton Review)

Fiske Guide to Colleges (Sourcebooks)

Peterson's Four-Year Colleges (Thomson Peterson's)

Peterson's Two-Year Colleges (Thomson Peterson's)

Peterson's College & University Almanac (Thomson Peterson's)

Peterson's Graduate & Professional Programs

Profiles of American College (Barron's Educational Series)

CAREER AND EDUCATION INFORMATION SOURCES

The following internet addresses represent a mix of professional and trade organizations, as well as government agencies, making career, education, and credentialing information available to the public. These sites also provide current information on industry and setting issues and trends.

Advertising, Marketing, and Public Relations Careers

American Association of Advertising Agencies, www.aaaa.org

Public Relations Society of America, www.prsa.org

Agriculture and Agribusiness Careers

American Society of Agricultural and Biological Engineers, www .asabe.org

National Future Farmers of America, www.ffa.org

Business, Finance, and Management Careers
American Bankers Association, www.aba.com

American Institute of Certified Public Accountants, www.aicpa.org

American Management Association, www.amanet.org

Bank Administration Institute, www.bai.org

Financial Management Association International, www.fma.org

Institute of Internal Auditors, www.theiia.org

Institute of Management Accountants, www.imanet.org

National Management Association, www.nma1.org

Society for Human Resource Management, www.shrm.org

Building and Construction Careers
American Builders and Contractors, www.abc.org

American Council for Construction Education, www.acce-hq.org

American Institute of Architects, www.aia.org

American Institute of Constructors, https://aic-builds.org

American Society of Heating, Refrigerating, and Air-Conditioning Engineers, www.ashrae.org

Associated General Contractors of America, www.agc.org

Home Builders Institute, www.hbi.org

International Brotherhood of Electrical Workers, www.ibew.org

International Masonry Institute, www.imiweb.org

International Union of Painters and Allied Trades, www.iupat.org

Mechanical Contractors Association of America, www.mcaa.org

National Center for Construction Education & Research, www
.nccer.org

National Electrical Contractors Association, www.necanet.org

Painting Contractors Association, www.pcapainted.org

Plumbing-Heating-Cooling Contractors Association, www.phc-
cweb.org

United Brotherhood of Carpenters and Joiners of America, www
.carpenters.org

United Association of Journeymen and Apprentices of the Plumbing and Pipefitting Industry, www.ua.org

Communications and Media Careers
National Association of Broadcast Employees and Technicians,
www.nabetcwa.org

National Association of Broadcasters, www.nab.org

Professional Photographers of America, www.ppa.com

Society of Broadcast Engineers, www.sbe.org

Computer and Technology Careers
Accreditation Board for Engineering and Technology, www.abet
.org

Association for Computing Machinery, www.acm.org

IEEE Computer Society, www.computer.org

Education and Public Service Careers
American Association of School Librarians, www.ala.org/aasl

American Association of School Administrators, www.aasa.org

American Association of University Professors, www.aaup.org

American Council for the Teaching of Foreign Languages, www
.actfl.org

American Counseling Association, www.counseling.org

American Library Association, www.ala.org

American School Counselor Association, www.schoolcounselor.org

Council for Accreditation of Counseling and Related Educational
Programs, www.cacrep.org

Council for the Accreditation of Educator Preparation, http://
caepnet.org

Council on Social Work Education, www.cswe.org

Modern Language Association, www.mla.org

National Association for Music Education, www.nafme.org

National Association of Elementary School Principals, www.naesp
.org

National Association of Secondary School Principals, www.nassp
.org

National Association of Social Workers, www.socialworkers.org

National Board for Certified Counselors, www.nbcc.org

National Council of Teachers of Mathematics, www.nctm.org

National Council for the Social Studies, www.socialstudies.org

National Council of Teachers of English, www.ncte.org

National Education Association, www.nea.org

National Science Teaching Association, www.nsta.org

Society of Health and Physical Educators, www.shapeamerica.org//

Special Libraries Association, www.sla.org

Engineering and Science Careers

Accreditation Board for Engineering and Technology, www.abet.org

Aerospace Industries Association, www.aia-aerospace.org

American Academy of Environmental Engineers, www.aaee.net

American Chemical Society, www.chemistry.org

American Geosciences Institute, www.agiweb.org

American Institute of Chemical Engineers, www.aiche.org

American Institute of Aeronautics and Astronautics, www.aiaa.org

American Nuclear Society, www.ans.org

American Society of Civil Engineers, www.asce.org

American Society of Mechanical Engineers, www.asme.org

American Society for Engineering Education, www.asee.org

Institute of Electrical and Electronics Engineers USA, www.ieeeusa.org

Institute of Industrial and Systems Engineers, https://iise.ie

Minerals, Metals & Materials Society, www.tms.org

National Society of Professional Engineers, www.nspe.org

Society of Naval Architects and Marine Engineers, www.sname.org

Society of Petroleum Engineers, www.spe.org

Society for Mining, Metallurgy & Exploration, www.smenet.org

Health Careers

American Association of Colleges of Nursing, www.aacnnursing.org

American Association of Medical Assistants, www.aama-ntl.org

American Association of Nurse Practitioners, www.aanp.org

American Dental Assistants Association, www.adaausa.org

American Dental Association, www.ada.org

American Dental Education Association, www.adea.org

American Hospital Association, www.aha.org

American Medical Technologists, www.americanmedtech.org

American Nurses Association, www.nursingworld.org

American Occupational Therapy Association, www.aota.org

American Pharmacists Association, www.pharmacist.com

American Psychiatric Association, www.psych.org

American Psychological Association, www.apa.org

American Physical Therapy Association, www.apta.org

American Society of Podiatric Medical Assistants, www.aspma.org

American Speech-Language-Hearing Association, www.asha.org

Association of Medical Illustrators, www.ami.org

Biomedical Engineering Society, www.bmes.org

Commission on Accreditation of Allied Health Education Programs, www.caahep.org

International Joint Commission on Allied Health Personnel in Ophthalmology, www.jcahpo.org

National Association of Licensed Professional Nurses, nalpn.org

National League for Nursing, www.nln.org

Hospitality, Leisure, and Recreation Careers

American Camp Association, www.acacamps.org

American Culinary Federation, www.acfchefs.org

American Hotel & Lodging Association, www.ahla.com

American Society of Travel Advisors, www.asta.org

National Recreation and Park Association, www.nrpa.org

National Restaurant Association, www.restaurant.org

Military Careers

The branches of the U.S. military represent an incredible number of opportunities for both educational and career experiences. You can learn about the opportunities available for both officers and enlisted personnel in each branch of military service by contacting the following websites:

- General military, www.todaysmilitary.com
- Air Force, www.airforce.com
- Army, www.goarmy.com
- Coast Guard, www.uscg.mil
- Marine Corps, www.marines.com
- Navy, www.navy.com

Personal Services Careers

American Association of Veterinary Medical Colleges, www.aavmc .org

American Bar Association, www.americanbar.org

American Counseling Association, www.counseling.org

American Psychological Association, www.apa.org

American Veterinary Medical Association, www.avma.org

Law School Admission Council, www.lsac.org

National Association of Personnel Services, www.recruitinglife.com

Security and Protection Service Careers

American Correctional Association, www.aca.org

Drug Enforcement Agency, www.dea.gov

Federal Bureau of Investigation, www.fbi.gov

International Association of Fire Fighters, www.iaff.org

International Association of Chiefs of Police, www.theiacp.org

National Association of Police Organizations, www.napo.org

National Sheriffs' Association, www.sheriffs.org

U.S. Secret Service, www.secretservice.gov

U.S. Bureau of Alcohol, Tobacco, Firearms and Explosives, www.atf.gov

U.S. Customs and Border Protection, www.cbp.gov

U.S. Department of Homeland Security, www.dhs.gov

U.S. Marshals Service, www.usmarshals.gov

Sales and Distribution Careers

Independent Insurance Agents & Brokers of America, www.independentagent.com

National Retail Federation, www.nrf.com

National Sales Network, www.salesnetwork.org

Transportation Careers

    Air Line Pilots Association, www.alpa.org

    Association of Flight Attendants, www.afanet.org

    Federal Aviation Administration, www.faa.gov

    International Air Transport Association, www.iata.org

    Society of Automotive Engineers, www.sae.org

AGENCIES AND ORGANIZATIONS SUPPORTING ENTREPRENEURS

    General, www.score.org

    Veterans, www.sba.gov/content/veterans

    Seniors, www.sba.gov/encore

    Women, www.sba.gov/content/women-owned-businesses

Note: Websites and addresses often change, and your author has attempted to offer the most current communication tools for contacting the source of the information in this appendix and the book. When not successful, use a general search engine to research the name or topic.

Index

older workers, 113, 271
onboarding, 48, 197–98, 198,
    200–203
orientation, 7, 85, 138, 168, 197,
    203, 212, 245
overaspiring, 6, 74–75

Palmer, Thomas, 175
Parker, Dorothy, 159
PayScale, 189
Penn, William, 91
personality and personality traits,
    4, 9, 11–12, 22, 44, 59, 64, 98,
    150, 153, 176–77, 181, 213–14,
    239, 248, 283
Pew Internet and American Life
    Study, Pew Research Center,
    125, 127, 271, 290
placement, 35, 71, 79, 103, 105,
    115, 128–130, 225
planning, 92–93, 96, 100, 116,
    173, 263–64, 296, 303, 305
Post, Diane, 299
power, 24–26, 49, 62, 98–99, 124,
    141, 159, 186–87, 277
Priestley, Joseph, 16
probationary period or status, 188,
    203, 238
procrastination and indecision,
    96–97, 187
professional and trade associations,
    33, 53, 67–68, 84, 122, 127–28,
    215, 253

Quinn, Jane Bryant, 269

**resume, resume construction,
and resume types, 7, 25, 124, 131,
133–44, 153, 159–60, 163, 165,
176–77, 179–80, 216, 239, 243**
retention, 114, 171, 198, 215, 220,
    221–22, 227–28, 235, 291
retirement and retirement
    planning, 45, 48, 87, 92, 95,
    168, 172, 174, 261–72, 275–76
Rometty, Virginia, 281

**salary, compensation, and
benefits, 33, 45, 56, 121–122,
153–54, 170–71, 185, 191, 192,
194, 209, 221, 223, 230, 235,
242–43, 245–46, 263, 287, 304**
Schultz, Charles, 219
science, technology, engineering,
    mathematics (STEM), 43, 77,
    115, 282
search and staffing professionals/
    firms and recruiters, 139, 170,
    182, 215, 216
self-awareness, 4–5, 9, 11, 21,
    25–26, 75, 92, 109, 173, 228,
    249, 264, 303
shadowing, 33, 84, 88, 105
Sheehy, Gail, 167, 251
skill set mastery, 283
social media, 30, 122, 125–27, 129,
    132, 138, 141, 179
Society for Human Resource
    Management, 171
Sotomayor, Sonia Maria, 47
supply and demand, 45, 181

ABOUT THE AUTHOR

Dr. Frank Burtnett is a veteran counselor, teacher, student service administrator, education association officer, and consultant who founded and served as the president and principal consultant of Education Now, an education and human resource development consulting firm located in Springfield, Virginia, and Rockport, Maine. At various times in his personal career, Frank served as the executive director of the National Association for College Admission Counseling (NACAC), associate executive director of the American Counseling Association (ACA), and certification and education consultant for the National Association of Personnel Services (NAPS). During the early stages of his career development, he served as a teacher, counselor, and student services director with the Fairfax County Public Schools in Virginia and counseling consultant with the Pennsylvania Department of Education.

Frank's personal career honors include being named an ACA Fellow by the American Counseling Association in 2016 for his lifetime contributions to the field of professional counseling and his recognition as a member of the NAPS Hall of Fame in 2013 for distinguished service to the professional development of members of the search and staffing industry. He was also honored by Shippensburg University with the Jesse B. Heiges Distinguished Alumni Award.

He is the author of *The Bound-for-College Guidebook* (third edition) and the *Bound-for-Career Guidebook* (second edition), both written for career and education explorers and published by Rowman & Littlefield Education. Previously, he wrote the *Parent's Guide to the College Admission Process*, a publication of the National Association for College Admission Counseling, and developed the early online information bank used by the more than 400,000 student members of the National Beta Club.

Frank is author of *The Career Mechanic*, an ongoing treatment of career issues and concerns that is featured regularly in EMInfo, the Employment Marketplace Information eNewsletter and read by more than 20,000 search and staffing professionals. He coauthored the AT&T publication, *Selecting the Right College*, which has been distributed to more than one million students nationally. He also wrote and edited numerous college and career guidance guides for the *Careers & Colleges* and *Futures* magazines and the Family Education Network.

Frank has served on the counselor education faculty of the School of Counseling, College of Health and Education of Marymount University in Arlington, Virginia, for more than a decade. He has also presented live seminars and professional development programs, as well as distance learning webinars, on career and education development topics for numerous businesses, institutions, agencies, organizations, and private sector entities.

He holds a bachelor of science degree in education from Shippensburg University (Pennsylvania) and master of arts and doctor of education degrees in counseling from the George Washington University (Washington, DC). He has achieved the National Certified Counselor (NCC) and National Certified Career Counselor (NCCC) credentials of the National Board for Certified Counselors and the Certified Personnel Consultant (CPC) credential of the NAPS. Frank is also a registered counselor (RC2478) in the state of Maine.

Other Rowman & Littlefield books by the author:

Bound-for-College Guidebook, Third Edition (2022)

Bound-for-Career Guidebook, Second Edition (2021)